The Ultimate Air Fryer Cookbook for Beginners and Advanced Users

1000 Days of Easy, Healthy, and Affordable Recipes for Master Air Frying and Make Delicious Food Within Reach.

Sarah Rabago

Table of Contents

Chapter 5: Vegetable Side Dishes Recipes 34

Chapter 6: Vegetarians Recipes 46

Chapter 7: Poultry Recipes 55

Chapter 8: Fish And Seafood Recipes 69

Chapter 9: Beef, pork & Lamb Recipes 80

Chapter 10: Desserts And Sweets 94

Recipes Index 105

Chapter 1: Introduction

In the ever-evolving landscape of kitchen appliances, the air fryer has emerged as a game-changer that revolutionizes the way we cook and enjoy our favorite foods. This versatile appliance utilizes hot air circulation to create crispy and delicious dishes with a fraction of the oil traditionally used for frying. In this comprehensive introduction, we will explore the history, benefits, features, usage tips, and maintenance guidelines of the air fryer.

History of the Air Fryer

The concept of cooking with hot air to achieve the texture and flavor of deep-fried foods without the excessive use of oil dates back several decades. However, the modern air fryer as we know it today has its roots in the early 21st century. The first patent for an air fryer-like device was filed in 2005 by Philips Electronics, a renowned name in the world of consumer electronics and appliances.

Philips introduced its "Airfryer" in 2010, marking a significant milestone in the evolution of air frying technology. This innovative appliance utilized rapid air technology to circulate hot air around food items, creating a crispy outer layer while preserving the moisture within. It quickly gained popularity for its ability to produce healthier versions of traditionally fried foods.

As consumer demand for healthier cooking options continued to grow, other companies began developing their own air fryer models, leading to a diverse range of options in the market today. The air fryer has since become a staple in kitchens around the world, offering a healthier and more convenient way to prepare fried and crispy dishes.

Benefits of the Air Fryer

The air fryer has gained immense popularity due to its numerous benefits, which cater to modern lifestyles and health-conscious consumers:

1.   **Healthier Cooking:** Perhaps the most significant advantage of the air fryer is its ability to cook with significantly less oil compared to traditional deep frying methods. This results in lower calorie counts and reduced intake of unhealthy fats.
2.   **Reduced Health Risks:** By minimizing oil use, the air fryer helps reduce the risks associated with consuming excessive fried foods, such as obesity, heart disease, and high cholesterol.
3.   **Versatility:** Beyond frying, the air fryer can also bake, roast, grill, and even dehydrate, making it a versatile appliance that can handle a wide range of recipes.
4.   **Time Efficiency:** Air fryers cook food faster and more evenly than conventional ovens, making them a time-saving option for busy individuals and families.
5.   **Energy Efficiency:** Air fryers typically consume less energy compared to traditional ovens, contributing to reduced electricity bills and environmental sustainability.
6.   **Delicious Results:** Despite using less oil, air-fried dishes come out crispy and flavorful, often rivaling the taste and texture of their deep-fried counterparts.

Features of the Air Fryer

Air fryers are equipped with a variety of features that enhance their functionality and user experience:

- **Adjustable Temperature Control:** Most air fryers offer a range of temperature settings to accommodate different cooking needs, allowing precise control over the cooking process.
- **Timer Function:** A timer with an audible alert ensures that your food is cooked to perfection without the risk of overcooking.
- **Cooking Basket:** The cooking basket with a perforated base allows hot air to circulate around the food, ensuring even cooking and crispiness.
- **Non-Stick Coating:** Many air fryer baskets and trays have a non-stick coating, making them easy to clean and maintain.
- **Digital Display:** User-friendly digital displays and control panels simplify the selection of cooking settings and adjustments.

Tips for Using the Air Fryer

To make the most of your air fryer and achieve delicious results, consider these practical tips:

1. **Preheat:** Preheat the air fryer for a few minutes before adding your food to ensure even cooking and better texture.
2. **Single Layer:** Avoid overcrowding the cooking basket to allow hot air to circulate evenly around the food. Cook in batches if necessary.
3. **Oil Application:** Lightly coat your ingredients with oil using a spray bottle or brush to achieve a crispy exterior.
4. **Shake or Flip:** Shake the basket or flip food halfway through cooking to ensure uniform results.
5. **Experiment:** Don't be afraid to experiment with different recipes and cooking times to find your preferred results.

Cleaning and Maintenance of the Air Fryer

Proper cleaning and maintenance are essential to keep your air fryer in excellent condition:

- **Regular Cleaning:** After each use, allow the appliance to cool, then remove the cooking basket and any removable parts for cleaning. Most components are dishwasher-safe for easy cleanup.
- **Exterior Cleaning:** Wipe down the exterior of the air fryer with a damp cloth to remove any grease or residue.
- **Filter Maintenance:** Some air fryer models have removable air filters. Clean or replace them as needed to maintain efficient air circulation.
- **Storage:** Store your air fryer in a dry place when not in use to prevent dust and debris from accumulating.

In conclusion, the air fryer has transformed the way we approach cooking, offering a healthier, more efficient, and versatile alternative to traditional frying methods. With its remarkable features, practical usage tips, and straightforward maintenance guidelines, the air fryer has earned its place as a kitchen essential for those seeking convenient, delicious, and health-conscious meal preparation. Explore the world of air frying and discover a culinary experience that redefines how you enjoy your favorite dishes.

Chapter 2: Measurement Conversions

BASIC KITCHEN CONVERSIONS & EQUIVALENTS

DRY MEASUREMENTS CONVERSION CHART
3 TEASPOONS = 1 TABLESPOON = 1/16 CUP
6 TEASPOONS = 2 TABLESPOONS = 1/8 CUP
12 TEASPOONS = 4 TABLESPOONS = 1/4 CUP
24 TEASPOONS = 8 TABLESPOONS = 1/2 CUP
36 TEASPOONS = 12 TABLESPOONS = 3/4 CUP
48 TEASPOONS = 16 TABLESPOONS = 1 CUP

METRIC TO US COOKING CONVER SIONS
OVEN TEMPERATURES
120 °C = 250 °F
160 °C = 320 °F
180° C = 360 °F
205 °C = 400 °F
220 °C = 425 °F

LIQUID MEASUREMENTS CONVERSION CHART
8 FLUID OUNCES = 1 CUP = 1/2 PINT = 1/4 QUART
16 FLUID OUNCES = 2 CUPS = 1 PINT = 1/2 QUART
32 FLUID OUNCES = 4 CUPS = 2 PINTS = 1 QUART = 1/4 GALLON
128 FLUID OUNCES = 16 CUPS = 8 PINTS = 4 QUARTS = 1 GALLON

BAKING IN GRAMS
1 CUP FLOUR = 140 GRAMS
1 CUP SUGAR = 150 GRAMS
1 CUP POWDERED SUGAR = 160 GRAMS
1 CUP HEAVY CREAM = 235 GRAMS

VOLUME
1 MILLILITER = 1/5 TEASPOON
5 ML = 1 TEASPOON
15 ML = 1 TABLESPOON
240 ML = 1 CUP OR 8 FLUID OUNCES
1 LITER = 34 FL. OUNCES

WEIGHT
1 GRAM = .035 OUNCES
100 GRAMS = 3.5 OUNCES
500 GRAMS = 1.1 POUNDS
1 KILOGRAM = 35 OUNCES

US TO METRIC COOKING CONVERSIONS
1/5 TSP = 1 ML
1 TSP = 5 ML
1 TBSP = 15 ML
1 FL OUNCE = 30 ML
1 CUP = 237 ML
1 PINT (2 CUPS) = 473 ML
1 QUART (4 CUPS) = .95 LITER
1 GALLON (16 CUPS) = 3.8 LITERS
1 OZ = 28 GRAMS
1 POUND = 454 GRAMS

BUTTER
1 CUP BUTTER = 2 STICKS = 8 OUNCES = 230 GRAMS = 8 TABLESPOONS

WHAT DOES 1 CUP EQUAL
1 CUP = 8 FLUID OUNCES
1 CUP – 16 TABLESPOONS
1 CUP = 48 TEASPOONS
1 CUP = 1/2 PINT
1 CUP = 1/4 QUART
1 CUP = 1/16 GALLON
1 CUP = 240 ML

BAKING PAN CONVERSIONS
1 CUP ALL-PURPOSE FLOUR = 4.5 OZ
1 CUP ROLLED OATS = 3 OZ 1 LARGE EGG = 1.7 OZ
1 CUP BUTTER = 8 OZ 1 CUP MILK = 8 OZ
1 CUP HEAVY CREAM = 8.4 OZ
1 CUP GRANULATED SUGAR = 7.1 OZ
1 CUP PACKED BROWN SUGAR = 7.75 OZ
1 CUP VEGETABLE OIL = 7.7 OZ
1 CUP UNSIFTED POWDERED SUGAR = 4.4 OZ

BAKING PAN CONVERSIONS
9-INCH ROUND CAKE PAN = 12 CUPS
10-INCH TUBE PAN =16 CUPS
11-INCH BUNDT PAN = 12 CUPS
9-INCH SPRINGFORM PAN = 10 CUPS
9 X 5 INCH LOAF PAN = 8 CUPS
9-INCH SQUARE PAN = 8 CUPS

Chapter 3: Bread And Breakfast

Egg Soufflé With Mushroom And Broccoli

Servings: 4
Cooking Time: 20 Minutes
Ingredients:
- 4 large eggs
- 1 teaspoon onion powder
- 1 teaspoon garlic powder
- 1 teaspoon red pepper, crushed
- ½ cup broccoli florets, chopped
- ½ cup mushrooms, chopped

Directions:
1. Sprinkle 4 ramekins with cooking spray and set aside.
2. In a suitable bowl, whisk eggs with onion powder, garlic powder, and red pepper.
3. Add mushrooms and broccoli and stir well.
4. Pour egg mixture into the prepared ramekins and place ramekins into the air fryer basket.
5. Cook at almost 350 degrees F/ 175 degrees C for almost 15 minutes. Make sure soufflé is cooked if soufflé is not cooked then cook for 5 minutes more.
6. Serve and enjoy.

Grilled Steak With Parsley Salad

Servings:4
Cooking Time: 45 Minutes
Ingredients:
- 1 ½ pounds flatiron steak
- 3 tablespoons olive oil
- Salt and pepper to taste
- 2 cups parsley leaves
- ½ cup parmesan cheese, grated
- 1 tablespoon fresh lemon juice

Directions:
1. Preheat the air fryer at 390°F.
2. Place the grill pan accessory in the air fryer.
3. Mix together the steak, oil, salt and pepper.
4. Grill for 15 minutes per batch and make sure to flip the meat halfway through the cooking time.
5. Meanwhile, prepare the salad by combining in a bowl the parsley leaves, parmesan cheese and lemon juice. Season with salt and pepper.

Strawberry Tarts

Servings: 6
Cooking Time: 10 Minutes
Ingredients:
- 2 refrigerated piecrusts
- ½ cup strawberry preserves
- 1 teaspoon cornstarch
- Cooking oil spray
- ½ cup low-fat vanilla yogurt
- 1-ounce cream cheese, at room temperature
- 3 tablespoons confectioners' sugar

- Rainbow sprinkles, for decorating

Directions:
1. Place the piecrusts on a flat surface.
2. Cut each piecrust into 3 rectangles using a knife or pizza cutter, for 6 in total.
3. In a suitable bowl, mix cornstarch and the preserves. Mix well.
4. Scoop 1 tablespoon of the strawberry filling onto the top ½ of each piece of piecrust.
5. Fold the bottom of each piece to enclose the filling inside.
6. Press along the edges of each tart to seal using the back of a fork.
7. At 350 degrees F/ 175 degrees C, preheat your air fryer.
8. Once your air fryer is preheated, spray the crisper plate with cooking oil.
9. Work in batches, spray the breakfast tarts with cooking oil and place them into the basket in a single layer.
10. Set the air fryer's temperature to 375 degrees F/ 190 degrees C, and set the time to 10 minutes.
11. 1
12. Repeat the same steps with remaining ingredients. 1
13. In a suitable bowl, stir together the cream cheese, yogurt, and confectioners' sugar. 1
14. Top the breakfast tarts with the frosting and garnish with sprinkles.

Quick And Easy Blueberry Muffins

Servings:8
Cooking Time: 12 Minutes
Ingredients:
- 1⅓ cups flour
- ½ cup sugar
- 2 teaspoons baking powder
- ¼ teaspoon salt
- ⅓ cup canola oil
- 1 egg
- ½ cup milk
- ⅔ cup blueberries, fresh or frozen and thawed

Directions:
1. Preheat the air fryer to 330°F (166°C).
2. In a medium bowl, stir together flour, sugar, baking powder, and salt.
3. In a separate bowl, combine oil, egg, and milk and mix well.
4. Add egg mixture to dry ingredients and stir just until moistened.
5. Gently stir in the blueberries.
6. Spoon batter evenly into parchment-paper-lined muffin cups.
7. Put 4 muffin cups in air fryer basket and bake for 12 minutes or until tops spring back when touched lightly.
8. Repeat previous step to bake remaining muffins.
9. Serve immediately.

Morning Burrito

Servings: 4
Cooking Time: 15 Minutes
Ingredients:

- 2 oz cheddar cheese, torn into pieces
- 2 hard-boiled eggs, chopped
- 1 avocado, chopped
- 1 red bell pepper, chopped
- 3 tbsp salsa
- 4 flour tortillas

Directions:

1. Whisk the eggs, avocado, red bell pepper, salsa, and cheese. Pout the tortillas on a clean surface and divide the egg mix between them. Fold the edges and roll up; poke a toothpick through so they hold. Preheat air fryer to 390°F. Place the burritos in the frying basket and Air Fry for 3-5 minutes until crispy and golden. Serve hot.

Banana-strawberry Cakecups

Servings: 6
Cooking Time: 25 Minutes
Ingredients:

- ½ cup mashed bananas
- ¼ cup maple syrup
- ½ cup Greek yogurt
- 1 tsp vanilla extract
- 1 egg
- 1 ½ cups flour
- 1 tbsp cornstarch
- ½ tsp baking soda
- ½ tsp baking powder
- ½ tsp salt
- ½ cup strawberries, sliced

Directions:

1. Preheat air fryer to 360°F. Place the mashed bananas, maple syrup, yogurt, vanilla, and egg in a large bowl and mix until smooth. Sift in 1 ½ cups of the flour, baking soda, baking powder, and salt, then stir to combine.
2. In a small bowl, toss the strawberries with the cornstarch. Fold the mixture into the muffin batter. Divide the mixture evenly between greased muffin cups and place into the air frying basket. Bake for 12-15 minutes until golden brown on top and a toothpick inserted into the middle of one of the muffins comes out clean. Leave to cool for 5 minutes. Serve and enjoy!

Cream Cheese Danish

Servings:4
Cooking Time: 10 Minutes
Ingredients:

- 1 sheet frozen puff pastry dough, thawed
- 1 large egg, beaten
- 4 ounces full-fat cream cheese, softened
- ¼ cup confectioners' sugar
- 1 teaspoon vanilla extract
- ½ teaspoon lemon juice

Directions:

1. Preheat the air fryer to 320°F.

2. Unfold puff pastry and cut into four equal squares. For each pastry, fold all four corners partway to the center, leaving a 1" square in the center.
3. Brush egg evenly over folded puff pastry.
4. In a medium bowl, mix cream cheese, confectioners' sugar, vanilla, and lemon juice. Scoop 2 tablespoons of mixture into the center of each pastry square.
5. Place danishes directly in the air fryer basket and cook 10 minutes until puffy and golden brown. Cool 5 minutes before serving.

Strawberry Pastry

Servings:8
Cooking Time: 15 Minutes Per Batch
Ingredients:

- 1 package refrigerated piecrust
- 1 cup strawberry jam
- 1 large egg, whisked
- ½ cup confectioners' sugar
- 2 tablespoons whole milk
- ½ teaspoon vanilla extract

Directions:

1. Preheat the air fryer to 320°F. Cut parchment paper to fit the air fryer basket.
2. On a lightly floured surface, lay piecrusts out flat. Cut each piecrust round into six 4" × 3" rectangles, reserving excess dough.
3. Form remaining dough into a ball, then roll out and cut four additional 4" × 3" rectangles, bringing the total to sixteen.
4. For each pastry, spread 2 tablespoons jam on a pastry rectangle, leaving a 1" border around the edges. Top with a second pastry rectangle and use a fork to gently press all four edges together. Repeat with remaining jam and pastry.
5. Brush tops of each pastry with egg and cut an X in the center of each to prevent excess steam from building up.
6. Place pastries on parchment in the air fryer basket, working in batches as necessary. Cook 12 minutes, then carefully flip and cook an additional 3 minutes until each side is golden brown. Let cool 10 minutes.
7. In a small bowl, whisk confectioners' sugar, milk, and vanilla. Brush each pastry with glaze, then place in the refrigerator 5 minutes to set before serving.

Sweet And Spicy Breakfast Sausage

Servings:6
Cooking Time: 10 Minutes
Ingredients:

- 1 pound 84% lean ground pork
- 2 tablespoons brown sugar
- 1 teaspoon salt
- ½ teaspoon ground black pepper
- ½ teaspoon garlic powder
- ½ teaspoon dried fennel
- ½ teaspoon crushed red pepper flakes

Directions:

1. Preheat the air fryer to 400°F.
2. In a large bowl, mix all ingredients until well combined. Divide mixture into eight portions and form into patties.
3. Spritz patties with cooking spray and place in the air fryer basket. Cook 10 minutes until patties are brown and internal temperature reaches at least 145°F. Serve warm.

Egg & Bacon Pockets

Servings: 4
Cooking Time: 50 Minutes
Ingredients:
- 2 tbsp olive oil
- 4 bacon slices, chopped
- ¼ red bell pepper, diced
- 1/3 cup scallions, chopped
- 4 eggs, beaten
- 1/3 cup grated Swiss cheese
- 1 cup flour
- 1 ½ tsp baking powder
- ½ tsp salt
- 1 cup Greek yogurt
- 1 egg white, beaten
- 2 tsp Italian seasoning
- 1 tbsp Tabasco sauce

Directions:
1. Warm the olive oil in a skillet over medium heat and add the bacon. Stir-fry for 3-4 minutes or until crispy. Add the bell pepper and scallions and sauté for 3-4 minutes. Pour in the beaten eggs and stir-fry to scramble them, 3 minutes. Stir in the Swiss cheese and set aside to cool.
2. Sift the flour, baking powder, and salt in a bowl. Add yogurt and mix together until combined. Transfer the dough to a floured workspace. Knead it for 3 minutes or until smooth. Form the dough into 4 equal balls. Roll out the balls into round discs. Divide the bacon-egg mixture between the rounds. Fold the dough over the filling and seal the edges with a fork. Brush the pockets with egg white and sprinkle with Italian seasoning.
3. Preheat air fryer to 350°F. Arrange the pockets on the greased frying basket and Bake for 9-11 minutes, flipping once until golden. Serve with Tabasco sauce.

Canadian Bacon And Cheese English Muffins

Servings: 4
Cooking Time: 10 Minutes
Ingredients:
- 4 English muffins
- 8 slices Canadian bacon
- 4 slices cheese
- Cooking oil

Directions:
1. Split each English muffin. Assemble the breakfast sandwiches by layering 2 slices of Canadian bacon and 1 slice of cheese onto each English muffin bottom. Top with the other half of the English muffin.

2. Place the sandwiches in the air fryer. Spray the top of each with cooking oil. Cook for 4 minutes.
3. Open the air fryer and flip the sandwiches. Cook for an additional 4 minutes.
4. Cool before serving.

Parsley Omelet

Servings: 4
Cooking Time: 15 Minutes
Ingredients:
- 4 eggs, whisked
- 1 tablespoon parsley, chopped
- ½ teaspoons cheddar cheese, shredded
- 1 avocado, peeled, pitted and cubed
- Cooking spray

Directions:
1. In a bowl, mix all the ingredients except the cooking spray and whisk well. Grease a baking pan that fits the Air Fryer with the cooking spray, pour the omelet mix, spread, introduce the pan in the machine and cook at 370°F for 15 minutes. Serve for breakfast.

Simple Scotch Eggs

Servings:4
Cooking Time: 25 Minutes
Ingredients:
- 4 large hard boiled eggs
- 1 (12-ounce / 340-g) package pork sausage
- 8 slices thick-cut bacon
- Special Equipment:
- 4 wooden toothpicks, soaked in water for at least 30 minutes

Directions:
1. Slice the sausage into four parts and place each part into a large circle.
2. Put an egg into each circle and wrap it in the sausage. Put in the refrigerator for 1 hour.
3. Preheat the air fryer to 450°F (235°C).
4. Make a cross with two pieces of thick-cut bacon. Put a wrapped egg in the center, fold the bacon over top of the egg, and secure with a toothpick.
5. Air fry in the preheated air fryer for 25 minutes.
6. Serve immediately.

Pita And Pepperoni Pizza

Servings:1
Cooking Time: 6 Minutes
Ingredients:
- 1 teaspoon olive oil
- 1 tablespoon pizza sauce
- 1 pita bread
- 6 pepperoni slices
- ¼ cup grated Mozzarella cheese
- ¼ teaspoon garlic powder
- ¼ teaspoon dried oregano

Directions:
1. Preheat the air fryer to 350°F (177°C). Grease the air fryer basket with olive oil.

2. Spread the pizza sauce on top of the pita bread. Put the pepperoni slices over the sauce, followed by the Mozzarella cheese.
3. Season with garlic powder and oregano.
4. Put the pita pizza inside the air fryer and place a trivet on top.
5. Bake in the preheated air fryer for 6 minutes and serve.

Canadian Bacon & Cheese Sandwich

Servings: 1
Cooking Time: 30 Minutes
Ingredients:
- 1 English muffin, halved
- 1 egg
- 1 Canadian bacon slice
- 1 slice provolone cheese

Directions:
1. Preheat air fryer to 350°F. Put the muffin, crusty side up, in the frying basket. Place a slice of bacon next to the muffins and Bake for 5 minutes. Flip the bacon and muffins, and lay a slice of provolone cheese on top of the muffins. Beat the egg in a small heatproof bowl.
2. Add the bowl in the frying basket next to the bacon and muffins and Bake for 15 minutes, or until the cheese melts, bacon is crispy and eggs set. Remove the muffin to a plate, layer a slice of bacon, then the egg and top with the second toasted muffin.

Avocado Quesadillas

Servings:4
Cooking Time: 11 Minutes
Ingredients:
- 4 eggs
- 2 tablespoons skim milk
- Salt and ground black pepper, to taste
- Cooking spray
- 4 flour tortillas
- 4 tablespoons salsa
- 2 ounces (57 g) Cheddar cheese, grated
- ½ small avocado, peeled and thinly sliced

Directions:
1. Preheat the air fryer to 270°F (132°C).
2. Beat together the eggs, milk, salt, and pepper.
3. Spray a baking pan lightly with cooking spray and add egg mixture.
4. Bake for 8 minutes, stirring every 1 to 2 minutes, until eggs are scrambled to the liking. Remove and set aside.
5. Spray one side of each tortilla with cooking spray. Flip over.
6. Divide eggs, salsa, cheese, and avocado among the tortillas, covering only half of each tortilla.
7. Fold each tortilla in half and press down lightly. Increase the temperature of the air fryer to 390°F (199°C).
8. Put 2 tortillas in air fryer basket and air fry for 3 minutes or until cheese melts and outside feels slightly crispy. Repeat with remaining two tortillas.

9. Cut each cooked tortilla into halves. Serve warm.

Potato Bread Rolls

Servings:5
Cooking Time: 20 Minutes
Ingredients:
- 5 large potatoes, boiled and mashed
- Salt and ground black pepper, to taste
- ½ teaspoon mustard seeds
- 1 tablespoon olive oil
- 2 small onions, chopped
- 2 sprigs curry leaves
- ½ teaspoon turmeric powder
- 2 green chilis, seeded and chopped
- 1 bunch coriander, chopped
- 8 slices bread, brown sides discarded

Directions:
1. Preheat the air fryer to 400°F (204°C).
2. Put the mashed potatoes in a bowl and sprinkle on salt and pepper. Set to one side.
3. Fry the mustard seeds in olive oil over a medium-low heat in a skillet, stirring continuously, until they sputter.
4. Add the onions and cook until they turn translucent. Add the curry leaves and turmeric powder and stir. Cook for a further 2 minutes until fragrant.
5. Remove the pan from the heat and combine with the potatoes. Mix in the green chilies and coriander.
6. Wet the bread slightly and drain of any excess liquid.
7. Spoon a small amount of the potato mixture into the center of the bread and enclose the bread around the filling, sealing it entirely. Continue until the rest of the bread and filling is used up. Brush each bread roll with some oil and transfer to the basket of the air fryer.
8. Air fry for 15 minutes, gently shaking the air fryer basket at the halfway point to ensure each roll is cooked evenly.
9. Serve immediately.

Sweet-hot Pepperoni Pizza

Servings: 2
Cooking Time: 18 Minutes
Ingredients:
- 1 (6- to 8-ounce) pizza dough ball*
- olive oil
- ½ cup pizza sauce
- ¾ cup grated mozzarella cheese
- ½ cup thick sliced pepperoni
- ⅓ cup sliced pickled hot banana peppers
- ¼ teaspoon dried oregano
- 2 teaspoons honey

Directions:
1. Preheat the air fryer to 390°F.
2. Cut out a piece of aluminum foil the same size as the bottom of the air fryer basket. Brush the foil circle with olive oil. Shape the dough into a circle and place it on top of the foil. Dock the dough by piercing it several times with a fork. Brush the dough lightly with olive oil

and transfer it into the air fryer basket with the foil on the bottom.

3. Air-fry the plain pizza dough for 6 minutes. Turn the dough over, remove the aluminum foil and brush again with olive oil. Air-fry for an additional 4 minutes.

4. Spread the pizza sauce on top of the dough and sprinkle the mozzarella cheese over the sauce. Top with the pepperoni, pepper slices and dried oregano. Lower the temperature of the air fryer to 350°F and cook for 8 minutes, until the cheese has melted and lightly browned. Transfer the pizza to a cutting board and drizzle with the honey. Slice and serve.

Home-made Potatoes With Paprika

Servings: 4
Cooking Time: 25 Minutes
Ingredients:
- 3 large russet potatoes
- 1 tablespoon canola oil
- 1 tablespoon extra-virgin olive oil
- 1 teaspoon paprika
- Salt
- Black pepper
- 1 cup chopped onion
- 1 cup chopped red bell pepper
- 1 cup chopped green bell pepper

Directions:
1. Cut the potatoes into ½-inch cubes.
2. Place the potatoes in a suitable bowl of cold water and allow them to soak for about 30 to 60 minutes.
3. Dry out the potatoes and wipe thoroughly with paper towels.
4. Return them to the empty bowl.
5. Add the canola and olive oils, paprika, and black pepper and salt to flavor.
6. Toss to fully coat the potatoes.
7. Transfer the potatoes to the air fryer.
8. Cook for 20 minutes, shaking the air fryer basket every 5 minutes a total of 4 times.
9. Put the onion and red and green bell peppers to the air fryer basket. Fry for an additional 3 to 4 minutes, or until the potatoes are cooked through and the black peppers are soft.
10. Cool before serving.

Scrambled Eggs

Servings: 2
Cooking Time: 6 Minutes
Ingredients:
- 4 eggs
- 1/4 tsp garlic powder
- 1/4 tsp onion powder
- 1 tbsp parmesan cheese
- Pepper
- Salt

Directions:
1. Whisk eggs with garlic powder, onion powder, parmesan cheese, pepper, and salt.

2. Pour egg mixture into the air fryer baking dish.
3. Place dish in the air fryer and cook at 360°F for 2 minutes. Stir quickly and cook for 3-4 minutes more.
4. Stir well and serve.

Classical French Frittata

Servings: 3
Cooking Time: 18 Minutes
Ingredients:
- 3 eggs
- 1 tablespoon heavy cream
- 1 teaspoon Herbs de Provence
- 1 teaspoon almond butter, softened
- 2 ounces Provolone cheese, grated

Directions:
1. Before cooking, heat your air fryer to 365 degrees F/ 185 degrees C.
2. Whisk the 3 eggs together in a medium bowl and then add the heavy cream. Whisk again with a hand whisker until smooth.
3. Then add herbs de Provence and the grated cheese.
4. Gently stir the egg mixture.
5. Using almond butter, grease the baking pan.
6. Then pour the egg mixture evenly on the baking pan.
7. Cook in the preheated air fryer for 18 minutes.
8. When it has preheated, cool to room temperature, and slice and serve.

Blueberry Applesauce Oat Cake

Servings: 4
Cooking Time: 65 Minutes
Ingredients:
- 1 cup applesauce
- 2/3 cup quick-cooking oats
- ½ tsp baking powder
- A pinch of salt
- ½ cup almond milk
- 5 tbsp almond flour
- 1 tbsp honey
- 1 egg
- 1 tsp vanilla extract
- ½ cup blueberries
- 4 tbsp grape preserves

Directions:
1. In a bowl, combine oats, baking powder, and salt. In a larger bowl, combine milk, almond flour, honey, egg, and vanilla with a whisk until well mixed. Add the applesauce until combined, then add the oat mixture. Gently fold in blueberries. Pour the mixture into a greased baking dish. Spoon jelly over the top, but do not stir it in.
2. Preheat air fryer to 300°F. Put the baking dish into the air fryer. Bake until the top is golden and the oatmeal is set, 25 minutes. Remove and allow to cool for 10-15 minutes. Slice four ways and serve warm.

Dill Eggs In Wonton

Servings: 4
Cooking Time: 4 Minutes
Ingredients:
- 2 eggs, hard-boiled, peeled
- 1 tablespoon cream cheese
- 1 tablespoon fresh dill, chopped
- 1 teaspoon ground black pepper
- 4 wontons wrap
- 1 egg white, whisked
- 1 teaspoon sesame oil

Directions:
1. Before cooking, heat your air fryer to 395 degrees F/ 200 degrees C.
2. Grease the air fryer basket with sesame oil.
3. Chop the hard-boiled eggs and in a bowl, mix together with dill, ground pepper, and cream cheese.
4. Separate the egg mixture onto wonton wraps and roll them into rolls.
5. Use the whisked egg white to brush the wontons.
6. Arrange the wontons evenly on the greased air fryer basket.
7. Cook in your air fryer at 395 degrees F/ 200 degrees C for 2 minutes from each side or until golden brown flip to the other side.

Almond Oatmeal

Servings: 4
Cooking Time: 15 Minutes
Ingredients:
- 2 cups almond milk
- 1 cup coconut, shredded
- 2 teaspoons stevia
- 2 teaspoons vanilla extract

Directions:
1. In a pan that fits your air fryer, mix all the ingredients, stir well, introduce the pan in the machine and cook at 360°F for 15 minutes. Divide into bowls and serve for breakfast.

Greek Frittata

Servings:4 (makes 2 Frittatas)
Cooking Time: 20 Minutes
Ingredients:
- Olive oil
- 5 eggs
- ¼ teaspoon salt
- ⅛ teaspoon freshly ground black pepper
- 1 cup baby spinach leaves, shredded
- ½ cup halved grape tomatoes
- ½ cup crumbled feta cheese

Directions:
1. Spray a small round air fryer-friendly pan with olive oil.
2. In a medium bowl, whisk together eggs, salt, and pepper and whisk to combine.
3. Add the spinach and stir to combine.
4. Pour ½ cup of the egg mixture into the pan.
5. Sprinkle ¼ cup of the tomatoes and ¼ cup of the feta on top of the egg mixture.
6. Cover the pan with aluminum foil and secure it around the edges.
7. Place the pan carefully into the fryer basket.
8. Air fry for 12 minutes.
9. Remove the foil from the pan and cook until the eggs are set, 5 to 7 minutes.
10. Remove the frittata from the pan and place on a serving platter. Repeat with the remaining ingredients.

Inside-out Cheeseburgers

Servings: 3
Cooking Time: 9-11 Minutes
Ingredients:
- 1 pound 2 ounces 90% lean ground beef
- ¾ teaspoon Dried oregano
- ¾ teaspoon Table salt
- ¾ teaspoon Ground black pepper
- ¼ teaspoon Garlic powder
- 6 tablespoons Shredded Cheddar, Swiss, or other semi-firm cheese, or a purchased blend of shredded cheeses
- 3 Hamburger buns (gluten-free, if a concern), split open

Directions:
1. Preheat the air fryer to 375°F .
2. Gently mix the ground beef, oregano, salt, pepper, and garlic powder in a bowl until well combined without turning the mixture to mush. Form it into two 6-inch patties for the small batch, three for the medium, or four for the large.
3. Place 2 tablespoons of the shredded cheese in the center of each patty. With clean hands, fold the sides of the patty up to cover the cheese, then pick it up and roll it gently into a ball to seal the cheese inside. Gently press it back into a 5-inch burger without letting any cheese squish out. Continue filling and preparing more burgers, as needed.
4. Place the burgers in the basket in one layer and air-fry undisturbed for 8 minutes for medium or 10 minutes for well-done.
5. Use a nonstick-safe spatula, and perhaps a flatware fork for balance, to transfer the burgers to a cutting board. Set the buns cut side down in the basket in one layer and air-fry undisturbed for 1 minute, to toast a bit and warm up. Cool the burgers a few minutes more, then serve them warm in the buns.

Cheddar Biscuits With Nutmeg

Servings: 4
Cooking Time: 8 Minutes
Ingredients:
- ½ cup almond flour
- ¼ cup Cheddar cheese, shredded
- ¾ teaspoon salt
- 1 egg, beaten
- 1 tablespoon mascarpone
- 1 tablespoon coconut oil, melted

- ¾ teaspoon baking powder
- ½ teaspoon apple cider vinegar
- ¼ teaspoon ground nutmeg

Directions:
1. Mix the almond flour, baking powder, salt, and ground nutmeg in a big bowl.
2. Place apple cider vinegar, egg, mascarpone, and coconut oil inside the bowl.
3. Add in cheese and make a dough. Knead until soft.
4. Divide into small balls to make the biscuits.
5. Before cooking, heat your air fryer to 400 degrees F/ 205 degrees C.
6. Prepare your air fryer basket by lining it with parchment paper.
7. Transfer the cheese biscuits onto the parchment paper. Cook the cheese biscuits in your air fryer at 400 degrees F/ 205 degrees C until golden brown, for 8 minutes or more.
8. Halfway cooking, check the biscuits to avoid burning.
9. Serve.

Scrambled Eggs With Mushrooms

Servings: 4
Cooking Time: 11 Minutes
Ingredients:
- 4 eggs
- 4 strips of bacon
- 2 mushrooms
- black pepper, to taste
- salt, to taste

Directions:
1. Slice the mushrooms, season with salt, black pepper and sprinkle with oil.
2. Fry in an air fryer at about 360 degrees F/ 180 degrees C, shaking halfway.
3. Fry the bacon strips for 5-6 minutes, shaking halfway.
4. Now we are preparing the scramble. Beat the eggs, mix well, add black pepper and salt to taste. Sprinkle the bottom of the air fryer or a cooking dish with olive oil.
5. Cook the scramble at 360 degrees F/ 180 degrees C for 5 minutes, stirring every minute.
6. Serve and enjoy.

Crispy Parmesan Asparagus

Servings: 4
Cooking Time: 10 Minutes
Ingredients:
- 1 pound asparagus spears
- 2 tablespoons butter
- ½ cup Parmesan cheese, grated
- Salt/Black pepper
- 1 teaspoon lemon zest

Directions:
1. Prepare all the recipe ingredients. Peel the asparagus, wash and dry.
2. Season the asparagus spears with black pepper and salt and brush with butter.

3. Arrange them in a deep air fryer basket and cook at 370 degrees F/ 185 degrees C, for about 8 to 10 minutes. Shake a couple of times while cooking.
4. Serve with parmesan and lemon zest.

Mozzarella Eggs With Basil Pesto

Servings: 4
Cooking Time: 20 Minutes
Ingredients:
- 2 tablespoons butter, melted
- 6 teaspoons basil pesto
- 1 cup mozzarella cheese, grated
- 6 eggs, whisked
- 1 tablespoons basil, chopped
- A pinch of salt and black pepper

Directions:
1. Before cooking, heat your air fryer to 360 degrees F/ 180 degrees C.
2. Mix the basil pesto, mozzarella cheese, the whisked egg, basil, salt, and black pepper together in a bowl. Whisk.
3. Drizzle the baking pan with butter and then add the mixture.
4. Cook in your air fryer at 360 degrees F/ 180 degrees C for 20 minutes.
5. When the cooking time is up, transfer from the air fryer and serve on plates.
6. Enjoy your breakfast.

Honey Oatmeal

Servings: 6
Cooking Time: 35 Minutes
Ingredients:
- 2 cups rolled oats
- 2 cups oat milk
- ¼ cup honey
- ½ cup Greek yogurt
- 1 tsp vanilla extract
- ½ tsp ground cinnamon
- ¼ tsp salt
- 1 ½ cups diced mango

Directions:
1. Preheat air fryer to 380°F. Stir together the oats, milk, honey, yogurt, vanilla, cinnamon, and salt in a large bowl until well combined. Fold in ¾ cup of the mango and then pour the mixture into a greased cake pan. Sprinkle the remaining manog across the top of the oatmeal mixture. Bake in the air fryer for 30 minutes. Leave to set and cool for 5 minutes. Serve and enjoy!

Banana Bread Pudding

Servings:4
Cooking Time: 20 Minutes
Ingredients:
- Olive oil
- 2 medium ripe bananas, mashed
- ½ cup low-fat milk
- 2 tablespoons peanut butter
- 2 tablespoons maple syrup

- 1 teaspoon ground cinnamon
- 1 teaspoon vanilla extract
- 2 slices whole-grain bread, torn into bite-sized pieces
- ¼ cup quick oats

Directions:
1. Lightly spray four individual ramekins or one air fryer–safe baking dish with olive oil.
2. In a large mixing bowl, combine the bananas, milk, peanut butter, maple syrup, cinnamon, and vanilla. Using an electric mixer or whisk, mix until fully combined.
3. Add the bread pieces and stir to coat in the liquid mixture.
4. Add the oats and stir until everything is combined.
5. Transfer the mixture to the baking dish or divide between the ramekins. Cover with aluminum foil.
6. Place 2 ramekins in the fryer basket and air fry until heated through, 10 to 12 minutes.
7. Remove the foil and cook for 6 to 8 more minutes.
8. Repeat with the remaining 2 ramekins.

Green Egg Quiche

Servings: 4
Cooking Time: 30 Minutes
Ingredients:
- 1 cup broccoli florets
- 2 cups baby spinach
- 2 garlic cloves, minced
- ¼ tsp ground nutmeg
- 1 tbsp olive oil
- Salt and pepper to taste
- 4 eggs
- 2 scallions, chopped
- 1 red onion, chopped
- 1 tbsp sour cream
- ½ cup grated fontina cheese

Directions:
1. Preheat air fryer to 375°F. Combine broccoli, spinach, onion, garlic, nutmeg, olive oil, and salt in a medium bowl, tossing to coat. Arrange the broccoli in a single layer in the parchment-lined frying basket and cook for 5 minutes. Remove and set to the side.
2. Use the same medium bowl to whisk eggs, salt, pepper, scallions, and sour cream. Add the roasted broccoli and ¼ cup fontina cheese until all ingredients are well combined. Pour the mixture into a greased baking dish and top with cheese. Bake in the air fryer for 15-18 minutes until the center is set. Serve and enjoy.

Sausage And Egg Breakfast Burrito

Servings: 6
Cooking Time: 30 Minutes
Ingredients:
- 6 eggs
- Salt
- Pepper
- Cooking oil
- ½ cup chopped red bell pepper

- ½ cup chopped green bell pepper
- 8 ounces ground chicken sausage
- ½ cup salsa
- 6 medium (8-inch) flour tortillas
- ½ cup shredded Cheddar cheese

Directions:
1. In a medium bowl, whisk the eggs. Add salt and pepper to taste.
2. Place a skillet on medium-high heat. Spray with cooking oil. Add the eggs. Scramble for 2 to 3 minutes, until the eggs are fluffy. Remove the eggs from the skillet and set aside.
3. If needed, spray the skillet with more oil. Add the chopped red and green bell peppers. Cook for 2 to 3 minutes, until the peppers are soft.
4. Add the ground sausage to the skillet. Break the sausage into smaller pieces using a spatula or spoon. Cook for 3 to 4 minutes, until the sausage is brown.
5. Add the salsa and scrambled eggs. Stir to combine. Remove the skillet from heat.
6. Spoon the mixture evenly onto the tortillas.
7. To form the burritos, fold the sides of each tortilla in toward the middle and then roll up from the bottom. You can secure each burrito with a toothpick. Or you can moisten the outside edge of the tortilla with a small amount of water. I prefer to use a cooking brush, but you can also dab with your fingers.
8. Spray the burritos with cooking oil and place them in the air fryer. Do not stack. Cook the burritos in batches if they do not all fit in the basket. Cook for 8 minutes.
9. Open the air fryer and flip the burritos. Cook for an additional 2 minutes or until crisp.
10. If necessary, repeat steps 8 and 9 for the remaining burritos.
11. Sprinkle the Cheddar cheese over the burritos. Cool before serving.

Egg And Bacon Muffins

Servings: 1
Cooking Time: 15 Minutes
Ingredients:
- 2 eggs
- Salt and ground black pepper, to taste
- 1 tablespoon green pesto
- 3 ounces (85 g) shredded Cheddar cheese
- 5 ounces (142 g) cooked bacon
- 1 scallion, chopped

Directions:
1. Preheat the air fryer to 350°F (177°C). Line a cupcake tin with parchment paper.
2. Beat the eggs with pepper, salt, and pesto in a bowl. Mix in the cheese.
3. Pour the eggs into the cupcake tin and top with the bacon and scallion.
4. Bake in the preheated air fryer for 15 minutes, or until the egg is set.
5. Serve immediately.

Spinach-bacon Rollups

Servings: 4
Cooking Time: 9 Minutes
Ingredients:
- 4 flour tortillas
- 4 slices Swiss cheese
- 1 cup baby spinach leaves
- 4 slices turkey bacon

Directions:
1. Preheat air fryer to 390°F.
2. On each tortilla, place one slice of cheese and ¼ cup of spinach.
3. Roll up tortillas and wrap each with a strip of bacon. Secure each end with a toothpick.
4. Place rollups in air fryer basket, leaving a little space in between them.
5. Cook for 4minutes. Turn and rearrange rollups and cook for 5minutes longer, until bacon is crisp.

Asparagus Strata

Servings:4
Cooking Time: 17 Minutes
Ingredients:
- 6 asparagus spears, cut into 2-inch pieces
- 2 slices whole-wheat bread, cut into ½-inch cubes
- 4 eggs
- 3 tablespoons whole milk
- ½ cup grated Havarti or Swiss cheese
- 2 tablespoons chopped flat-leaf parsley
- Pinch salt
- Freshly ground black pepper

Directions:
1. Place the asparagus spears and 1 tablespoon water in a 6-inch baking pan and place in the air fryer basket. Bake for 3 to 5 minutes or until crisp and tender. Remove the asparagus from the pan and drain it. Spray the pan with nonstick cooking spray.
2. Arrange the bread cubes and asparagus into the pan and set aside.
3. In a medium bowl, beat the eggs with the milk until combined. Add the cheese, parsley, salt, and pepper. Pour into the baking pan.
4. Bake for 11 to 14 minutes or until the eggs are set and the top starts to brown.

Oat Muffins With Blueberries

Servings: 6
Cooking Time: 25 Minutes
Ingredients:
- ¾ cup old-fashioned rolled oats
- 1 ½ cups flour
- ½ cup evaporated cane sugar
- 1 tbsp baking powder
- 1 tsp ground cinnamon
- ¼ tsp ground chia seeds
- ¼ tsp ground sesame seeds
- ½ tsp salt
- 1 cup vanilla almond milk
- 4 tbsp butter, softened
- 2 eggs
- 1 tsp vanilla extract
- 1 cup blueberries
- 2 tbsp powdered sugar

Directions:
1. Preheat air fryer to 350°F. Combine flour oats, sugar, baking powder, chia seeds, sesame seeds, cinnamon, and salt in a bowl. Mix the almond milk, butter, eggs, and vanilla in another bowl until smooth. Pour in dry ingredients and stir to combine. Fold in blueberries.Fill 12 silicone muffin cups about halfway and place them in the frying basket. Bake for 12-15 minutes until just browned, and a toothpick in the center comes out clean. Cool for 5 minutes. Serve topped with powdered sugar.

Jalapeño And Bacon Breakfast Pizza

Servings:2
Cooking Time: 10 Minutes
Ingredients:
- 1 cup shredded mozzarella cheese
- 1 ounce cream cheese, broken into small pieces
- 4 slices cooked sugar-free bacon, chopped
- ¼ cup chopped pickled jalapeños
- 1 large egg, whisked
- ¼ teaspoon salt

Directions:
1. Place mozzarella in a single layer on the bottom of an ungreased 6" round nonstick baking dish. Scatter cream cheese pieces, bacon, and jalapeños over mozzarella, then pour egg evenly around baking dish.
2. Sprinkle with salt and place into air fryer basket. Adjust the temperature to 330°F and set the timer for 10 minutes. When cheese is brown and egg is set, pizza will be done.
3. Let cool on a large plate 5 minutes before serving.

Chocolate Chip Scones

Servings:8
Cooking Time:15 Minutes
Ingredients:
- ½ cup cold salted butter, divided
- 2 cups all-purpose flour
- ½ cup brown sugar
- ½ teaspoon baking powder
- 1 large egg
- ¾ cup buttermilk
- ½ cup semisweet chocolate chips

Directions:
1. Preheat the air fryer to 320°F. Cut parchment paper to fit the air fryer basket.
2. Chill 6 tablespoons butter in the freezer 10 minutes. In a small microwave-safe bowl, microwave remaining 2 tablespoons butter 30 seconds until melted, and set aside.
3. In a large bowl, mix flour, brown sugar, and baking powder.
4. Remove butter from freezer and grate into bowl. Use a wooden spoon to evenly distribute.

5. Add egg and buttermilk and stir gently until a soft, sticky dough forms. Gently fold in chocolate chips.

6. Turn dough out onto a lightly floured surface. Fold a couple of times and gently form into a 6" round. Cut into eight triangles.

7. Place scones on parchment in the air fryer basket, leaving at least 2" space between each, working in batches as necessary.

8. Brush each scone with melted butter. Cook 15 minutes until scones are dark golden brown and crispy on the edges, and a toothpick inserted into the center comes out clean. Serve warm.

Shakshuka-style Pepper Cups

Servings:4
Cooking Time: 35 Minutes
Ingredients:
- 2 tbsp ricotta cheese crumbles
- 1 tbsp olive oil
- ½ yellow onion, diced
- 2 cloves garlic, minced
- ¼ tsp turmeric
- 1 can diced tomatoes
- 1 tbsp tomato paste
- ½ tsp smoked paprika
- ½ tsp salt
- ½ tsp granular sugar
- ¼ tsp ground cumin
- ¼ tsp ground coriander
- ⅛ tsp cayenne pepper
- 4 bell peppers
- 4 eggs
- 2 tbsp chopped basil

Directions:
1. Warm the olive oil in a saucepan over medium heat. Stir-fry the onion for 10 minutes or until softened. Stir in the garlic and turmeric for another 1 minute. Add diced tomatoes, tomato paste, paprika, salt, sugar, cumin, coriander, and cayenne. Remove from heat and stir.

2. Preheat air fryer to 350°F. Slice the tops off the peppers, and carefully remove the core and seeds. Put the bell peppers in the frying basket. Divide the tomato mixture among bell peppers. Crack 1 egg into tomato mixture in each pepper. Bake for 8-10 minutes. Sprinkle with ricotta cheese and cook for 1 more minute. Let rest 5 minutes. Garnish with fresh basil and serve immediately.

Parmesan Sausage Egg Muffins

Servings:4
Cooking Time: 20 Minutes
Ingredients:
- 6 ounces (170 g) Italian sausage, sliced
- 6 eggs
- ⅛ cup heavy cream
- Salt and ground black pepper, to taste
- 3 ounces (85 g) Parmesan cheese, grated

Directions:

1. Preheat the air fryer to 350ºF (177ºC). Grease a muffin pan.
2. Put the sliced sausage in the muffin pan.
3. Beat the eggs with the cream in a bowl and season with salt and pepper.
4. Pour half of the mixture over the sausages in the pan.
5. Sprinkle with cheese and the remaining egg mixture.
6. Bake in the preheated air fryer for 20 minutes or until set.
7. Serve immediately.

Ham & Cheese Sandwiches

Servings: 2
Cooking Time: 15 Minutes
Ingredients:
- 1 tsp butter
- 4 bread slices
- 4 deli ham slices
- 4 Cheddar cheese slices
- 4 thick tomato slices
- 1 tsp dried oregano

Directions:
1. Preheat air fryer to 370°F. Smear ½ tsp of butter on only one side of each slice of bread and sprinkle with oregano. On one of the slices, layer 2 slices of ham, 2 slices of cheese, and 2 slices of tomato on the unbuttered side. Place the unbuttered side of another piece of bread onto the toppings. Place the sandwiches butter side down into the air fryer. Bake for 8 minutes, flipping once until crispy. Let cool slightly, cut in half and serve.

Puffed Egg Tarts

Servings:4
Cooking Time:42 Minutes
Ingredients:
- 1 sheet frozen puff pastry half, thawed and cut into 4 squares
- ¾ cup Monterey Jack cheese, shredded and divided
- 4 large eggs
- 1 tablespoon fresh parsley, minced
- 1 tablespoon olive oil

Directions:
1. Preheat the Air fryer to 390°F
2. Place 2 pastry squares in the air fryer basket and cook for about 10 minutes.
3. Remove Air fryer basket from the Air fryer and press each square gently with a metal tablespoon to form an indentation.
4. Place 3 tablespoons of cheese in each hole and top with 1 egg each.
5. Return Air fryer basket to Air fryer and cook for about 11 minutes.
6. Remove tarts from the Air fryer basket and sprinkle with half the parsley.
7. Repeat with remaining pastry squares, cheese and eggs.
8. Dish out and serve warm.

Omelette In Bread Cups

Servings:4
Cooking Time: 11 Minutes
Ingredients:
- 4 (3-by-4-inch) crusty rolls
- 4 thin slices Gouda or Swiss cheese mini wedges
- 5 eggs
- 2 tablespoons heavy cream
- ½ teaspoon dried thyme
- 3 strips precooked bacon, chopped
- Pinch salt
- Freshly ground black pepper

Directions:
1. Cut the tops off the rolls and remove the insides with your fingers to make a shell with about ½-inch of bread remaining. Line the rolls with a slice of cheese, pressing down gently so the cheese conforms to the inside of the roll.
2. In a medium bowl, beat the eggs with the heavy cream until combined. Stir in the thyme, bacon, and salt and pepper.
3. Spoon the egg mixture into the rolls over the cheese.
4. Bake for 8 to 12 minutes or until the eggs are puffy and starting to brown on top.

Chapter 4: Appetizers And Snacks

Parmesan Breaded Zucchini Chips

Servings: 5
Cooking Time: 20 Minutes
Ingredients:
- For the zucchini chips
- 2 medium zucchini
- 2 eggs
- ⅓ cup bread crumbs
- ⅓ cup grated Parmesan cheese
- Salt
- Pepper
- Cooking oil
- For the lemon aioli
- ½ cup mayonnaise
- ½ tablespoon olive oil
- Juice of ½ lemon
- 1 teaspoon minced garlic
- Salt
- Pepper

Directions:
1. Slice the zucchini into thin chips (about ⅛ inch thick) using a knife or mandoline.
2. In a small bowl, beat the eggs. In another small bowl, combine the bread crumbs, Parmesan cheese, and salt and pepper to taste.
3. Spray the air fryer basket with cooking oil.
4. Dip the zucchini slices one at a time in the eggs and then the bread crumb mixture. You can also sprinkle the bread crumbs onto the zucchini slices with a spoon.
5. Place the zucchini chips in the air fryer basket, but do not stack. Cook in batches. Spray the chips with cooking oil from a distance (otherwise, the breading may fly off). Cook for 10 minutes.
6. Remove the cooked zucchini chips from the air fryer, then repeat step 5 with the remaining zucchini.
7. While the zucchini is cooking, combine the mayonnaise, olive oil, lemon juice, and garlic in a small bowl, adding salt and pepper to taste. Mix well until fully combined.
8. Cool the zucchini and serve alongside the aioli.

Sweet Apple Fries

Servings: 3
Cooking Time: 8 Minutes
Ingredients:
- 2 Medium-size sweet apple(s), such as Gala or Fuji
- 1 Large egg white(s)
- 2 tablespoons Water
- 1½ cups Finely ground gingersnap crumbs (gluten-free, if a concern)
- Vegetable oil spray

Directions:
1. Preheat the air fryer to 375°F .
2. Peel and core an apple, then cut it into 12 slices. Repeat with more apples as necessary.
3. Whisk the egg white(s) and water in a medium bowl until foamy. Add the apple slices and toss well to coat.

4. Spread the gingersnap crumbs across a dinner plate. Using clean hands, pick up an apple slice, let any excess egg white mixture slip back into the rest, and dredge the slice in the crumbs, coating it lightly but evenly on all sides. Set it aside and continue coating the remaining apple slices.
5. Lightly coat the slices on all sides with vegetable oil spray, then set them curved side down in the basket in one layer. Air-fry undisturbed for 6 minutes, or until browned and crisp. You may need to air-fry the slices for 2 minutes longer if the temperature is at 360°F.
6. Use kitchen tongs to transfer the slices to a wire rack. Cool for 2 to 3 minutes before serving.

Zucchini And Potato Tots

Servings:4
Cooking Time: 20 Minutes
Ingredients:
- 1 large zucchini, grated
- 1 medium baked potato, skin removed and mashed
- ¼ cup shredded Cheddar cheese
- 1 large egg, beaten
- ½ teaspoon kosher salt
- Cooking spray

Directions:
1. Preheat the air fryer to 390ºF (199ºC).
2. Wrap the grated zucchini in a paper towel and squeeze out any excess liquid, then combine the zucchini, baked potato, shredded Cheddar cheese, egg, and kosher salt in a large bowl.
3. Spray a baking pan with cooking spray, then place individual tablespoons of the zucchini mixture in the pan and air fry for 10 minutes. Repeat this process with the remaining mixture.
4. Remove the tots and allow to cool on a wire rack for 5 minutes before serving.

Bacon Smokies With Tomato Sauce

Servings:10
Cooking Time: 10 Minutes
Ingredients:
- 12 oz. pork and beef smokies
- 3 oz. bacon, sliced
- 1 teaspoon keto tomato sauce
- 1 teaspoon Erythritol
- 1 teaspoon avocado oil
- ½ teaspoon cayenne pepper

Directions:
1. Use the cayenne pepper and tomato sauce to sprinkle the smokies, then repeat the step with the Erythritol and olive oil.
2. After that, wrap every smokie in the bacon and use the toothpick to secure each roll.
3. Arrange the bacon smokies in the air fryer and cook for 10 minutes at 400 degrees F/ 205 degrees C.
4. During cooking, to avoid over cooking, shake them gently.
5. When done, serve and enjoy.

Buttered Bacon

Servings: 5
Cooking Time: 10 Minutes
Ingredients:
- ½ cup butter
- 3 ounces bacon, chopped

Directions:
1. At 400 degrees F/ 205 degrees C, preheat your air fryer and put the bacon inside.
2. Cook it for 8 minutes. Stir the bacon every 2 minutes.
3. Meanwhile, soften the butter in the air fryer and put it in the butter mold.
4. Add cooked bacon and churn the butter. Refrigerate the butter for 30 minutes.
5. Serve.

Zucchini Fritters With Olives

Servings: 6
Cooking Time: 12 Minutes
Ingredients:
- Cooking spray
- ½ cup parsley, chopped
- 1 egg
- ½ cup almond flour
- Black pepper and salt to the taste
- 3 spring onions, chopped
- ½ cup Kalamata olives, pitted and minced
- 3 zucchinis, grated

Directions:
1. In a suitable bowl, mix all the recipe ingredients except the cooking spray, stir well and shape medium fritters out of this mixture.
2. Place the fritters in your air fryer basket, grease them with cooking spray and cook at almost 380 degrees F/ 195 degrees C for 6 minutes on each side.
3. Serve them as an appetizer.

Warm Spinach Dip With Pita Chips

Servings: 6
Cooking Time: 40 Minutes
Ingredients:
- Pita Chips:
- 4 pita breads
- 1 tablespoon olive oil
- ½ teaspoon paprika
- salt and freshly ground black pepper
- Spinach Dip:
- 8 ounces cream cheese, softened at room , Temperature: 1 cup ricotta cheese
- 1 cup grated Fontina cheese
- ½ teaspoon Italian seasoning
- ½ teaspoon garlic powder
- ¾ teaspoon salt
- freshly ground black pepper
- 16 ounces frozen chopped spinach, thawed and squeezed dry
- ¼ cup grated Parmesan cheese
- ½ tomato, finely diced
- ¼ teaspoon dried oregano

Directions:
1. Preheat the air fryer to 390°F.
2. Split the pita breads open so you have 2 circles. Cut each circle into 8 wedges. Place all the wedges into a large bowl and toss with the olive oil. Season with the paprika, salt and pepper and toss to coat evenly. Air-fry the pita triangles in two batches for 5 minutes each, shaking the basket once or twice while they cook so they brown and crisp evenly.
3. Combine the cream cheese, ricotta cheese, Fontina cheese, Italian seasoning, garlic powder, salt and pepper in a large bowl. Fold in the spinach and mix well.
4. Transfer the spinach-cheese mixture to a 7-inch ceramic baking dish or cake pan. Sprinkle the Parmesan cheese on top and wrap the dish with aluminum foil. Transfer the dish to the basket of the air fryer, lowering the dish into the basket using a sling made of aluminum foil (fold a piece of aluminum foil into a strip about 2-inches wide by 24-inches long). Fold the ends of the aluminum foil over the top of the dish before returning the basket to the air fryer. Air-fry for 30 minutes at 390°F. With 4 minutes left on the air fryer timer, remove the foil and let the cheese brown on top.
5. Sprinkle the diced tomato and oregano on the warm dip and serve immediately with the pita chips.

Air Fried Shrimp & Bacon

Servings: 4-6
Cooking Time: 10 Minutes
Ingredients:
- 16 ounces sliced bacon
- 20 ounces peeled shrimp, deveined

Directions:
1. Prepare your clean air fryer.
2. Preheat the air fryer for 4 to 5 minutes at 390 degrees F/ 200 degrees C.
3. Make the shrimps under the bacon regularly. Put them in the refrigerator and cool for 15 to 20 minutes.
4. After that, take out the shrimps and place them in the air-frying basket.
5. Let the shrimps be cooked for 6 minutes in the air fryer.
6. Serve and enjoy!

Crispy Prawns

Servings:4
Cooking Time: 8 Minutes
Ingredients:
- 1 egg
- ½ pound nacho chips, crushed
- 18 prawns, peeled and deveined

Directions:
1. In a shallow dish, crack the egg, and beat well.
2. Put the crushed nacho chips in another dish.
3. Now, dip the prawn into beaten egg and then, coat with the nacho chips.
4. Set the temperature of Air Fryer to 355°F.

5. Place the prawns in an Air Fryer basket in a single layer.
6. Air Fry for about 8 minutes.
7. Serve hot.

Spiced Roasted Pepitas

Servings:4
Cooking Time: 25 Minutes
Ingredients:
- 2 cups pumpkin seeds
- 1 tbsp butter, melted
- Salt and pepper to taste
- ½ tsp shallot powder
- ½ tsp smoked paprika
- ½ tsp dried parsley
- ½ tsp garlic powder
- ¼ tsp dried chives
- ¼ tsp dry mustard
- ¼ tsp celery seed

Directions:
1. Preheat air fryer to 325ºF. Combine the pumpkin seeds, butter, and salt in a bowl. Place the seed mixture in the frying basket and Roast for 13 minutes, turning once. Transfer to a medium serving bowl. Stir in shallot powder, paprika, parsley, garlic powder, chives, dry mustard, celery seed, and black pepper. Serve right away.

Easy-to-make Cheese Rounds

Servings:4
Cooking Time: 6 Minutes
Ingredients:
- 1 cup Cheddar cheese, shredded

Directions:
1. Preheat the air fryer to 400 degrees F/ 205 degrees C.
2. Prepare the air fryer basket by lining it with baking paper.
3. Sprinkle the cheese on the baking paper in the shape of small rounds.
4. Cook them for 6 minutes or until the cheese is melted and starts to be crispy.
5. Serve and enjoy!

Buffalo Cauliflower Wings

Servings:4
Cooking Time: 14 Minutes
Ingredients:
- 1 cauliflower head, cut into florets
- 1 tbsp butter, melted
- 1/2 cup buffalo sauce
- Pepper
- Salt

Directions:
1. Spray air fryer basket with cooking spray.
2. In a bowl, mix together buffalo sauce, butter, pepper, and salt.
3. Add cauliflower florets into the air fryer basket and cook at 400 °F for 7 minutes.

4. Transfer cauliflower florets into the buffalo sauce mixture and toss well.
5. Again, add cauliflower florets into the air fryer basket and cook for 7 minutes more at 400 °F.
6. Serve and enjoy.

Poutine

Servings: 2
Cooking Time: 25 Minutes
Ingredients:
- 2 russet potatoes, scrubbed and cut into ½-inch sticks
- 2 teaspoons vegetable oil
- 2 tablespoons butter
- ¼ onion, minced (about ¼ cup)
- 1 clove garlic, smashed
- ¼ teaspoon dried thyme
- 3 tablespoons flour
- 1 teaspoon tomato paste
- 1½ cups strong beef stock
- salt and lots of freshly ground black pepper
- a few dashes of Worcestershire sauce
- ⅔ cup chopped string cheese or cheese curds

Directions:
1. Bring a large saucepan of salted water to a boil on the stovetop while you peel and cut the potatoes. Blanch the potatoes in the boiling salted water for 4 minutes while you Preheat the air fryer to 400°F. Strain the potatoes and rinse them with cold water. Dry them well with a clean kitchen towel.
2. Toss the dried potato sticks gently with the oil and place them in the air fryer basket. Air-fry for 25 minutes, shaking the basket a few times while the fries cook to help them brown evenly.
3. While the fries are cooking, make the gravy. Melt the butter in a small saucepan over medium heat. Add the onion, garlic and thyme and cook for five minutes, until soft and just starting to brown. Stir in the flour and cook for another two minutes, stirring regularly. Finally, add the tomato paste and continue to cook for another minute or two. Whisk in the beef stock and bring the mixture to a boil to thicken. Season to taste with salt, lots of freshly ground black pepper and a few dashes of Worcestershire sauce. Keep the gravy warm.
4. As soon as the fries are done, season them with salt and transfer to a plate or basket. Top the fries with the cheese curds or string cheese, and pour the warm gravy over the top.

Hot Cauliflower Bites

Servings: 4
Cooking Time: 35 Minutes
Ingredients:
- 1 head cauliflower, cut into florets
- 1 cup all-purpose flour
- 1 tsp garlic powder
- 1/3 cup cayenne sauce

Directions:

1. Preheat air fryer to 370°F. Mix the flour, 1 cup of water, and garlic powder in a large bowl until a batter forms. Coat cauliflower in the batter, then transfer to a large bowl to drain excess. Place the cauliflower in the greased frying basket without stacking. Spray with cooking, then Bake for 6 minutes. Remove from the air fryer and transfer to a large bowl. Top with cayenne sauce. Return to the fryer and cook for 6 minutes or until crispy. Serve.

Mexican Muffins

Servings:4
Cooking Time: 15 Minutes
Ingredients:
- 1 cup ground beef
- 1 teaspoon taco seasonings
- 2 oz Mexican blend cheese, shredded
- 1 teaspoon keto tomato sauce
- Cooking spray

Directions:
1. Preheat the air fryer to 375°F. Meanwhile, in the mixing bowl mix up ground beef and taco seasonings. Spray the muffin molds with cooking spray. Then transfer the ground beef mixture in the muffin molds and top them with cheese and tomato sauce. Transfer the muffin molds in the preheated air fryer and cook them for 15 minutes.

Potato Chips With Sour Cream And Onion Dip

Servings: 2
Cooking Time: 20 Minutes
Ingredients:
- 2 large potatoes (Yukon Gold or russet)
- vegetable or olive oil in a spray bottle
- sea salt and freshly ground black pepper
- Sour Cream and Onion Dip:
- ½ cup sour cream
- 1 tablespoon olive oil
- 2 scallions, white part only minced
- ¼ teaspoon salt
- freshly ground black pepper
- a squeeze of lemon juice (about ¼ teaspoon)

Directions:
1. Wash the potatoes well, but leave the skins on. Slice them into ⅛-inch thin slices, using a mandolin or food processor. Rinse the potatoes under cold water until the water runs clear and then let them soak in a bowl of cold water for at least 10 minutes. Drain and dry the potato slices really well in a single layer on a clean kitchen towel.
2. Preheat the air fryer to 300°F. Spray the potato chips with the oil so that both sides are evenly coated, or rub the slices between your hands with some oil if you don't have a spray bottle.
3. Air-fry in two batches at 300°F for 20 minutes, shaking the basket a few times during the cooking process so the chips crisp and brown more evenly.

Season the finished chips with sea salt and freshly ground black pepper while they are still hot.
4. While the chips are air-frying, make the sour cream and onion dip by mixing together the sour cream, olive oil, scallions, salt, pepper and lemon juice. Serve the chips warm or at room temperature along with the dip.

Mustard Greens Chips With Curried Sauce

Servings: 4
Cooking Time: 20 Minutes
Ingredients:
- 1 cup plain yogurt
- 1 tbsp lemon juice
- 1 tbsp curry powder
- 1 bunch of mustard greens
- 2 tsp olive oil
- Sea salt to taste

Directions:
1. Preheat air fryer to 390°F. Using a sharp knife, remove and discard the ribs from the mustard greens. Slice the leaves into 2-3-inch pieces. Transfer them to a large bowl, then pour in olive oil and toss to coat. Air Fry for 5-6 minutes. Shake at least once. The chips should be crispy when finished. Sprinkle with a little bit of sea salt. Mix the yogurt, lemon juice, salt, and curry in a small bowl. Serve the greens with the sauce.

Crabby Fries

Servings: 2
Cooking Time: 30 Minutes
Ingredients:
- 2 to 3 large russet potatoes, peeled and cut into ½-inch sticks
- 2 tablespoons vegetable oil
- 2 tablespoons butter
- 2 tablespoons flour
- 1 to 1½ cups milk
- ½ cup grated white Cheddar cheese
- pinch of nutmeg
- ½ teaspoon salt
- freshly ground black pepper
- 1 tablespoon Old Bay® Seasoning

Directions:
1. Bring a large saucepan of salted water to a boil on the stovetop while you peel and cut the potatoes. Blanch the potatoes in the boiling salted water for 4 minutes while you Preheat the air fryer to 400°F. Strain the potatoes and rinse them with cold water. Dry them well with a clean kitchen towel.
2. Toss the dried potato sticks gently with the oil and place them in the air fryer basket. Air-fry for 25 minutes, shaking the basket a few times while the fries cook to help them brown evenly.
3. While the fries are cooking, melt the butter in a medium saucepan. Whisk in the flour and cook for one minute. Slowly add 1 cup of milk, whisking constantly. Bring the mixture to a simmer and continue to whisk

until it thickens. Remove the pan from the heat and stir in the Cheddar cheese. Add a pinch of nutmeg and season with salt and freshly ground black pepper. Transfer the warm cheese sauce to a serving dish. Thin with more milk if you want the sauce a little thinner.

4. As soon as the French fries have finished air-frying transfer them to a large bowl and season them with the Old Bay® Seasoning. Return the fries to the air fryer basket and air-fry for an additional 3 to 5 minutes. Serve immediately with the warm white Cheddar cheese sauce.

Cheesy Jalapeño Poppers

Servings:4
Cooking Time: 10 Minutes
Ingredients:
*   8 jalapeño peppers
*   ½ cup whipped cream cheese
*   ¼ cup shredded Cheddar cheese
Directions:
1. Preheat the air fryer to 360ºF (182ºC).
2. Use a paring knife to carefully cut off the jalapeño tops, then scoop out the ribs and seeds. Set aside.
3. In a medium bowl, combine the whipped cream cheese and shredded Cheddar cheese. Place the mixture in a sealable plastic bag, and using a pair of scissors, cut off one corner from the bag. Gently squeeze some cream cheese mixture into each pepper until almost full.
4. Place a piece of parchment paper on the bottom of the air fryer basket and place the poppers on top, distributing evenly. Air fry for 10 minutes.
5. Allow the poppers to cool for 5 to 10 minutes before serving.

Chicken Shawarma Bites

Servings: 6
Cooking Time: 22 Minutes
Ingredients:
*   1½ pounds Boneless skinless chicken thighs, trimmed of any fat and cut into 1-inch pieces
*   1½ tablespoons Olive oil
*   Up to 1½ tablespoons Minced garlic
*   ½ teaspoon Table salt
*   ¼ teaspoon Ground cardamom
*   ¼ teaspoon Ground cinnamon
*   ¼ teaspoon Ground cumin
*   ¼ teaspoon Mild paprika
*   Up to a ¼ teaspoon Grated nutmeg
*   ¼ teaspoon Ground black pepper
Directions:
1. Preheat the air fryer to 400°F.
2. Mix all the ingredients in a large bowl until the chicken is thoroughly and evenly coated in the oil and spices.
3. When the machine is at temperature, scrape the coated chicken pieces into the basket and spread them out into one layer as much as you can. Air-fry for 22 minutes, shaking the basket at least three times during

cooking to rearrange the pieces, until well browned and crisp.
4. Pour the chicken pieces onto a wire rack. Cool for 5 minutes before serving.

Crispy Okra Fries

Servings: 4
Cooking Time: 25 Minutes
Ingredients:
*   ½ lb trimmed okra, cut lengthways
*   ¼ tsp deggi mirch chili powder
*   3 tbsp buttermilk
*   2 tbsp chickpea flour
*   2 tbsp cornmeal
*   Salt and pepper to taste
Directions:
1. Preheat air fryer to 380°F. Set out 2 bowls. In one, add buttermilk. In the second, mix flour, cornmeal, chili powder, salt, and pepper. Dip the okra in buttermilk, then dredge in flour and cornmeal. Transfer to the frying basket and spray the okra with oil. Air Fry for 10 minutes, shaking once halfway through cooking until crispy. Let cool for a few minutes and serve warm.

Chicken Bites With Coconut

Servings: 4
Cooking Time: 20 Minutes
Ingredients:
*   2 teaspoons garlic powder
*   2 eggs
*   Salt and black pepper to the taste
*   ¾ cup coconut flakes
*   Cooking spray
*   1 pound chicken breasts, skinless, boneless, and cubed
Directions:
1. In a bowl, put the coconut in and mix the eggs with garlic powder, salt and pepper in a second one.
2. Dredge the chicken cubes in eggs and then in coconut.
3. Arrange all the prepared chicken cubes to the basket.
4. Grease with cooking spray and cook them at 370 degrees F/ 185 degrees C for 20 minutes.
5. When cooked, place the chicken bites on a platter and serve as an appetizer.

Crunchy Tortellini Bites

Servings: 5
Cooking Time: 10 Minutes
Ingredients:
*   10 ounces Cheese tortellini
*   ⅓ cup Yellow cornmeal
*   ⅓ cup Seasoned Italian-style dried bread crumbs
*   ⅓ cup Finely grated Parmesan cheese
*   1 Large egg
*   Olive oil spray
Directions:

1. Bring a large pot of water to a boil over high heat. Add the tortellini and cook for 3 minutes. Drain in a colander set in the sink, then spread out the tortellini on a large baking sheet and cool for 15 minutes.
2. Preheat the air fryer to 400°F.
3. Mix the cornmeal, bread crumbs, and cheese in a large zip-closed plastic bag.
4. Whisk the egg in a medium bowl until uniform. Add the tortellini and toss well to coat, even along the inside curve of the pasta. Use a slotted spoon or kitchen tongs to transfer 5 or 6 tortellini to the plastic bag, seal, and shake gently to coat thoroughly and evenly. Set the coated tortellini aside on a cutting board and continue coating the rest in the same way.
5. Generously coat the tortellini on all sides with the olive oil spray, then set them in one layer in the basket. Air-fry undisturbed for 10 minutes, gently tossing the basket and rearranging the tortellini at the 4- and 7-minute marks, until brown and crisp.
6. Pour the contents of the basket onto a wire rack. Cool for 5 minutes before serving.

Potato Pastries

Servings: 8
Cooking Time: 37 Minutes
Ingredients:
- 2 large potatoes, peeled
- 1 tablespoon olive oil
- ½ cup carrot, peeled and chopped
- ½ cup onion, chopped
- 2 garlic cloves, minced
- 1 tablespoon fresh ginger, minced
- ½ cup green peas, shelled
- Salt and ground black pepper, as needed
- 3 puff pastry sheets

Directions:
1. Boil water in a suitable pan, then put the potatoes and cook for about 15-20 minutes
2. Drain the potatoes well and then mash the potatoes.
3. Heat the oil over medium heat in a skillet, then add the carrot, onion, ginger, garlic and sauté for about 4-5 minutes.
4. Then drain all the fat from the skillet.
5. Stir in the mashed potatoes, peas, salt and black pepper. Continue to cook for about 1-2 minutes.
6. Remove the potato mixture from heat and set aside to cool completely.
7. After placing the puff pastry onto a smooth surface, cut each puff pastry sheet into four pieces and cut each piece into a round shape.
8. Add about 2 tablespoons of veggie filling over each pastry round.
9. Use your wet finger to moisten the edges.
10. To seal the filling, fold each pastry round in half.
11. Firmly press the edges with a fork.
12. Set the temperature setting to 390 degrees F/ 200 degrees C.

13. Arrange the pastries in the basket of your air fryer and air fry for about 5 minutes at 390 minutes.
14. Work in 2 batches.
15. Serve.

Roasted Chickpeas

Servings: 1
Cooking Time: 15 Minutes
Ingredients:
- 1 15-ounce can chickpeas, drained
- 2 teaspoons curry powder
- ¼ teaspoon salt
- 1 tablespoon olive oil

Directions:
1. Drain chickpeas thoroughly and spread in a single layer on paper towels. Cover with another paper towel and press gently to remove extra moisture. Don't press too hard or you'll crush the chickpeas.
2. Mix curry powder and salt together.
3. Place chickpeas in a medium bowl and sprinkle with seasonings. Stir well to coat.
4. Add olive oil and stir again to distribute oil.
5. Cook at 390°F for 15 minutes, stopping to shake basket about halfway through cooking time.
6. Cool completely and store in airtight container.

Ranch Kale Chips

Servings: 4
Cooking Time: 5 Minutes
Ingredients:
- 4 cups kale, stemmed
- 1 tablespoon nutritional yeast flakes
- 2 teaspoons ranch seasoning
- 2 tablespoons olive oil
- ¼ teaspoon salt

Directions:
1. Add all the recipe ingredients into the suitable mixing bowl and toss well.
2. Grease its air fryer basket with cooking spray.
3. Add kale in air fryer basket and cook for 4 to 5 minutes at 370 degrees F/ 185 degrees C. Shake halfway through.
4. Serve and enjoy.

Cauliflower "tater" Tots

Servings: 6
Cooking Time: 10 Minutes
Ingredients:
- 1 head of cauliflower
- 2 eggs
- ¼ cup all-purpose flour*
- ½ cup grated Parmesan cheese
- 1 teaspoon salt
- freshly ground black pepper
- vegetable or olive oil, in a spray bottle

Directions:
1. Grate the head of cauliflower with a box grater or finely chop it in a food processor. You should have about

3½ cups. Place the chopped cauliflower in the center of a clean kitchen towel and twist the towel tightly to squeeze all the water out of the cauliflower.

2. Place the squeezed cauliflower in a large bowl. Add the eggs, flour, Parmesan cheese, salt and freshly ground black pepper. Shape the cauliflower into small cylinders or "tater tot" shapes, rolling roughly one tablespoon of the mixture at a time. Place the tots on a cookie sheet lined with paper towel to absorb any residual moisture. Spray the cauliflower tots all over with oil.

3. Preheat the air fryer to 400°F.

4. Air-fry the tots at 400°F, one layer at a time for 10 minutes, turning them over for the last few minutes of the cooking process for even browning. Season with salt and black pepper. Serve hot with your favorite dipping sauce.

Bacon-wrapped Dates

Servings:6
Cooking Time: 10 To 14 Minutes
Ingredients:
*   12 dates, pitted
*   6 slices high-quality bacon, cut in half
*   Cooking spray

Directions:
1. Preheat the air fryer to 360ºF (182ºC).
2. Wrap each date with half a bacon slice and secure with a toothpick.
3. Spray the air fryer basket with cooking spray, then place 6 bacon-wrapped dates in the basket and bake for 5 to 7 minutes or until the bacon is crispy. Repeat this process with the remaining dates.
4. Remove the dates and allow to cool on a wire rack for 5 minutes before serving.

Buffalo Bites

Servings: 16
Cooking Time: 12 Minutes
Ingredients:
*   1 pound ground chicken
*   8 tablespoons buffalo wing sauce
*   2 ounces Gruyère cheese, cut into 16 cubes
*   1 tablespoon maple syrup

Directions:
1. Mix 4 tablespoons buffalo wing sauce into all the ground chicken.
2. Shape chicken into a log and divide into 16 equal portions.
3. With slightly damp hands, mold each chicken portion around a cube of cheese and shape into a firm ball. When you have shaped 8 meatballs, place them in air fryer basket.
4. Cook at 390°F for approximately 5minutes. Shake basket, reduce temperature to 360°F, and cook for 5 minutes longer.
5. While the first batch is cooking, shape remaining chicken and cheese into 8 more meatballs.
6. Repeat step 4 to cook second batch of meatballs.

7. In a medium bowl, mix the remaining 4 tablespoons of buffalo wing sauce with the maple syrup. Add all the cooked meatballs and toss to coat.
8. Place meatballs back into air fryer basket and cook at 390°F for 2 minutes to set the glaze. Skewer each with a toothpick and serve.

Grilled Cheese Sandwiches

Servings:2
Cooking Time:5 Minutes
Ingredients:
*   4 white bread slices
*   ½ cup melted butter, softened
*   ½ cup sharp cheddar cheese, grated
*   1 tablespoon mayonnaise

Directions:
1. Preheat the Air fryer to 355°F and grease an Air fryer basket.
2. Spread the mayonnaise and melted butter over one side of each bread slice.
3. Sprinkle the cheddar cheese over the buttered side of the 2 slices.
4. Cover with the remaining slices of bread and transfer into the Air fryer basket.
5. Cook for about 5 minutes and dish out to serve warm.

Salmon Bites With Coconut

Servings: 12
Cooking Time: 10 Minutes
Ingredients:
*   2 avocados, peeled, pitted and mashed
*   4 ounces smoked salmon, skinless, boneless and chopped
*   2 tablespoons coconut cream
*   1 teaspoon avocado oil
*   1 teaspoon dill, chopped
*   A pinch of salt and black pepper

Directions:
1. Mix the avocados, smoked salmon, coconut cream, avocado oil, the chopped dill, salt, and black pepper well in a clean bowl.
2. Shape medium balls out of this mix.
3. Place the balls in the basket of your air fryer.
4. Cook at 350 degrees F/ 175 degrees C for 10 minutes.
5. Serve as an appetizer.

Panko Crusted Chicken Tenders

Servings: 4
Cooking Time: 10 Minutes
Ingredients:
*   12 ounces chicken breasts, cut into tenders
*   1 egg white
*   ⅛ cup flour
*   ½ cup panko bread crumbs
*   Black pepper and salt, to taste

Directions:
1. At 350 degrees F/ 175 degrees C, preheat your air fryer. and grease its air fryer basket.

2. Season the chicken tenders with some black pepper and salt.
3. Coat the chicken tenders with flour, then dip in egg whites and then dredge in the panko bread crumbs.
4. Arrange the prepared tender in the air fryer basket and cook for about 10 minutes.
5. Dish out in a platter and serve warm.

Ham And Cheese Sliders

Servings:3
Cooking Time: 10 Minutes
Ingredients:
- 6 Hawaiian sweet rolls
- 12 slices thinly sliced Black Forest ham
- 6 slices sharp Cheddar cheese
- ⅓ cup salted butter, melted
- 1 ½ teaspoons minced garlic

Directions:
1. Preheat the air fryer to 350°F.
2. For each slider, slice horizontally through the center of a roll without fully separating the two halves. Place 2 slices ham and 2 slices cheese inside roll and close. Repeat with remaining rolls, ham, and cheese.
3. In a small bowl, mix butter and garlic and brush over all sides of rolls.
4. Place in the air fryer and cook 10 minutes until rolls are golden on top and cheese is melted. Serve warm.

Jalapeño & Mozzarella Stuffed Mushrooms

Servings: 4
Cooking Time: 30 Minutes
Ingredients:
- 16 button mushrooms
- 1/3 cup salsa
- 3 garlic cloves, minced
- 1 onion, finely chopped
- 1 jalapeño pepper, minced
- ⅛ tsp cayenne pepper
- 3 tbsp shredded mozzarella
- 2 tsp olive oil

Directions:
1. Preheat air fryer to 350°F. Cut the stem off the mushrooms, then slice them finely. Set the caps aside. Combine the salsa, garlic, onion, jalapeño, cayenne, and mozzarella cheese in a bowl, then add the stems. Fill the mushroom caps with the mixture, making sure to overfill so the mix is coming out of the top. Drizzle with olive oil. Place the caps in the air fryer and Bake for 8-12 minutes. The filling should be hot and the mushrooms soft. Serve warm.

Bacon-wrapped Goat Cheese Poppers

Servings: 10
Cooking Time: 10 Minutes
Ingredients:
- 10 large jalapeño peppers

- 8 ounces goat cheese
- 10 slices bacon

Directions:
1. Preheat the air fryer to 380°F.
2. Slice the jalapeños in half. Carefully remove the veins and seeds of the jalapeños with a spoon.
3. Fill each jalapeño half with 2 teaspoons goat cheese.
4. Cut the bacon in half lengthwise to make long strips. Wrap the jalapeños with bacon, trying to cover the entire length of the jalapeño.
5. Place the bacon-wrapped jalapeños into the air fryer basket. Cook the stuffed jalapeños for 10 minutes or until bacon is crispy.

Hearty Greens Chips With Curried Yogurt Sauce

Servings: 4
Cooking Time:5 To 6 Minutes
Ingredients:
- 1 cup low-fat Greek yogurt
- 1 tablespoon freshly squeezed lemon juice
- 1 tablespoon curry powder
- ½ bunch curly kale, stemmed, ribs removed and discarded, leaves cut into 2- to 3-inch pieces
- ½ bunch chard, stemmed, ribs removed and discarded, leaves cut into 2- to 3-inch pieces
- 1½ teaspoons olive oil

Directions:
1. In a small bowl, stir together the yogurt, lemon juice, and curry powder. Set aside.
2. In a large bowl, toss the kale and chard with the olive oil, working the oil into the leaves with your hands. This helps break up the fibers in the leaves so the chips are tender.
3. Air-fry the greens in batches for 5 to 6 minutes, until crisp, shaking the basket once during cooking. Serve with the yogurt sauce.

Oregano Cheese Rolls

Servings: 4
Cooking Time: 25 Minutes
Ingredients:
- ¼ cup grated cheddar cheese
- ¼ cup blue cheese, crumbled
- 8 flaky pastry dough sheets
- 1 tbsp vegetable oil
- 1 tsp dry oregano

Directions:
1. Preheat air fryer to 350°F. Mix the cheddar cheese, blue cheese, and oregano in a bowl. Divide the cheese mixture between pastry sheets and seal the seams with a touch of water. Brush the pastry rolls with vegetable oil. Arrange them on the greased frying basket and Bake for 15 minutes or until the pastry crust is golden brown and the cheese is melted. Serve hot.

Kale Chips With Tex-mex Dip

Servings: 8
Cooking Time:5 To 6 Minutes
Ingredients:

- 1 cup Greek yogurt
- 1 tablespoon chili powder
- ⅓ cup low-sodium salsa, well drained
- 1 bunch curly kale
- 1 teaspoon olive oil
- ¼ teaspoon coarse sea salt

Directions:

1. In a small bowl, combine the yogurt, chili powder, and drained salsa; refrigerate.
2. Rinse the kale thoroughly, and pat dry. Remove the stems and ribs from the kale, using a sharp knife. Cut or tear the leaves into 3-inch pieces.
3. Toss the kale with the olive oil in a large bowl.
4. Air-fry the kale in small batches until the leaves are crisp. This should take 5 to 6 minutes. Shake the basket once during cooking time.
5. As you remove the kale chips, sprinkle them with a bit of the sea salt.
6. When all of the kale chips are done, serve with the dip.

Turkey Spring Rolls

Servings: 4
Cooking Time: 20 Minutes
Ingredients:

- 1 lb turkey breast, grilled, cut into chunks
- 1 celery stalk, julienned
- 1 carrot, grated
- 1 tsp fresh ginger, minced
- 1 tsp sugar
- 1 tsp chicken stock powder
- 1 egg
- 1 tsp corn starch
- 6 spring roll wrappers

Directions:

1. Preheat the air fryer to 360°F. Mix the turkey, celery, carrot, ginger, sugar, and chicken stock powder in a large bowl. Combine thoroughly and set aside. In another bowl, beat the egg, and stir in the cornstarch. On a clean surface, spoon the turkey filling into each spring roll, roll up and seal the seams with the egg-cornstarch mixture. Put each roll in the greased frying basket and Air Fry for 7-8 minutes, flipping once until golden brown. Serve hot.

Savory Ranch Chicken Bites

Servings:6
Cooking Time: 15 Minutes
Ingredients:

- 2 boneless, skinless chicken breasts, cut into 1" cubes
- 1 tablespoon coconut oil
- ½ teaspoon salt
- ¼ teaspoon ground black pepper
- ⅓ cup ranch dressing
- ½ cup shredded Colby cheese
- 4 slices cooked sugar-free bacon, crumbled

Directions:

1. Drizzle chicken with coconut oil. Sprinkle with salt and pepper, and place into an ungreased 6" round nonstick baking dish.
2. Place dish into air fryer basket. Adjust the temperature to 370°F and set the timer for 10 minutes, stirring chicken halfway through cooking.
3. When timer beeps, drizzle ranch dressing over chicken and top with Colby and bacon. Adjust the temperature to 400°F and set the timer for 5 minutes. When done, chicken will be browned and have an internal temperature of at least 165°F. Serve warm.

Pepperoni Rolls

Servings:12
Cooking Time: 8 Minutes
Ingredients:

- 2½ cups shredded mozzarella cheese
- 2 ounces cream cheese, softened
- 1 cup blanched finely ground almond flour
- 48 slices pepperoni
- 2 teaspoons Italian seasoning

Directions:

1. In a large microwave-safe bowl, combine mozzarella, cream cheese, and flour. Microwave on high 90 seconds until cheese is melted.
2. Using a wooden spoon, mix melted mixture 2 minutes until a dough forms.
3. Once dough is cool enough to work with your hands, about 2 minutes, spread it out into a 12" × 4" rectangle on ungreased parchment paper. Line dough with pepperoni, divided into four even rows. Sprinkle Italian seasoning evenly over pepperoni.
4. Starting at the long end of the dough, roll up until a log is formed. Slice the log into twelve even pieces.
5. Place pizza rolls in an ungreased 6" nonstick baking dish. Adjust the temperature to 375°F and set the timer for 8 minutes. Rolls will be golden and firm when done. Allow cooked rolls to cool 10 minutes before serving.

Tomato & Basil Bruschetta

Servings: 4
Cooking Time: 15 Minutes
Ingredients:

- 3 red tomatoes, diced
- ½ ciabatta loaf
- 1 garlic clove, minced
- 1 fresh mozzarella ball, sliced
- 1 tbsp olive oil
- 10 fresh basil, chopped
- 1 tsp balsamic vinegar
- Pinch of salt

Directions:

1. Preheat air fryer to 370°F.Mix tomatoes, olive oil, salt, vinegar, basil, and garlic in a bowl until well combined. Cut the loaf into 6 slices, about 1-inch thick.

Spoon the tomato mixture over the bread and top with one mozzarella slice. Repeat for all bruschettas. Put the bruschettas in the foil-lined frying basket and Bake for 5 minutes until golden. Serve.

Lemon Tofu Cubes

Servings:2
Cooking Time: 7 Minutes
Ingredients:
- ½ teaspoon ground coriander
- 1 tablespoon avocado oil
- 1 teaspoon lemon juice
- ½ teaspoon chili flakes
- 6 oz tofu

Directions:
1. In the shallow bowl mix up ground coriander, avocado oil, lemon juice, and chili flakes. Chop the tofu into cubes and sprinkle with coriander mixture. Shake the tofu. After this, preheat the air fryer to 400°F and put the tofu cubes in it. Cook the tofu for 4 minutes. Then flip the tofu on another side and cook for 3 minutes more.

Cinnamon Pita Chips

Servings: 4
Cooking Time: 6 Minutes
Ingredients:
- 2 tablespoons sugar
- 2 teaspoons cinnamon
- 2 whole 6-inch pitas, whole grain or white
- oil for misting or cooking spray

Directions:
1. Mix sugar and cinnamon together.
2. Cut each pita in half and each half into 4 wedges. Break apart each wedge at the fold.
3. Mist one side of pita wedges with oil or cooking spray. Sprinkle them all with half of the cinnamon sugar.
4. Turn the wedges over, mist the other side with oil or cooking spray, and sprinkle with the remaining cinnamon sugar.
5. Place pita wedges in air fryer basket and cook at 330°F for 2minutes.
6. Shake basket and cook 2 more minutes. Shake again, and if needed cook 2 more minutes, until crisp. Watch carefully because at this point they will cook very quickly.

Brie-currant & Bacon Spread

Servings: 6
Cooking Time: 30 Minutes
Ingredients:
- 4 oz cream cheese, softened
- 3 tbsp mayonnaise
- 1 cup diced Brie cheese
- ½ tsp dried thyme
- 4 oz cooked bacon, crumbled
- 1/3 cup dried currants

Directions:
1. Preheat the air fryer to 350°F. Beat the cream cheese with the mayo until well blended. Stir in the Brie, thyme,

bacon, and currants and pour the dip mix in a 6-inch round pan. Put the pan in the fryer and Air Fry for 10-12 minutes, stirring once until the dip is melting and bubbling. Serve warm.

Crab Cake Bites

Servings: 6
Cooking Time: 20 Minutes
Ingredients:
- 8 oz lump crab meat
- 1 diced red bell pepper
- 1 spring onion, diced
- 1 garlic clove, minced
- 1 tbsp capers, minced
- 1 tbsp cream cheese
- 1 egg, beaten
- ¼ cup bread crumbs
- ¼ tsp salt
- 1 tbsp olive oil
- 1 lemon, cut into wedges

Directions:
1. Preheat air fryer to 360°F. Combine the crab, bell pepper, spring onion, garlic, and capers in a bowl until combined. Stir in the cream cheese and egg. Mix in the bread crumbs and salt. Divide this mixture into 6 equal portions and pat out into patties. Put the crab cakes into the frying basket in a single layer. Drizzle the tops of each patty with a bit of olive oil and Bake for 10 minutes. Serve with lemon wedges on the side. Enjoy!

Chipotle Sunflower Seeds

Servings:4
Cooking Time: 20 Minutes
Ingredients:
- 2 cups sunflower seeds
- 2 tsp olive oil
- ½ tsp chipotle powder
- 1 garlic clove, minced
- ¼ tsp salt
- 1 tsp granulated sugar

Directions:
1. Preheat air fryer to 325ºF. In a bowl, mix the sunflower seeds, olive oil, chipotle powder, garlic, salt, and sugar until well coated. Place the mixture in the frying basket and Air Fry for 10 minutes, shaking once. Serve chilled.

Beef Meatballs With Chives

Servings: 6
Cooking Time: 20 Minutes
Ingredients:
- 1 pound beef meat, ground
- 1 teaspoon onion powder
- 1 teaspoon garlic powder
- A pinch of salt and black pepper
- 2 tablespoons chives, chopped Cooking spray

Directions:

1. In addition to the cooking spray, mix the other ingredients well in a bowl and shape medium meatballs out of this mix.
2. Place the balls in the basket of your air fryer and oil them.
3. Cook for 20 minutes at 360 degrees F/ 180 degrees C.
4. When done, serve as an appetizer.

Beef Steak Sliders

Servings: 8
Cooking Time: 22 Minutes
Ingredients:
- 1 pound top sirloin steaks, about ¾-inch thick
- salt and pepper
- 2 large onions, thinly sliced
- 1 tablespoon extra-light olive oil
- 8 slider buns
- Horseradish Mayonnaise
- 1 cup light mayonnaise
- 4 teaspoons prepared horseradish
- 2 teaspoons Worcestershire sauce
- 1 teaspoon coarse brown mustard

Directions:
1. Place steak in air fryer basket and cook at 390°F for 6minutes. Turn and cook 6 more minutes for medium rare. If you prefer your steak medium, continue cooking for 3 minutes.
2. While the steak is cooking, prepare the Horseradish Mayonnaise by mixing all ingredients together.
3. When steak is cooked, remove from air fryer, sprinkle with salt and pepper to taste, and set aside to rest.
4. Toss the onion slices with the oil and place in air fryer basket. Cook at 390°F for 7 minutes, until onion rings are soft and browned.
5. Slice steak into very thin slices.
6. Spread slider buns with the horseradish mayo and pile on the meat and onions. Serve with remaining horseradish dressing for dipping.

Cayenne-spiced Roasted Pecans

Servings: 4
Cooking Time: 15 Minutes
Ingredients:
- ¼ tsp chili powder
- Salt and pepper to taste
- ⅛ tsp cayenne pepper
- 1 tsp cumin powder
- 1 tsp cinnamon powder
- ⅛ tsp garlic powder
- ⅛ tsp onion powder
- 1 cup raw pecans
- 2 tbsp butter, melted
- 1 tsp honey

Directions:
1. Preheat air fryer to 300°F. Whisk together black pepper, chili powder, salt, cayenne pepper, cumin, garlic powder, cinnamon, and onion powder. Set to the side. Toss pecans, butter, and honey in a medium bowl, then toss in the spice mixture. Pour pecans in the frying basket and toast for 3 minutes. Stir the pecans and toast for another 3 to 5 minutes until the nuts are crisp. Cool and serve.

Chapter 5: Vegetable Side Dishes Recipes

Crispy Breaded Bell Pepper Strips

Servings:4
Cooking Time: 7 Minutes
Ingredients:
- Olive oil
- ⅔ cup whole-wheat panko bread crumbs
- ½ teaspoon paprika
- ½ teaspoon garlic powder
- ½ teaspoon salt
- 1 egg, beaten
- 2 red, orange, or yellow bell peppers, cut into ½-inch-thick slices

Directions:
1. Spray a fryer basket lightly with olive oil.
2. In a medium shallow bowl, mix together the panko bread crumbs, paprika, garlic powder, and salt.
3. In a separate small shallow bowl, whisk the egg with 1½ teaspoons of water to make an egg wash.
4. Dip the bell pepper slices in the egg wash to coat, then dredge them in the panko bread crumbs until evenly coated.
5. Place the bell pepper slices in the fryer basket in a single layer. Lightly spray the bell pepper strips with oil. You may need to cook these in batches.
6. Air fry until lightly browned, 4 to 7 minutes.
7. Carefully remove from fryer basket to ensure the that the coating does not come off. Serve immediately.

Chipotle Chickpea Tacos

Servings: 4
Cooking Time: 10 Minutes
Ingredients:
- 2 cans chickpeas, drained and rinsed
- ¼ cup adobo sauce
- ¾ teaspoon salt
- ¼ teaspoon ground black pepper
- 8 medium flour tortillas, warmed
- 1 ½ cups chopped avocado
- ½ cup chopped fresh cilantro

Directions:
1. Preheat the air fryer to 375°F.
2. In a large bowl, toss chickpeas, adobo, salt, and pepper to fully coat.
3. Using a slotted spoon, place chickpeas in the air fryer basket and cook 10 minutes, shaking the basket twice during cooking, until tender.
4. To assemble, scoop ¼ cup chickpeas into a tortilla, then top with avocado and cilantro. Repeat with remaining tortillas and filling. Serve warm.

Butternut Medallions With Honey Butter And Sage

Servings: 2
Cooking Time: 15 Minutes
Ingredients:
- 1 butternut squash, peeled
- olive oil, in a spray bottle
- salt and freshly ground black pepper
- 2 tablespoons butter, softened
- 2 tablespoons honey
- pinch ground cinnamon
- pinch ground nutmeg
- chopped fresh sage

Directions:
1. Preheat the air fryer to 370°F.
2. Cut the neck of the butternut squash into disks about ½-inch thick. (Use the base of the butternut squash for another use.) Brush or spray the disks with oil and season with salt and freshly ground black pepper.
3. Transfer the butternut disks to the air fryer in one layer (or just ever so slightly overlapping). Air-fry at 370°F for 5 minutes.
4. While the butternut squash is cooking, combine the butter, honey, cinnamon and nutmeg in a small bowl. Brush this mixture on the butternut squash, flip the disks over and brush the other side as well. Continue to air-fry at 370°F for another 5 minutes. Flip the disks once more, brush with more of the honey butter and air-fry for another 5 minutes. The butternut should be browning nicely around the edges.
5. Remove the butternut squash from the air-fryer and repeat with additional batches if necessary. Transfer to a serving platter, sprinkle with the fresh sage and serve.

Patatas Bravas

Servings: 4
Cooking Time: 35 Minutes
Ingredients:
- 1 lb baby potatoes
- 1 onion, chopped
- 4 garlic cloves, minced
- 2 jalapeno peppers, minced
- 2 tsp olive oil
- 2 tsp Chile de Árbol, ground
- ½ tsp ground cumin
- ½ tsp dried oregano

Directions:
1. Preheat air fryer to 370°F. Put the baby potatoes, onion, garlic, and jalapeños in a bowl, stir, then pour in the olive oil and stir again to coat. Season with ground chile de Árbol, cumin, and oregano, and stir once again. Put the bowl in the air fryer and Air Fry for 22-28 minutes, shake the bowl once. Serve hot.

Cheese Spinach

Servings: 6
Cooking Time: 16 Minutes
Ingredients:
- 1-pound fresh spinach
- 6 ounces gouda cheese, shredded
- 8 ounces cream cheese
- 1 teaspoon garlic powder
- 1 tablespoon onion, minced
- Black pepper
- Salt

Directions:
1. At 370 degrees F/ 185 degrees C, preheat your air fryer.
2. Grease its air fryer basket with cooking spray and set aside.
3. Spray a large pan with cooking spray and heat over medium heat.
4. Add spinach to the same pan and cook until wilted.
5. Add cream cheese, garlic powder, and onion and stir until cheese is melted.
6. Remove pan from heat and add Gouda cheese and season with black pepper and salt.
7. Transfer spinach mixture to the prepared baking dish and place into the air fryer.
8. Cook for 16 minutes.
9. Serve and enjoy.

Sage & Thyme Potatoes

Servings: 4
Cooking Time: 30 Minutes
Ingredients:
- 2 red potatoes, peeled and cubed
- ¼ cup olive oil
- 1 tsp dried sage
- ½ tsp dried thyme
- ½ tsp salt
- 2 tbsp grated Parmesan

Directions:
1. Preheat air fryer to 360°F. Coat the red potatoes with olive oil, sage, thyme and salt in a bowl. Pour the potatoes into the air frying basket and Roast for 10 minutes. Stir the potatoes and sprinkle the Parmesan over the top. Continue roasting for 8 more minutes. Serve hot.

Steakhouse Baked Potatoes

Servings: 3
Cooking Time: 55 Minutes
Ingredients:
- 3 10-ounce russet potatoes
- 2 tablespoons Olive oil
- 1 teaspoon Table salt

Directions:
1. Preheat the air fryer to 375°F.
2. Poke holes all over each potato with a fork. Rub the skin of each potato with 2 teaspoons of the olive oil, then sprinkle ¼ teaspoon salt all over each potato.
3. When the machine is at temperature, set the potatoes in the basket in one layer with as much air space between them as possible. Air-fry for 50 minutes, turning once, or until soft to the touch but with crunchy skins. If the machine is at 360°F, you may need to add up to 5 minutes to the cooking time.
4. Use kitchen tongs to gently transfer the baked potatoes to a wire rack. Cool for 5 or 10 minutes before serving.

Yellow Squash

Servings: 4
Cooking Time: 10 Minutes

Ingredients:
- 1 large yellow squash
- 2 eggs
- ¼ cup buttermilk
- 1 cup panko breadcrumbs
- ¼ cup white cornmeal
- ½ teaspoon salt
- oil for misting or cooking spray

Directions:
1. Preheat air fryer to 390°F.
2. Cut the squash into ¼-inch slices.
3. In a shallow dish, beat together eggs and buttermilk.
4. In sealable plastic bag or container with lid, combine ¼ cup panko crumbs, white cornmeal, and salt. Shake to mix well.
5. Place the remaining ¾ cup panko crumbs in a separate shallow dish.
6. Dump all the squash slices into the egg/buttermilk mixture. Stir to coat.
7. Remove squash from buttermilk mixture with a slotted spoon, letting excess drip off, and transfer to the panko/cornmeal mixture. Close bag or container and shake well to coat.
8. Remove squash from crumb mixture, letting excess fall off. Return squash to egg/buttermilk mixture, stirring gently to coat. If you need more liquid to coat all the squash, add a little more buttermilk.
9. Remove each squash slice from egg wash and dip in a dish of ¾ cup panko crumbs.
10. Mist squash slices with oil or cooking spray and place in air fryer basket. Squash should be in a single layer, but it's okay if the slices crowd together and overlap a little.
11. Cook at 390°F for 5minutes. Shake basket to break up any that have stuck together. Mist again with oil or spray.
12. Cook 5minutes longer and check. If necessary, mist again with oil and cook an additional two minutes, until squash slices are golden brown and crisp.

Buttered Kale Mix

Servings: 2
Cooking Time: 12 Minutes
Ingredients:
- 3 tablespoons butter, melted
- 2 cups kale leaves
- Black pepper and salt to taste
- ½ cup yellow onion, chopped
- 2 teaspoons turmeric powder

Directions:
1. Place all the recipe ingredients in a pan that fits your air fryer and mix well.
2. Put the pan in the air fryer and cook at almost 250 degrees F/ 120 degrees C for 12 minutes.
3. Divide between plates and serve.

Turmeric Cauliflower Rice

Servings: 4

Cooking Time: 20 Minutes

Ingredients:

- 1 big cauliflower, florets separated and riced
- 1 and ½ cups chicken stock
- 1 tablespoon olive oil
- Salt and black pepper to the taste
- ½ teaspoon turmeric powder

Directions:

1. In a pan that fits the air fryer, combine the cauliflower with the oil and the rest of the ingredients, toss, introduce in the air fryer and cook at 360ºF for 20 minutes. Divide between plates and serve as a side dish.

Vegetable Medley

Servings: 4

Cooking Time: 15 Minutes

Ingredients:

- 1 head broccoli, chopped (about 2 cups)
- 2 medium carrots, cut into 1-inch pieces
- Salt
- Pepper
- Cooking oil
- 1 zucchini, cut into 1-inch chunks
- 1 medium red bell pepper, seeded and thinly sliced

Directions:

1. In a large bowl, combine the broccoli and carrots. Season with salt and pepper to taste. Spray with cooking oil.
2. Transfer the broccoli and carrots to the air fryer basket. Cook for 6 minutes.
3. Place the zucchini and red pepper in the bowl. Season with salt and pepper to taste. Spray with cooking oil.
4. Add the zucchini and red pepper to the broccoli and carrots in the air fryer basket. Cook for 6 minutes.
5. Cool before serving.

Roasted Brussels Sprouts With Bacon

Servings: 4

Cooking Time: 20 Minutes

Ingredients:

- 4 slices thick-cut bacon, chopped (about ¼ pound)
- 1 pound Brussels sprouts, halved (or quartered if large)
- freshly ground black pepper

Directions:

1. Preheat the air fryer to 380°F.
2. Air-fry the bacon for 5 minutes, shaking the basket once or twice during the cooking time.
3. Add the Brussels sprouts to the basket and drizzle a little bacon fat from the bottom of the air fryer drawer into the basket. Toss the sprouts to coat with the bacon fat. Air-fry for an additional 15 minutes, or until the Brussels sprouts are tender to a knifepoint.
4. Season with freshly ground black pepper.

Mini Spinach And Sweet Pepper Poppers

Servings:16

Cooking Time: 8 Minutes

Ingredients:

- 4 ounces cream cheese, softened
- 1 cup chopped fresh spinach leaves
- ½ teaspoon garlic powder
- 8 mini sweet bell peppers, tops removed, seeded, and halved lengthwise

Directions:

1. In a medium bowl, mix cream cheese, spinach, and garlic powder. Place 1 tablespoon mixture into each sweet pepper half and press down to smooth.
2. Place poppers into ungreased air fryer basket. Adjust the temperature to 400°F and set the timer for 8 minutes. Poppers will be done when cheese is browned on top and peppers are tender-crisp. Serve warm.

Garlic Sautéed Artichokes

Servings: 4

Cooking Time: 15 Minutes

Ingredients:

- 10 ounces artichoke hearts, halved
- 3 garlic cloves
- 2 cups baby spinach
- ¼ cup veggie stock
- 2 teaspoons lime juice
- Black pepper and salt to the taste

Directions:

1. In a suitable pan that fits your air fryer, mix all the recipe ingredients, toss, introduce in the fryer and cook at almost 370 degrees F/ 185 degrees C for almost 15 minutes.
2. Divide the mixture between plates and serve as a side dish.

Zucchini Boats With Ham And Cheese

Servings: 4

Cooking Time: 12 Minutes

Ingredients:

- 2 6-inch-long zucchini
- 2 ounces Thinly sliced deli ham, any rind removed, meat roughly chopped
- 4 Dry-packed sun-dried tomatoes, chopped
- ⅓ cup Purchased pesto
- ¼ cup Packaged mini croutons
- ¼ cup (about 1 ounce) Shredded semi-firm mozzarella cheese

Directions:

1. Preheat the air fryer to 375°F .
2. Split the zucchini in half lengthwise and use a flatware spoon or a serrated grapefruit spoon to scoop out the insides of the halves, leaving at least a ¼-inch border all around the zucchini half. (You can save the scooped out insides to add to soups and stews—or even freeze it for a much later use.)

3. Mix the ham, sun-dried tomatoes, pesto, croutons, and half the cheese in a bowl until well combined. Pack this mixture into the zucchini "shells." Top them with the remaining cheese.

4. Set them stuffing side up in the basket without touching (even a fraction of an inch between them is enough room). Air-fry undisturbed for 12 minutes, or until softened and browned, with the cheese melted on top.

5. Use a nonstick-safe spatula to transfer the zucchini boats stuffing side up on a wire rack. Cool for 5 or 10 minutes before serving.

Dijon Roast Cabbage

Servings:4
Cooking Time: 10 Minutes
Ingredients:
- 1 small head cabbage, cored and sliced into 1"-thick slices
- 2 tablespoons olive oil, divided
- ½ teaspoon salt
- 1 tablespoon Dijon mustard
- 1 teaspoon apple cider vinegar
- 1 teaspoon granular erythritol

Directions:
1. Drizzle each cabbage slice with 1 tablespoon olive oil, then sprinkle with salt. Place slices into ungreased air fryer basket, working in batches if needed. Adjust the temperature to 350°F and set the timer for 10 minutes. Cabbage will be tender and edges will begin to brown when done.

2. In a small bowl, whisk remaining olive oil with mustard, vinegar, and erythritol. Drizzle over cabbage in a large serving dish. Serve warm.

Lemony Green Bean Sautée

Servings: 6
Cooking Time: 15 Minutes
Ingredients:
- 1 tbsp cilantro, chopped
- 1 lb green beans, trimmed
- ½ red onion, sliced
- 2 tbsp olive oil
- Salt and pepper to taste
- 1 tbsp grapefruit juice
- 6 lemon wedges

Directions:
1. Preheat air fryer to 360°F. Coat the green beans, red onion, olive oil, salt, pepper, cilantro and grapefruit juice in a bowl. Pour the mixture into the air fryer and Bake for 5 minutes. Stir well and cook for 5 minutes more. Serve with lemon wedges. Enjoy!

Mozzarella Eggplant Gratin

Servings: 2
Cooking Time: 30 Minutes
Ingredients:
- ¼ cup chopped red pepper
- ¼ cup chopped green pepper
- ¼ cup chopped onion
- ⅓ cup chopped tomatoes
- 1 clove garlic, minced
- 1 tablespoon sliced pimiento-stuffed olives
- 1 teaspoon capers
- ¼ teaspoon dried basil
- ¼ teaspoon dried marjoram
- Salt and pepper to taste
- Cooking spray
- ¼ cup grated mozzarella cheese
- 1 tablespoon breadcrumbs

Directions:
1. Before cooking, heat your air fryer to 300 degrees F/ 150 degrees C.
2. Add the green pepper, red pepper, eggplant, onion, olives, garlic, capers, basil marjoram, salt, tomatoes, and pepper in a large bowl.
3. Using olive oil cooking spray, lightly grease a suitable baking dish.
4. Evenly line the eggplant mixture into the baking dish.
5. Then flatten the mixture.
6. Add the mozzarella cheese on the top and spread over with breadcrumbs.
7. Cook in your air fryer for 20 minutes.

Potatoes With Zucchinis

Servings:4
Cooking Time: 45 Minutes
Ingredients:
- 2 potatoes, peeled and cubed
- 4 carrots, cut into chunks
- 1 head broccoli, cut into florets
- 4 zucchinis, sliced thickly
- Salt and ground black pepper, to taste
- ¼ cup olive oil
- 1 tablespoon dry onion powder

Directions:
1. Preheat the air fryer to 400°F (204°C).
2. In a baking dish, add all the ingredients and combine well.
3. Bake for 45 minutes in the air fryer, ensuring the vegetables are soft and the sides have browned before serving.

Potato And Broccoli With Tofu Scramble

Servings:3
Cooking Time: 30 Minutes
Ingredients:
- 2½ cups chopped red potato
- 2 tablespoons olive oil, divided
- 1 block tofu, chopped finely
- 2 tablespoons tamari
- 1 teaspoon turmeric powder
- ½ teaspoon onion powder
- ½ teaspoon garlic powder
- ½ cup chopped onion

- 4 cups broccoli florets

Directions:
1. Preheat the air fryer to 400ºF (204ºC).
2. Toss together the potatoes and 1 tablespoon of the olive oil.
3. Air fry the potatoes in a baking dish for 15 minutes, shaking once during the cooking time to ensure they fry evenly.
4. Combine the tofu, the remaining 1 tablespoon of the olive oil, turmeric, onion powder, tamari, and garlic powder together, stirring in the onions, followed by the broccoli.
5. Top the potatoes with the tofu mixture and air fry for an additional 15 minutes. Serve warm.

Double Cheese-broccoli Tots

Servings:4
Cooking Time: 30 Minutes
Ingredients:
- 1/3 cup grated sharp cheddar cheese
- 1 cup riced broccoli
- 1 egg
- 1 oz herbed Boursin cheese
- 1 tbsp grated onion
- 1/3 cup bread crumbs
- ½ tsp salt
- ¼ tsp garlic powder

Directions:
1. Preheat air fryer to 375ºF. Mix the riced broccoli, egg, cheddar cheese, Boursin cheese, onion, bread crumbs, salt, and garlic powder in a bowl. Form into 12 rectangular mounds. Cut a piece of parchment paper to fit the bottom of the frying basket, place the tots, and Air Fry for 9 minutes. Let chill for 5 minutes before serving.

Cheddar Tomatillos With Lettuce

Servings: 4
Cooking Time: 4 Minutes
Ingredients:
- 2 tomatillos
- ¼ cup coconut flour
- 2 eggs, beaten
- ¼ teaspoon ground nutmeg
- ¼ teaspoon chili flakes
- 1 ounce Cheddar cheese, shredded
- 4 lettuce leaves

Directions:
1. Cut the tomatillos into slices.
2. Mix ground nutmeg, chili flakes, and beaten eggs in a bowl.
3. Brush the tomatillo slices with the egg mixture. Then coat with coconut flour.
4. Repeat above steps with the rest slices.
5. Before cooking, heat your air fryer to 400 degrees F/ 205 degrees C.
6. Place the coated tomatillo slices in the air fryer basket in a single layer.
7. Cook in your air fryer for 2 minutes from each side.

8. When cooked, add the lettuce leaves on the top of the tomatillos.
9. To serve, sprinkle with shredded cheese.

Mediterranean Air Fried Veggies

Servings:4
Cooking Time: 6 Minutes
Ingredients:
- 1 large zucchini, sliced
- 1 cup cherry tomatoes, halved
- 1 parsnip, sliced
- 1 green pepper, sliced
- 1 carrot, sliced
- 1 teaspoon mixed herbs
- 1 teaspoon mustard
- 1 teaspoon garlic purée
- 6 tablespoons olive oil
- Salt and ground black pepper, to taste

Directions:
1. Preheat the air fryer to 400ºF (204ºC).
2. Combine all the ingredients in a bowl, making sure to coat the vegetables well.
3. Transfer to the air fryer and air fry for 6 minutes, ensuring the vegetables are tender and browned.
4. Serve immediately.

Roasted Baby Carrots

Servings: 6
Cooking Time: 20 Minutes
Ingredients:
- 1 lb baby carrots
- 2 tbsp olive oil
- ¼ cup raw honey
- ¼ tsp ground cinnamon
- ¼ tsp ground nutmeg
- ¼ cup pecans, chopped

Directions:
1. Preheat air fryer to 360°F. Place the baby carrots with olive oil, honey, nutmeg and cinnamon in a bowl and toss to coat. Pour into the air fryer and Roast for 6 minutes. Shake the basket, sprinkle the pecans on top, and roast for 6 minutes more. Serve and enjoy!

Sweet And Spicy Tofu

Servings: 3
Cooking Time: 23 Minutes
Ingredients:
- For Tofu:
- 1 (14-ounce) block firm tofu, pressed and cubed
- ½ cup arrowroot flour
- ½ teaspoon sesame oil
- For Sauce:
- 4 tablespoons low-sodium soy sauce
- 1½ tablespoons rice vinegar
- 1½ tablespoons chili sauce
- 1 tablespoon agave nectar
- 2 large garlic cloves, minced
- 1 teaspoon fresh ginger, peeled and grated

- 2 scallions (green part), chopped

Directions:
1. Mix arrowroot flour, sesame oil, and tofu together in a bowl.
2. Before cooking, heat your air fryer to 360 degrees F/ 180 degrees C.
3. Gently grease an air fryer basket.
4. Place the tofu evenly on the air fryer basket in a layer.
5. Cook in your air fryer for 20 minutes. Halfway through cooking, shake the air fryer basket once.
6. To make the sauce, add soy sauce, rice vinegar, chili sauce, agave nectar, garlic, and ginger in a bowl. Beat the mixture to combine well.
7. When the tofu has cooked, remove from the air fryer and transfer to a skillet.
8. Add the sauce and heat the skillet over medium heat. Cook for about 3 minutes. Stir the meal from time to time.
9. Add the scallions to garnish and serve hot.

Thyme Sweet Potato Wedges

Servings: 4
Cooking Time: 30 Minutes
Ingredients:
- 2 peeled sweet potatoes, cubed
- ¼ cup grated Parmesan
- 1 tbsp olive oil
- Salt and pepper to taste
- ½ tsp dried thyme
- ½ tsp ground cumin

Directions:
1. Preheat air fryer to 330°F. Add sweet potato cubes to the frying basket, then drizzle with oil. Toss to gently coat. Season with salt, pepper, thyme, and cumin. Roast the potatoes for about 10 minutes. Shake the basket and continue roasting for another 10 minutes. Shake the basket again, this time adding Parmesan cheese. Shake and return to the air fryer. Roast until the potatoes are tender, 4-6 minutes. Serve and enjoy!

Blistered Green Beans

Servings: 3
Cooking Time: 10 Minutes
Ingredients:
- ¾ pound Green beans, trimmed on both ends
- 1½ tablespoons Olive oil
- 3 tablespoons Pine nuts
- 1½ tablespoons Balsamic vinegar
- 1½ teaspoons Minced garlic
- ¾ teaspoon Table salt
- ¾ teaspoon Ground black pepper

Directions:
1. Preheat the air fryer to 400°F.
2. Toss the green beans and oil in a large bowl until all the green beans are glistening.
3. When the machine is at temperature, pile the green beans into the basket. Air-fry for 10 minutes, tossing

often to rearrange the green beans in the basket, or until blistered and tender.
4. Dump the contents of the basket into a serving bowl. Add the pine nuts, vinegar, garlic, salt, and pepper. Toss well to coat and combine. Serve warm or at room temperature.

Grilled Lime Scallions

Servings:6
Cooking Time: 15 Minutes
Ingredients:
- 2 bunches of scallions
- 1 tbsp olive oil
- 2 tsp lime juice
- Salt and pepper to taste
- ¼ tsp Italian seasoning
- 2 tsp lime zest

Directions:
1. Preheat air fryer to 370ºF. Trim the scallions and cut them in half lengthwise. Place them in a bowl and add olive oil and lime juice. Toss to coat. Place the mix in the frying basket and Air Fry for 7 minutes, tossing once. Transfer to a serving dish and stir in salt, pepper, Italian seasoning and lime zest. Serve immediately.

Zucchinis And Arugula Salad

Servings: 4
Cooking Time: 20 Minutes
Ingredients:
- 1-pound zucchinis, sliced
- 1 tablespoon olive oil
- Salt and white pepper to the taste
- 4 ounces arugula leaves
- ¼ cup chives, chopped
- 1 cup walnuts, chopped

Directions:
1. Combine the chopped chives, zucchini, olive oil, salt, and white pepper in the air fryer basket. Toss well.
2. Cook in your air fryer at 360 degrees F/ 180 degrees C for 20 minutes.
3. Place the cooked veggies in a salad bowl and toss with the walnuts and arugula.
4. Serve as a side salad.

Mom´s Potatoes Au Gratin

Servings: 4
Cooking Time: 50 Minutes
Ingredients:
- 4 Yukon Gold potatoes, peeled
- 1cup shredded cheddar cheese
- 2 tbsp grated Parmesan cheese
- 2 garlic cloves, minced
- 1/3 cup heavy cream
- 1/3 cup whole milk
- ½ tsp dried marjoram
- Salt and pepper to taste

Directions:

1. Preheat the air fryer to 350°F. Spray a 7-inch round pan thoroughly with cooking oil. Cut the potatoes into ⅛-inch-thick slices and layer the potatoes inside the pan along with cheddar cheese and garlic. Mix the cream, milk, marjoram, salt, and pepper in a bowl, then slowly pour the mix over the potatoes. Sprinkle with Parmesan and put the pan in the fryer. Bake for 25-35 minutes or until the potatoes are tender, the sauce is bubbling, and the top is golden. Serve warm.

Air-fried Asparagus

Servings: 4
Cooking Time: 6 Minutes
Ingredients:
- 12 ounces asparagus, trimmed
- 2 eggs, beaten
- ¼ cup Swiss cheese, shredded
- ½ cup coconut flour
- 1 teaspoon olive oil
- 1 teaspoon salt

Directions:
1. In the mixing bowl, mix up Swiss cheese, coconut flour, and salt.
2. Then dip the asparagus in the beaten eggs and coat in the coconut flour mixture.
3. Repeat the same steps 1 more time and transfer the coated asparagus in the air fryer basket.
4. Cook the vegetables for 6 minutes at 395 degrees F/ 200 degrees C.
5. Serve.

Ricotta & Broccoli Cannelloni

Servings: 4
Cooking Time: 35 Minutes
Ingredients:
- 1 cup shredded mozzarella cheese
- ½ cup cooked broccoli, chopped
- ½ cup cooked spinach, chopped
- 4 cooked cannelloni shells
- 1 cup ricotta cheese
- ½ tsp dried marjoram
- 1 egg
- 1 cup passata
- 1 tbsp basil leaves

Directions:
1. Preheat air fryer to 360°F. Beat the egg in a bowl until fluffy. Add the ricotta, marjoram, half of the mozzarella, broccoli, and spinach and stir to combine. Cover the base of a baking dish with a layer of passata. Fill the cannelloni with the cheese mixture and place them on top of the sauce. Spoon the remaining passata over the tops and top with the rest of the mozzarella cheese. Put the dish in the frying basket and Bake for 25 minutes until the cheese is melted and golden. Top with basil.

Vegetable Fried Rice

Servings: 5
Cooking Time: 20 Minutes

Ingredients:
- 2 (9-ounce) packages precooked, microwavable rice
- 2 teaspoons sesame oil, divided
- 1 medium green bell pepper, seeded and chopped
- 1 cup peas
- 2 medium carrots, diced (about 1 cup)
- ½ cup chopped onion
- Salt
- Pepper
- 1 tablespoon soy sauce
- 2 medium eggs, scrambled

Directions:
1. Cook the rice in the microwave according to the package instructions and place in the refrigerator. The rice will need to cool for 15 to 20 minutes. You can also place it in the freezer until cold.
2. Add 1 teaspoon of sesame oil to the bottom of the barrel pan.
3. In a large bowl, combine the cold rice, green bell pepper, peas, carrots, and onion. Drizzle with the remaining 1 teaspoon of sesame oil and stir. Add salt and pepper to taste.
4. Transfer the mixture to the barrel pan. Cook for 15 minutes.
5. Remove the barrel pan. Drizzle the soy sauce all over and add the scrambled eggs. Stir to combine.
6. Serve warm.

Buttery Radish Wedges

Servings:2
Cooking Time: 20 Minutes
Ingredients:
- 2 tbsp butter, melted
- 2 cloves garlic, minced
- ¼ tsp salt
- 20 radishes, quartered
- 2 tbsp feta cheese crumbles
- 1 tbsp chopped parsley

Directions:
1. Preheat air fryer to 370°F. Mix the butter, garlic, and salt in a bowl. Stir in radishes. Place the radish wedges in the frying basket and Roast for 10 minutes, shaking once. Transfer to a large serving dish and stir in feta cheese. Scatter with parsley and serve.

Pungent Mushroom Pizza

Servings: 3-4
Cooking Time: 8 Minutes
Ingredients:
- 3 tablespoons olive oil
- 3 cleaned portabella mushroom caps, scooped
- 3 tablespoons tomato sauce
- 12 slices pepperoni
- 3 tablespoons mozzarella, shredded
- 1 pinch salt
- 1 pinch dried Italian seasonings

Directions:

1. On a flat kitchen surface, plug your air fryer and turn it on.
2. At 330 degrees F/ 165 degrees C, heat your air fryer for 4 to 5 minutes in advance.
3. Gently coat your air fryer basket with cooking oil or spray.
4. Toss the mushrooms with olive oil.
5. Season the inner side with Italian seasoning and salt.
6. Sprinkle the top with tomato sauce and cheese.
7. Arrange evenly the mushrooms onto the grease air fryer basket.
8. Cook in your air fryer at 330 degrees F/ 165 degrees C for 2 minutes.
9. When the cooking time is up, add the pepperoni slices and continue cooking for 4 to 5 minutes.
10. To serve, sprinkle the top with red pepper flakes and more cheese as you like.

Hawaiian Brown Rice

Servings: 4
Cooking Time: 12 Minutes
Ingredients:
- ¼ pound ground sausage
- 1 teaspoon butter
- ¼ cup minced onion
- ¼ cup minced bell pepper
- 2 cups cooked brown rice
- 1 8-ounce can crushed pineapple, drained

Directions:
1. Shape sausage into 3 or 4 thin patties. Cook at 390°F for 6 to 8minutes or until well done. Remove from air fryer, drain, and crumble. Set aside.
2. Place butter, onion, and bell pepper in baking pan. Cook at 390°F for 1 minute and stir. Cook 4 minutes longer or just until vegetables are tender.
3. Add sausage, rice, and pineapple to vegetables and stir together.
4. Cook at 390°F for 2 minutes, until heated through.

Acorn Squash Halves With Maple Butter Glaze

Servings: 2
Cooking Time: 33 Minutes
Ingredients:
- 1 medium Acorn squash
- Vegetable oil spray
- ¼ teaspoon Table salt
- 1½ tablespoons Butter, melted
- 1½ tablespoons Maple syrup

Directions:
1. Preheat the air fryer to 325°F.
2. Cut a squash in half through the stem end. Use a flatware spoon to scrape out and discard the seeds and membranes in each half. Use a paring knife to make a crisscross pattern of cuts about ½ inch apart and ¼ inch deep across the "meat" of the squash. If working with a second squash, repeat this step for that one.

3. Generously coat the cut side of the squash halves with vegetable oil spray. Sprinkle the halves with the salt. Set them in the basket cut side up with at least ¼ inch between them. Air-fry undisturbed for 30 minutes.
4. Increase the machine's temperature to 400°F. Mix the melted butter and syrup in a small bowl until uniform. Brush this mixture over the cut sides of the squash(es), letting it pool in the center. Air-fry undisturbed for 3 minutes, or until the glaze is bubbling.
5. Use a nonstick-safe spatula and kitchen tongs to transfer the squash halves cut side up to a wire rack. Cool for 5 to 10 minutes before serving.

Air Fried Brussels Sprouts

Servings: 4
Cooking Time: 20 Minutes
Ingredients:
- 1 pound Brussels sprouts, trimmed and halved
- Black pepper and salt to the taste
- 2 tablespoons ghee, melted
- ½ cup coconut cream
- 2 tablespoons. garlic, minced
- 1 tablespoon chives, chopped

Directions:
1. In your air fryer, mix the sprouts with the rest of the ingredients except the chives, toss well, introduce in the preheated air fryer and cook them at 370 degrees F/ 185 degrees C for 20 minutes.
2. Divide the Brussels sprouts between plates, sprinkle the chives on top and serve as a side dish.

Roasted Broccoli And Sesame Seeds

Servings: 2
Cooking Time: 10 Minutes
Ingredients:
- 1 pound broccoli florets
- 2 tablespoons sesame oil
- ½ teaspoon shallot powder
- ½ teaspoon porcini powder
- 1 teaspoon garlic powder
- Salt and black pepper, to taste
- ½ teaspoon cumin powder
- ¼ teaspoon paprika
- 2 tablespoons sesame seeds

Directions:
1. At 400 degrees F/ 205 degrees C, preheat your air fryer.
2. Blanch the broccoli florets in boiling water until al dente, about 3 to 4 minutes.
3. Drain well and transfer to the lightly greased air fryer basket.
4. Add the sesame oil, shallot powder, porcini powder, garlic powder, salt, black pepper, cumin powder, paprika, and sesame seeds.
5. Cook for almost 6 minutes, tossing halfway through the cooking time.
6. Serve

Balsamic Tomatoes With Garlic

Servings: 4
Cooking Time: 15 Minutes
Ingredients:
- 1 tablespoon olive oil
- 1 pound cherry tomatoes, halved
- 1 tablespoon dill, chopped
- 6 garlic cloves, minced
- 1 tablespoon balsamic vinegar
- Black pepper and salt to the taste

Directions:
1. In a pan that fits the air fryer, combine all the recipe ingredients, toss gently.
2. Put the pan in your preheated air fryer and air fryer at almost 380 degrees F/ 195 degrees C for almost 15 minutes.
3. Divide between plates and serve.

Hot Okra Wedges

Servings: 2
Cooking Time: 35 Minutes
Ingredients:
- 1 cup okra, sliced
- 1 cup breadcrumbs
- 2 eggs, beaten
- A pinch of black pepper
- 1 tsp crushed red peppers
- 2 tsp hot Tabasco sauce

Directions:
1. Preheat air fryer to 350°F. Place the eggs and Tabasco sauce in a bowl and stir thoroughly; set aside. In a separate mixing bowl, combine the breadcrumbs, crushed red peppers, and pepper. Dip the okra into the beaten eggs, then coat in the crumb mixture. Lay the okra pieces on the greased frying basket. Air Fry for 14-16 minutes, shaking the basket several times during cooking. When ready, the okra will be crispy and golden brown. Serve.

Fried Green Tomatoes

Servings: 4
Cooking Time:6 To 8 Minutes
Ingredients:
- 4 medium green tomatoes
- ⅓ cup all purpose flour
- 2 egg whites
- ¼ cup almond milk
- 1 cup ground almonds
- ½ cup panko bread crumbs
- 2 teaspoons olive oil
- 1 teaspoon paprika
- 1 clove garlic, minced

Directions:
1. Rinse the tomatoes and pat dry. Cut the tomatoes into ½-inch slices, discarding the thinner ends.
2. Put the flour on a plate. In a shallow bowl, beat the egg whites with the almond milk until frothy. And on another plate, combine the almonds, bread crumbs, olive oil, paprika, and garlic and mix well.
3. Dip the tomato slices into the flour, then into the egg white mixture, then into the almond mixture to coat.
4. Place four of the coated tomato slices in the air fryer basket. Air fry for 6 to 8 minutes or until the tomato coating is crisp and golden brown. Repeat with remaining tomato slices and serve immediately.

Roasted Eggplant Slices

Servings:1
Cooking Time: 15 Minutes
Ingredients:
- 1 large eggplant, sliced
- 2 tablespoons olive oil
- ¼ teaspoon salt
- ½ teaspoon garlic powder

Directions:
1. Preheat the air fryer to 390°F (199°C).
2. Apply the olive oil to the slices with a brush, coating both sides. Season each side with sprinklings of salt and garlic powder.
3. Put the slices in the air fryer and roast for 15 minutes.
4. Serve immediately.

Cinnamon Roasted Pumpkin

Servings: 2
Cooking Time: 25 Minutes
Ingredients:
- 1 lb pumpkin, halved crosswise and seeded
- 1 tsp coconut oil
- 1 tsp sugar
- ½ tsp ground nutmeg
- 1 tsp ground cinnamon

Directions:
1. Prepare the pumpkin by rubbing coconut oil on the cut sides. In a small bowl, combine sugar, nutmeg and cinnamon. Sprinkle over the pumpkin. Preheat air fryer to 325°F. Put the pumpkin in the greased frying basket, cut sides up. Bake until the squash is soft in the center, 15 minutes. Test with a knife to ensure softness. Serve.

Air Fried Potatoes With Olives

Servings:1
Cooking Time: 40 Minutes
Ingredients:
- 1 medium russet potato, scrubbed and peeled
- 1 teaspoon olive oil
- ¼ teaspoon onion powder
- ⅛ teaspoon salt
- Dollop of butter
- Dollop of cream cheese
- 1 tablespoon Kalamata olives
- 1 tablespoon chopped chives

Directions:
1. Preheat the air fryer to 400°F (204°C).
2. In a bowl, coat the potatoes with the onion powder, salt, olive oil, and butter.

3. Transfer to the air fryer and air fry for 40 minutes, turning the potatoes over at the halfway point.

4. Take care when removing the potatoes from the air fryer and serve with the cream cheese, Kalamata olives and chives on top.

Sweet Potato Puffs

Servings: 18
Cooking Time: 35 Minutes
Ingredients:
- 3 8- to 10-ounce sweet potatoes
- 1 cup Seasoned Italian-style dried bread crumbs
- 3 tablespoons All-purpose flour
- 3 tablespoons Instant mashed potato flakes
- ¾ teaspoon Onion powder
- ¾ teaspoon Table salt
- Olive oil spray

Directions:
1. Preheat the air fryer to 350°F .
2. Prick the sweet potatoes in four or five different places with the tines of a flatware fork.
3. When the machine is at temperature, set the sweet potatoes in the basket with as much air space between them as possible. Air-fry undisturbed for 20 minutes.
4. Use kitchen tongs to transfer the sweet potatoes to a wire rack. Cool for 10 to 15 minutes. Meanwhile, increase the machine's temperature to 400°F. Spread the bread crumbs on a dinner plate.
5. Peel the sweet potatoes. Shred them through the large holes of a box grater into a large bowl. Stir in the flour, potato flakes, onion powder, and salt until well combined.
6. Scoop up 2 tablespoons of the sweet potato mixture. Form it into a small puff, a cylinder about like a Tater Tot. Set this cylinder in the bread crumbs. Gently roll it around to coat on all sides, even the ends. Set aside on a cutting board and continue making more puffs: 11 more for a small batch, 17 more for a medium batch, or 23 more for a large batch.
7. Generously coat the puffs with olive oil spray on all sides. Set the puffs in the basket with as much air space between them as possible. They should not be touching, but even a fraction of an inch will work well. Air-fry undisturbed for 15 minutes, or until lightly browned and crunchy.
8. Gently turn the contents of the basket out onto a wire rack. Cool the puffs for a couple of minutes before serving.

Spicy Bean Stuffed Potatoes

Servings: 4
Cooking Time: 60 Minutes
Ingredients:
- 1 lb russet potatoes, scrubbed and perforated with a fork
- 1 can diced green chilies, including juice
- 1/3 cup grated Mexican cheese blend
- 1 green bell pepper, diced
- 1 yellow bell pepper, diced
- ¼ cup torn iceberg lettuce
- 2 tsp olive oil
- 2 tbsp sour cream
- ½ tsp chili powder
- 2-3 jalapeños, sliced
- 1 red bell pepper, chopped
- Salt and pepper to taste
- 1/3 cup canned black beans
- 4 grape tomatoes, sliced
- ¼ cup chopped parsley

Directions:
1. Preheat air fryer at 400°F. Brush olive oil over potatoes. Place them in the frying basket and Bake for 45 minutes, turning at 30 minutes mark. Let cool on a cutting board for 10 minutes until cool enough to handle. Slice each potato lengthwise and scoop out all but a ¼" layer of potato to form 4 boats.
2. Mash potato flesh, sour cream, green chilies, cheese, chili powder, jalapeños, green, yellow, and red peppers, salt, and pepper in a bowl until smooth. Fold in black beans. Divide between potato skin boats. Place potato boats in the frying basket and Bake for 2 minutes. Remove them to a serving plate. Top each boat with lettuce, tomatoes, and parsley. Sprinkle tops with salt and serve.

Mashed Potato Tots

Servings: 18
Cooking Time: 10 Minutes
Ingredients:
- 1 medium potato or 1 cup cooked mashed potatoes
- 1 tablespoon real bacon bits
- 2 tablespoons chopped green onions, tops only
- ¼ teaspoon onion powder
- 1 teaspoon dried chopped chives
- salt
- 2 tablespoons flour
- 1 egg white, beaten
- ½ cup panko breadcrumbs
- oil for misting or cooking spray

Directions:
1. If using cooked mashed potatoes, jump to step 4.
2. Peel potato and cut into ½-inch cubes. (Small pieces cook more quickly.) Place in saucepan, add water to cover, and heat to boil. Lower heat slightly and continue cooking just until tender, about 10minutes.
3. Drain potatoes and place in ice cold water. Allow to cool for a minute or two, then drain well and mash.
4. Preheat air fryer to 390°F.
5. In a large bowl, mix together the potatoes, bacon bits, onions, onion powder, chives, salt to taste, and flour. Add egg white and stir well.
6. Place panko crumbs on a sheet of wax paper.
7. For each tot, use about 2 teaspoons of potato mixture. To shape, drop the measure of potato mixture onto panko crumbs and push crumbs up and around potatoes to coat edges. Then turn tot over to coat other side with crumbs.

8. Mist tots with oil or cooking spray and place in air fryer basket, crowded but not stacked.
9. Cook at 390°F for 10 minutes, until browned and crispy.
10. Repeat steps 8 and 9 to cook remaining tots.

Yeast Rolls

Servings:16
Cooking Time: 1 Hour 10 Minutes
Ingredients:
- 4 tablespoons salted butter
- ¼ cup granulated sugar
- 1 cup hot water
- 1 tablespoon quick-rise yeast
- 1 large egg
- 1 teaspoon salt
- 2 ½ cups all-purpose flour, divided
- Cooking spray

Directions:
1. In a microwave-safe bowl, microwave butter 30 seconds until melted. Pour 2 tablespoons of butter into a large bowl. Add sugar, hot water, and yeast. Mix until yeast is dissolved.
2. Using a rubber spatula, mix in egg, salt, and 2 ¼ cups flour. Dough will be very sticky.
3. Cover bowl with plastic wrap and let rise in a warm place 1 hour.
4. Sprinkle remaining ¼ cup flour on dough and turn onto a lightly floured surface. Knead 2 minutes, then cut into sixteen even pieces.
5. Preheat the air fryer to 350°F. Spray a 6" round cake pan with cooking spray.
6. Sprinkle each roll with flour and arrange in pan. Brush with remaining melted butter. Place pan in the air fryer basket and cook 10 minutes until fluffy and golden on top. Serve warm.

Roasted Broccoli

Servings:4
Cooking Time: 8 Minutes
Ingredients:
- 12 ounces broccoli florets
- 2 tablespoons olive oil
- ½ teaspoon salt
- ¼ teaspoon ground black pepper

Directions:
1. Preheat the air fryer to 360°F.
2. In a medium bowl, place broccoli and drizzle with oil. Sprinkle with salt and pepper.
3. Place in the air fryer basket and cook 8 minutes, shaking the basket twice during cooking, until the edges are brown and the center is tender. Serve warm.

Chapter 6: Vegetarians Recipes

Crispy Apple Fries With Caramel Sauce

Servings: 4
Cooking Time: 15 Minutes
Ingredients:
- 4 medium apples, cored
- ¼ tsp cinnamon
- ¼ tsp nutmeg
- 1 cup caramel sauce

Directions:
1. Preheat air fryer to 350°F. Slice the apples to a 1/3-inch thickness for a crunchy chip. Place in a large bowl and sprinkle with cinnamon and nutmeg. Place the slices in the air fryer basket. Bake for 6 minutes. Shake the basket, then cook for another 4 minutes or until crunchy. Serve drizzled with caramel sauce and enjoy!

Buttered Broccoli

Servings:4
Cooking Time:7 Minutes
Ingredients:
- 4 cups fresh broccoli florets
- 2 tablespoons butter, melted
- ¼ cup water
- Salt and black pepper, to taste

Directions:
1. Preheat the Air fryer to 400°F and grease an Air fryer basket.
2. Mix broccoli, butter, salt, and black pepper in a bowl and toss to coat well.
3. Place water at the bottom of Air fryer pan and arrange the broccoli florets into the Air fryer basket.
4. Cook for about 7 minutes and dish out in a bowl to serve hot.

Balsamic Caprese Hasselback

Servings:4
Cooking Time: 15 Minutes
Ingredients:
- 4 tomatoes
- 12 fresh basil leaves
- 1 ball fresh mozzarella
- Salt and pepper to taste
- 1 tbsp olive oil
- 2 tsp balsamic vinegar
- 1 tbsp basil, torn

Directions:
1. Preheat air fryer to 325°F. Remove the bottoms from the tomatoes to create a flat surface. Make 4 even slices on each tomato, 3/4 of the way down. Slice the mozzarella and the cut into 12 pieces. Stuff 1 basil leaf and a piece of mozzarella into each slice. Sprinkle with salt and pepper. Place the stuffed tomatoes in the frying basket and Air Fry for 3 minutes. Transfer to a large serving plate. Drizzle with olive oil and balsamic vinegar and scatter the basil over. Serve and enjoy!

Cinnamon Sugar Tortilla Chips

Servings: 4
Cooking Time: 20 Minutes
Ingredients:
- 4 flour tortillas
- 1/4 cup vegan margarine, melted
- 1 ½ tablespoons ground cinnamon
- 1/4 cup caster sugar

Directions:
1. Slice each tortilla into eight slices. Brush the tortilla pieces with the melted margarine.
2. In a mixing bowl, thoroughly combine the cinnamon and sugar. Toss the cinnamon mixture with the tortillas.
3. Transfer to the cooking basket and cook at 360°F for 8 minutes or until lightly golden. Work in batches.
4. They will crisp up as they cool. Serve and enjoy!

Curried Eggplant

Servings:2
Cooking Time:10 Minutes
Ingredients:
- 1 large eggplant, cut into ½-inch thick slices
- 1 garlic clove, minced
- ½ fresh red chili, chopped
- 1 tablespoon vegetable oil
- ¼ teaspoon curry powder
- Salt, to taste

Directions:
1. Preheat the Air fryer to 300°F and grease an Air fryer basket.
2. Mix all the ingredients in a bowl and toss to coat well.
3. Arrange the eggplant slices in the Air fryer basket and cook for about 10 minutes, tossing once in between.
4. Dish out onto serving plates and serve hot.

Golden Fried Tofu

Servings: 4
Cooking Time: 20 Minutes
Ingredients:
- ¼ cup flour
- ¼ cup cornstarch
- 1 tsp garlic powder
- ¼ tsp onion powder
- Salt and pepper to taste
- 1 firm tofu, cubed
- 2 tbsp cilantro, chopped

Directions:
1. Preheat air fryer to 390°F. Combine the flour, cornstarch, salt, garlic, onion powder, and black pepper in a bowl. Stir well. Place the tofu cubes in the flour mix. Toss to coat. Spray the tofu with oil and place them in a single layer in the greased frying basket. Air Fry for 14-16 minutes, flipping the pieces once until golden and crunchy. Top with freshly chopped cilantro and serve immediately.

Zucchini Fries

Servings: 4 Servings
Cooking Time: 15 Minutes
Ingredients:
- 2 medium zucchini
- ½ cup of grated Parmesan cheese
- ½ cup of almond flour or panko bread crumbs
- 1 large egg
- 1 teaspoon of Italian seasoning
- ½ teaspoon of garlic powder
- Pinch of black pepper and salt, to taste

Directions:
1. Preheat your air fryer to 400°F. Spray some oil inside the air fryer basket.
2. Cut zucchini into ½-inch thick and 3–4 inches long.
3. Add almond flour (or bread crumbs), spices, Parmesan, salt, and pepper in a shallow bowl. Stir it until combined. Whisk the egg in a separate bowl.
4. Dip zucchini sticks in the egg mixture, then coat with the flour mixture. Transfer them in the preheated air fryer basket in a single layer and spray tops with olive oil. Cook at 400°F for 10 minutes, shaking halfway, until crispy. Repeat the last step with the remaining part of zucchinis.
5. Serve with the preferred sauce and enjoy your Zucchini Fries!

Twice-baked Broccoli-cheddar Potatoes

Servings:4
Cooking Time: 35 Minutes
Ingredients:
- 4 large russet potatoes
- 2 tablespoons plus 2 teaspoons ranch dressing
- 1 teaspoon salt
- ½ teaspoon ground black pepper
- ¼ cup chopped cooked broccoli florets
- 1 cup shredded sharp Cheddar cheese

Directions:
1. Preheat the air fryer to 400°F.
2. Using a fork, poke several holes in potatoes. Place in the air fryer basket and cook 30 minutes until fork-tender.
3. Once potatoes are cool enough to handle, slice lengthwise and scoop out the cooked potato into a large bowl, being careful to maintain the structural integrity of potato skins. Add ranch dressing, salt, pepper, broccoli, and Cheddar to potato flesh and stir until well combined.
4. Scoop potato mixture back into potato skins and return to the air fryer basket. Cook an additional 5 minutes until cheese is melted. Serve warm.

Green Bean Sautée

Servings: 4
Cooking Time: 25 Minutes
Ingredients:
- 1 ½ lb green beans, trimmed
- 1 tbsp olive oil
- ½ tsp garlic powder
- Salt and pepper to taste
- 4 garlic cloves, thinly sliced
- 1 tbsp fresh basil, chopped

Directions:
1. Preheat the air fryer to 375°F. Toss the beans with the olive oil, garlic powder, salt, and pepper in a bowl, then add to the frying basket. Air Fry for 6 minutes, shaking the basket halfway through the cooking time. Add garlic to the air fryer and cook for 3-6 minutes or until the green beans are tender and the garlic slices start to brown. Sprinkle with basil and serve warm.

Chicano Rice Bowls

Servings: 4
Cooking Time: 10 Minutes
Ingredients:
- 1 cup sour cream
- 2 tbsp milk
- 1 tsp ground cumin
- 1 tsp chili powder
- 1/8 tsp cayenne pepper
- 1 tbsp tomato paste
- 1 white onion, chopped
- 1 clove garlic, minced
- ½ tsp ground turmeric
- ½ tsp salt
- 1 cup canned black beans
- 1 cup canned corn kernels
- 1 tsp olive oil
- 4 cups cooked brown rice
- 3 tomatoes, diced
- 1 avocado, diced

Directions:
1. Whisk the sour cream, milk, cumin, ground turmeric, chili powder, cayenne pepper, and salt in a bowl. Let chill covered in the fridge until ready to use.
2. Preheat air fryer at 350°F. Combine beans, white onion, tomato paste, garlic, corn, and olive oil in a bowl. Transfer it into the frying basket and Air Fry for 5 minutes. Divide cooked rice into 4 serving bowls. Top each with bean mixture, tomatoes, and avocado and drizzle with sour cream mixture over. Serve immediately.

Broccoli & Parmesan Dish

Servings:4
Cooking Time: 25 Minutes
Ingredients:
- 1 tbsp olive oil
- 1 lemon, Juiced
- Salt and pepper to taste
- 1-ounce Parmesan cheese, grated

Directions:
1. In a bowl, mix all ingredients. Add the mixture to your air fryer and cook for 20 minutes at 360°F. Serve.

Sweet & Spicy Vegetable Stir-fry

Servings: 2

Cooking Time: 45 Minutes

Ingredients:

- ½ pineapple, cut into bite-size chunks
- ¼ cup Tabasco sauce
- ¼ cup lime juice
- 2 tsp allspice
- 5 oz cauliflower florets
- 1 carrot, thinly sliced
- 1 cup frozen peas, thawed
- 2 scallions, chopped

Directions:

1. Preheat air fryer to 400°F. Whisk Tabasco sauce, lime juice, and allspice in a bowl. Then toss in cauliflower, pineapple, and carrots until coated. Strain the remaining sauce; reserve it. Air Fry the veggies for 12 minutes, shake, and Air Fry for 10-12 more minutes until cooked. Once the veggies are ready, remove to a bowl. Combine peas, scallions, and reserved sauce until coated. Transfer to a pan and Air Fry them for 3 minutes. Remove them to the bowl and serve right away.

Broccoli Cheddar Stuffed Potatoes

Servings: 2

Cooking Time: 42 Minutes

Ingredients:

- 2 large russet potatoes, scrubbed
- 1 tablespoon olive oil
- salt and freshly ground black pepper
- 2 tablespoons butter
- ¼ cup sour cream
- 3 tablespoons half-and-half (or milk)
- 1¼ cups grated Cheddar cheese, divided
- ¾ teaspoon salt
- freshly ground black pepper
- 1 cup frozen baby broccoli florets, thawed and drained

Directions:

1. Preheat the air fryer to 400°F.
2. Rub the potatoes all over with olive oil and season generously with salt and freshly ground black pepper. Transfer the potatoes into the air fryer basket and air-fry for 30 minutes, turning the potatoes over halfway through the cooking process.
3. Remove the potatoes from the air fryer and let them rest for 5 minutes. Cut a large oval out of the top of both potatoes. Leaving half an inch of potato flesh around the edge of the potato, scoop the inside of the potato out and into a large bowl to prepare the potato filling. Mash the scooped potato filling with a fork and add the butter, sour cream, half-and-half, 1 cup of the grated Cheddar cheese, salt and pepper to taste. Mix well and then fold in the broccoli florets.
4. Stuff the hollowed out potato shells with the potato and broccoli mixture. Mound the filling high in the potatoes – you will have more filling than room in the potato shells.

5. Transfer the stuffed potatoes back to the air fryer basket and air-fry at 360°F for 10 minutes. Sprinkle the remaining Cheddar cheese on top of each stuffed potato, lower the heat to 330°F and air-fry for an additional minute or two to melt cheese.

Veggie Burgers

Servings: 4

Cooking Time: 15 Minutes

Ingredients:

- 2 cans black beans, rinsed and drained
- ½ cup cooked quinoa
- ½ cup shredded raw sweet potato
- ¼ cup diced red onion
- 2 teaspoons ground cumin
- 1 teaspoon coriander powder
- ½ teaspoon salt
- oil for misting or cooking spray
- 8 slices bread
- suggested toppings: lettuce, tomato, red onion, Pepper Jack cheese, guacamole

Directions:

1. In a medium bowl, mash the beans with a fork.
2. Add the quinoa, sweet potato, onion, cumin, coriander, and salt and mix well with the fork.
3. Shape into 4 patties, each ¾-inch thick.
4. Mist both sides with oil or cooking spray and also mist the basket.
5. Cook at 390°F for 15minutes.
6. Follow the recipe for Toast, Plain & Simple.
7. Pop the veggie burgers back in the air fryer for a minute or two to reheat if necessary.
8. Serve on the toast with your favorite burger toppings.

Roasted Vegetable Stromboli

Servings: 2

Cooking Time: 29 Minutes

Ingredients:

- ½ onion, thinly sliced
- ½ red pepper, julienned
- ½ yellow pepper, julienned
- olive oil
- 1 small zucchini, thinly sliced
- 1 cup thinly sliced mushrooms
- 1½ cups chopped broccoli
- 1 teaspoon Italian seasoning
- salt and freshly ground black pepper
- ½ recipe of Blue Jean Chef Pizza dough (page 231) OR 1 (14-ounce) tube refrigerated pizza dough
- 2 cups grated mozzarella cheese
- ¼ cup grated Parmesan cheese
- ½ cup sliced black olives, optional
- dried oregano
- pizza or marinara sauce

Directions:

1. Preheat the air fryer to 400°F.
2. Toss the onions and peppers with a little olive oil and air-fry the vegetables for 7 minutes, shaking the

basket once or twice while the vegetables cook. Add the zucchini, mushrooms, broccoli and Italian seasoning to the basket. Add a little more olive oil and season with salt and freshly ground black pepper. Air-fry for an additional 7 minutes, shaking the basket halfway through. Let the vegetables cool slightly while you roll out the pizza dough.

3.   On a lightly floured surface, roll or press the pizza dough out into a 13-inch by 11-inch rectangle, with the long side closest to you. Sprinkle half of the mozzarella and Parmesan cheeses over the dough leaving an empty 1-inch border from the edge farthest away from you. Spoon the roasted vegetables over the cheese, sprinkle the olives over everything and top with the remaining cheese.

4.   Start rolling the stromboli away from you and toward the empty border. Make sure the filling stays tightly tucked inside the roll. Finally, tuck the ends of the dough in and pinch the seam shut. Place the seam side down and shape the stromboli into a U-shape to fit into the air fryer basket. Cut 4 small slits with the tip of a sharp knife evenly in the top of the dough, lightly brush the stromboli with a little oil and sprinkle with some dried oregano.

5.   Preheat the air fryer to 360°F.

6.   Spray or brush the air fryer basket with oil and transfer the U-shaped stromboli to the air fryer basket. Air-fry for 15 minutes, flipping the stromboli over after the first 10 minutes. (Use a plate to invert the Stromboli out of the air fryer basket and then slide it back into the basket off the plate.)

7.   To remove, carefully flip the stromboli over onto a cutting board. Let it rest for a couple of minutes before serving. Cut it into 2-inch slices and serve with pizza or marinara sauce.

Black Bean And Rice Burrito Filling

Servings:4
Cooking Time: 20 Minutes
Ingredients:
- 1 cup uncooked instant long-grain white rice
- 1 cup salsa
- ½ cup vegetable broth
- 1 cup black beans
- ½ cup corn

Directions:
1.   Preheat the air fryer to 400°F.
2.   Mix all ingredients in a 3-quart baking dish until well combined.
3.   Cover with foil, being sure to tuck foil under the bottom of the pan to ensure the air fryer fan does not blow it off.
4.   Cook 20 minutes, stirring twice during cooking. Serve warm.

Spaghetti Squash And Kale Fritters With Pomodoro Sauce

Servings: 3
Cooking Time: 45 Minutes

Ingredients:
- 1½-pound spaghetti squash (about half a large or a whole small squash)
- olive oil
- ½ onion, diced
- ½ red bell pepper, diced
- 2 cloves garlic, minced
- 4 cups coarsely chopped kale
- salt and freshly ground black pepper
- 1 egg
- ⅓ cup breadcrumbs, divided*
- ⅓ cup grated Parmesan cheese
- ½ teaspoon dried rubbed sage
- pinch nutmeg
- Pomodoro Sauce:
- 2 tablespoons olive oil
- ½ onion, chopped
- 1 to 2 cloves garlic, minced
- 1 (28-ounce) can peeled tomatoes
- ¼ cup red wine
- 1 teaspoon Italian seasoning
- 2 tablespoons chopped fresh basil, plus more for garnish
- salt and freshly ground black pepper
- ½ teaspoon sugar (optional)

Directions:
1.   Preheat the air fryer to 370°F.
2.   Cut the spaghetti squash in half lengthwise and remove the seeds. Rub the inside of the squash with olive oil and season with salt and pepper. Place the squash, cut side up, into the air fryer basket and air-fry for 30 minutes, flipping the squash over halfway through the cooking process.
3.   While the squash is cooking, Preheat a large sauté pan over medium heat on the stovetop. Add a little olive oil and sauté the onions for 3 minutes, until they start to soften. Add the red pepper and garlic and continue to sauté for an additional 4 minutes. Add the kale and season with salt and pepper. Cook for 2 more minutes, or until the kale is soft. Transfer the mixture to a large bowl and let it cool.
4.   While the squash continues to cook, make the Pomodoro sauce. Preheat the large sauté pan again over medium heat on the stovetop. Add the olive oil and sauté the onion and garlic for 2 to 3 minutes, until the onion begins to soften. Crush the canned tomatoes with your hands and add them to the pan along with the red wine and Italian seasoning and simmer for 20 minutes. Add the basil and season to taste with salt, pepper and sugar (if using).
5.   When the spaghetti squash has finished cooking, use a fork to scrape the inside flesh of the squash onto a sheet pan. Spread the squash out and let it cool.
6.   Once cool, add the spaghetti squash to the kale mixture, along with the egg, breadcrumbs, Parmesan cheese, sage, nutmeg, salt and freshly ground black pepper. Stir to combine well and then divide the mixture

into 6 thick portions. You can shape the portions into patties, but I prefer to keep them a little random and unique in shape. Spray or brush the fritters with olive oil.

7. Preheat the air fryer to 370°F.

8. Brush the air fryer basket with a little olive oil and transfer the fritters to the basket. Air-fry the squash and kale fritters at 370°F for 15 minutes, flipping them over halfway through the cooking process.

9. Serve the fritters warm with the Pomodoro sauce spooned over the top or pooled on your plate. Garnish with the fresh basil leaves.

Cheesy Cauliflower Crust Pizza

Servings:2
Cooking Time: 12 Minutes Per Batch
Ingredients:
- 2 steamer bags cauliflower florets
- 1 large egg
- 1 cup grated vegetarian Parmesan cheese
- 3 cups shredded mozzarella cheese, divided
- 1 cup pizza sauce

Directions:
1. Preheat the air fryer to 375°F. Cut two pieces of parchment paper to fit the air fryer basket, one for each crust.

2. Cook cauliflower in the microwave according to package instructions, then drain in a colander. Run under cold water until cool to the touch. Use a cheesecloth to squeeze the excess water from cauliflower, removing as much as possible.

3. In a food processor, combine cauliflower, egg, Parmesan, and 1 cup mozzarella. Process on low about 15 seconds until a sticky ball forms.

4. Separate dough into two pieces. Working with damp hands to prevent dough from sticking, press each dough ball into a 6" round.

5. Place crust on parchment in the air fryer basket, working in batches as necessary. Cook 6 minutes, then flip over with a spatula and top the crust with ½ cup pizza sauce and 1 cup mozzarella. Cook an additional 6 minutes until edges are dark brown and cheese is brown and bubbling. Let cool at least 5 minutes before serving. The crust firms up as it cools.

Sicilian-style Vegetarian Pizza

Servings: 2
Cooking Time: 20 Minutes
Ingredients:
- 1 pizza pie crust
- ¼ cup ricotta cheese
- ½ tbsp tomato paste
- ½ white onion, sliced
- ½ tsp dried oregano
- ¼ cup Sicilian olives, sliced
- ¼ cup grated mozzarella

Directions:
1. Preheat air fryer to 350°F. Lay the pizza dough on a parchment paper sheet. Spread the tomato paste evenly over the pie crust, allowing at least ½ inch border.

Sprinkle with oregano and scatter the ricotta cheese on top. Cover with onion and Sicilian olive slices and finish with a layer of mozzarella cheese. Bake for 10 minutes until the cheese has melted and lightly crisped, and the crust is golden brown. Serve sliced and enjoy!

Cool Mini Zucchini's

Servings:4
Cooking Time: 25 Minutes
Ingredients:
- 4 large eggs, beaten
- 1 medium zucchini, sliced
- 4 ounces feta cheese, drained and crumbled
- 2 tbsp fresh dill, chopped
- Cooking spray
- Salt and pepper as needed

Directions:
1. Preheat the air fryer to 360°F, and un a bowl, add the beaten eggs and season with salt and pepper.

2. Stir in zucchini, dill and feta cheese. Grease 8 muffin tins with cooking spray. Roll pastry and arrange them to cover the sides of the muffin tins. Divide the egg mixture evenly between the holes. Place the prepared tins in your air fryer and cook for 15 minutes. Serve and enjoy!

Harissa Veggie Fries

Servings: 4
Cooking Time: 55 Minutes
Ingredients:
- 1 pound red potatoes, cut into rounds
- 1 onion, diced
- 1 green bell pepper, diced
- 1 red bell pepper, diced
- 2 tbsp olive oil
- Salt and pepper to taste
- ¾ tsp garlic powder
- ¾ tsp harissa seasoning

Directions:
1. Combine all ingredients in a large bowl and mix until potatoes are well coated and seasoned. Preheat air fryer to 350°F. Pour all of the contents in the bowl into the frying basket. Bake for 35 minutes, shaking every 10 minutes, until golden brown and soft. Serve hot.

Spinach And Feta Pinwheels

Servings:4
Cooking Time: 15 Minutes
Ingredients:
- 1 sheet frozen puff pastry, thawed
- 3 ounces full-fat cream cheese, softened
- 1 bag frozen spinach, thawed and drained
- ¼ teaspoon salt
- ⅓ cup crumbled feta cheese
- 1 large egg, whisked

Directions:
1. Preheat the air fryer to 320°F. Unroll puff pastry into a flat rectangle.

2. In a medium bowl, mix cream cheese, spinach, and salt until well combined.

3. Spoon cream cheese mixture onto pastry in an even layer, leaving a ½" border around the edges.

4. Sprinkle feta evenly across dough and gently press into filling to secure. Roll lengthwise to form a log shape.

5. Cut the roll into twelve 1" pieces. Brush with egg. Place in the air fryer basket and cook 15 minutes, turning halfway through cooking time.

6. Let cool 5 minutes before serving.

Crustless Spinach And Cheese Frittata

Servings:4
Cooking Time: 20 Minutes
Ingredients:
- 6 large eggs
- ½ cup heavy whipping cream
- 1 cup frozen chopped spinach, drained
- 1 cup shredded sharp Cheddar cheese
- ¼ cup peeled and diced yellow onion
- ½ teaspoon salt
- ¼ teaspoon ground black pepper

Directions:
1. In a large bowl, whisk eggs and cream together. Whisk in spinach, Cheddar, onion, salt, and pepper.

2. Pour mixture into an ungreased 6" round nonstick baking dish. Place dish into air fryer basket. Adjust the temperature to 320°F and set the timer for 20 minutes. Eggs will be firm and slightly browned when done. Serve immediately.

Pinto Bean Casserole

Servings: 2
Cooking Time: 15 Minutes
Ingredients:
- 1 can pinto beans
- ¼ cup tomato sauce
- 2 tbsp cornstarch
- 2 garlic cloves, minced
- ½ tsp dried oregano
- ½ tsp cumin
- 1 tsp smoked paprika
- Salt and pepper to taste

Directions:
1. Preheat air fryer to 390°F. Stir the beans, tomato sauce, cornstarch, garlic, oregano, cumin, smoked paprika, salt, and pepper in a bowl until combined. Pour the bean mix into a greased baking pan. Bake in the fryer for 4 minutes. Remove, stir, and Bake for 4 minutes or until the mix is thick and heated through. Serve hot.

Pizza Eggplant Rounds

Servings: 4
Cooking Time: 25 Minutes
Ingredients:
- 3 tsp olive oil
- ¼ cup diced onion
- ½ tsp garlic powder
- ½ tsp dried oregano
- ½ cup diced mushrooms
- ½ cup marinara sauce
- 1 eggplant, sliced
- 1 tsp salt
- 1 cup shredded mozzarella
- 2 tbsp Parmesan cheese
- ¼ cup chopped basil

Directions:
1. Warm 2 tsp of olive oil in a skillet over medium heat. Add in onion and mushrooms and cook for 5 minutes until the onions are translucent. Stir in marinara sauce, then add oregano and garlic powder. Turn the heat off.

2. Preheat air fryer at 375°F. Rub the remaining olive oil over both sides of the eggplant circles. Lay circles on a large plate and sprinkle with salt and black pepper. Top each circle with the marinara sauce mixture and shredded mozzarella and Parmesan cheese. Place eggplant circles in the frying basket and Bake for 5 minutes. Scatter with the basil and serve.

Pepper-pineapple With Butter-sugar Glaze

Servings:2
Cooking Time: 10 Minutes
Ingredients:
- 1 medium-sized pineapple, peeled and sliced
- 1 red bell pepper, seeded and julienned
- 1 teaspoon brown sugar
- 2 teaspoons melted butter
- Salt to taste

Directions:
1. Preheat the air fryer to 390°F.
2. Place the grill pan accessory in the air fryer.
3. Mix all ingredients in a Ziploc bag and give a good shake.
4. Dump onto the grill pan and cook for 10 minutes making sure that you flip the pineapples every 5 minutes.

Home-style Cinnamon Rolls

Servings: 4
Cooking Time: 40 Minutes
Ingredients:
- ½ pizza dough
- 1/3 cup dark brown sugar
- ¼ cup butter, softened
- ½ tsp ground cinnamon

Directions:
1. Preheat air fryer to 360°F. Roll out the dough into a rectangle. Using a knife, spread the brown sugar and butter, covering all the edges, and sprinkle with cinnamon. Fold the long side of the dough into a log, then cut it into 8 equal pieces, avoiding compression. Place the rolls, spiral-side up, onto a parchment-lined sheet. Let rise for 20 minutes. Grease the rolls with cooking spray and Bake for 8 minutes until golden brown. Serve right away.

Vegetarian Shepherd´s Pie

Servings: 4
Cooking Time: 40 Minutes
Ingredients:
- 1 russet potato, peeled and diced
- 1 tbsp olive oil
- 2 tbsp balsamic vinegar
- ¼ cup cheddar shreds
- 2 tbsp milk
- Salt and pepper to taste
- 2 tsp avocado oil
- 1 cup beefless grounds
- ½ onion, diced
- 3 cloves garlic
- 1 carrot, diced
- ¼ diced green bell peppers
- 1 celery stalk, diced
- 2/3 cup tomato sauce
- 1 tsp chopped rosemary
- 1 tbsp sesame seeds
- 1 tsp thyme leaves
- 1 lemon

Directions:
1. Add salted water to a pot over high heat and bring it to a boil. Add in diced potatoes and cook for 5 minutes until fork tender. Drain and transfer it to a bowl. Add in the olive oil cheddar shreds, milk, salt, and pepper and mash it until smooth. Set the potato topping aside.
2. Preheat air fryer at 350ºF. Place avocado oil, beefless grounds, garlic, onion, carrot, bell pepper, and celery in a skillet over medium heat and cook for 4 minutes until the veggies are tender. Stir in the remaining ingredients and turn the heat off. Spoon the filling into a greased cake pan. Top with the potato topping.
3. Using tines of a fork, create shallow lines along the top of mashed potatoes. Place cake pan in the frying basket and Bake for 12 minutes. Let rest for 10 minutes before serving sprinkled with sesame seeds and squeezed lemon.

General Tso's Cauliflower

Servings: 4
Cooking Time: 15 Minutes
Ingredients:
- 1 head cauliflower cut into florets
- ¾ cup all-purpose flour, divided*
- 3 eggs, lightly beaten
- 1 cup panko breadcrumbs*
- canola or peanut oil, in a spray bottle
- 2 tablespoons oyster sauce
- ¼ cup soy sauce
- 2 teaspoons chili paste
- 2 tablespoons rice wine vinegar
- 2 tablespoons sugar
- ¼ cup water
- white or brown rice for serving
- steamed broccoli

Directions:

1. Set up dredging station using three bowls. Place the cauliflower in a large bowl and sprinkle ¼ cup of the flour over the top. Place the eggs in a second bowl and combine the panko breadcrumbs and remaining ½ cup flour in a third bowl. Toss the cauliflower in the flour to coat all the florets thoroughly. Dip the cauliflower florets in the eggs and finally toss them in the breadcrumbs to coat on all sides. Place the coated cauliflower florets on a baking sheet and spray generously with canola or peanut oil.
2. Preheat the air fryer to 400°F.
3. Air-fry the cauliflower at 400°F for 15 minutes, flipping the florets over for the last 3 minutes of the cooking process and spraying again with oil.
4. While the cauliflower is air-frying, make the General Tso Sauce. Combine the oyster sauce, soy sauce, chili paste, rice wine vinegar, sugar and water in a saucepan and bring the mixture to a boil on the stove top. Lower the heat and let it simmer for 10 minutes, stirring occasionally.
5. When the timer is up on the air fryer, transfer the cauliflower to a large bowl, pour the sauce over it all and toss to coat. Serve with white or brown rice and some steamed broccoli.

Smoked Paprika Sweet Potato Fries

Servings: 4
Cooking Time: 35 Minutes
Ingredients:
- 2 sweet potatoes, peeled
- 1 ½ tbsp cornstarch
- 1 tbsp canola oil
- 1 tbsp olive oil
- 1 tsp smoked paprika
- 1 tsp garlic powder
- Salt and pepper to taste
- 1 cup cocktail sauce

Directions:
1. Cut the potatoes lengthwise to form French fries. Put in a resealable plastic bag and add cornstarch. Seal and shake to coat the fries. Combine the canola oil, olive oil, paprika, garlic powder, salt, and pepper fries in a large bowl. Add the sweet potato fries and mix to combine.
2. Preheat air fryer to 380°F. Place fries in the greased basket and fry for 20-25 minutes, shaking the basket once until crisp. Drizzle with Cocktail sauce to serve.

Bell Pepper & Lentil Tacos

Servings: 2
Cooking Time: 40 Minutes
Ingredients:
- 2 corn tortilla shells
- ½ cup cooked lentils
- ½ white onion, sliced
- ½ red pepper, sliced
- ½ green pepper, sliced
- ½ yellow pepper, sliced
- ½ cup shredded mozzarella
- ½ tsp Tabasco sauce

Directions:

1. Preheat air fryer to 320°F. Sprinkle half of the mozzarella cheese over one of the tortillas, then top with lentils, Tabasco sauce, onion, and peppers. Scatter the remaining mozzarella cheese, cover with the other tortilla and place in the frying basket. Bake for 6 minutes, flipping halfway through cooking. Serve and enjoy!

Vegetarian Paella

Servings: 3
Cooking Time: 50 Minutes
Ingredients:
- ½ cup chopped artichoke hearts
- ½ sliced red bell peppers
- 4 mushrooms, thinly sliced
- ½ cup canned diced tomatoes
- ½ cup canned chickpeas
- 3 tbsp hot sauce
- 2 tbsp lemon juice
- 1 tbsp allspice
- 1 cup rice

Directions:
1. Preheat air fryer to 400°F. Combine the artichokes, peppers, mushrooms, tomatoes and their juices, chickpeas, hot sauce, lemon juice, and allspice in a baking pan. Roast for 10 minutes. Pour in rice and 2 cups of boiling water, cover with aluminum foil, and Roast for 22 minutes. Discard the foil and Roast for 3 minutes until the top is crisp. Let cool slightly before stirring. Serve.

Tofu & Spinach Lasagna

Servings: 4
Cooking Time: 30 Minutes
Ingredients:
- 8 oz cooked lasagne noodles
- 1 tbsp olive oil
- 2 cups crumbled tofu
- 2 cups fresh spinach
- 2 tbsp cornstarch
- 1 tsp onion powder
- Salt and pepper to taste
- 2 garlic cloves, minced
- 2 cups marinara sauce
- ½ cup shredded mozzarella

Directions:
1. Warm the olive oil in a large pan over medium heat. Add the tofu and spinach and stir-fry for a minute. Add the cornstarch, onion powder, salt, pepper, and garlic. Stir until the spinach wilts. Remove from heat.
2. Preheat air fryer to 390°F. Pour a thin layer of pasta sauce in a baking pan. Layer 2-3 lasagne noodles on top of the marinara sauce. Top with a little more sauce and some of the tofu mix. Add another 2-3 noodles on top, then another layer of sauce, then another layer of tofu. Finish with a layer of noodles and a final layer of sauce. Sprinkle with mozzarella cheese on top. Place the pan in the air fryer and Bake for 15 minutes or until the noodle edges are browned and the cheese is melted. Cut and serve.

Spicy Vegetable And Tofu Shake Fry

Servings: 4
Cooking Time: 17 Minutes
Ingredients:
- 4 teaspoons canola oil, divided
- 2 tablespoons rice wine vinegar
- 1 tablespoon sriracha chili sauce
- ¼ cup soy sauce*
- ½ teaspoon toasted sesame oil
- 1 teaspoon minced garlic
- 1 tablespoon minced fresh ginger
- 8 ounces extra firm tofu
- ½ cup vegetable stock or water
- 1 tablespoon honey
- 1 tablespoon cornstarch
- ½ red onion, chopped
- 1 red or yellow bell pepper, chopped
- 1 cup green beans, cut into 2-inch lengths
- 4 ounces mushrooms, sliced
- 2 scallions, sliced
- 2 tablespoons fresh cilantro leaves
- 2 teaspoons toasted sesame seeds

Directions:
1. Combine 1 tablespoon of the oil, vinegar, sriracha sauce, soy sauce, sesame oil, garlic and ginger in a small bowl. Cut the tofu into bite-sized cubes and toss the tofu in with the marinade while you prepare the other vegetables. When you are ready to start cooking, remove the tofu from the marinade and set it aside. Add the water, honey and cornstarch to the marinade and bring to a simmer on the stovetop, just until the sauce thickens. Set the sauce aside.
2. Preheat the air fryer to 400°F.
3. Toss the onion, pepper, green beans and mushrooms in a bowl with a little canola oil and season with salt. Air-fry at 400°F for 11 minutes, shaking the basket and tossing the vegetables every few minutes. When the vegetables are cooked to your preferred doneness, remove them from the air fryer and set aside.
4. Add the tofu to the air fryer basket and air-fry at 400°F for 6 minutes, shaking the basket a few times during the cooking process. Add the vegetables back to the basket and air-fry for another minute. Transfer the vegetables and tofu to a large bowl, add the scallions and cilantro leaves and toss with the sauce. Serve over rice with sesame seeds sprinkled on top.

Italian Seasoned Easy Pasta Chips

Servings:2
Cooking Time:10 Minutes
Ingredients:
- ½ teaspoon salt
- 1 ½ teaspoon Italian seasoning blend
- 1 tablespoon nutritional yeast
- 1 tablespoon olive oil
- 2 cups whole wheat bowtie pasta

Directions:
1. Place the baking dish accessory in the air fryer.
2. Give a good stir.
3. Close the air fryer and cook for 10 minutes at 390°F.

Chapter 7: Poultry Recipes

Korean-style Chicken Bulgogi

Servings: 4
Cooking Time: 30 Minutes
Ingredients:
- 6 boneless, skinless chicken thighs, cubed
- 3 scallions, sliced, whites and green separated
- 2 carrots, grated
- ½ cup rice vinegar
- 2 tsp granulated sugar
- Salt to taste
- 2 tbsp tamari
- 2 tsp sesame oil
- 1 tbsp light brown sugar
- 1 tbsp lime juice
- 1 tbsp soy sauce
- 2 cloves garlic, minced
- ½ Asian pear
- 2 tsp minced ginger
- 4 cups cooked white rice
- 2 tsp sesame seeds

Directions:
1. In a bowl, combine the carrots, half of the rice vinegar, sugar, and salt. Let chill covered in the fridge until ready to use. Mix the tamari, sesame oil, soy sauce, brown sugar, remaining rice vinegar, lime juice, garlic, Asian pear, ginger, and scallion whites in a bowl. Toss in chicken thighs and let marinate for 10 minutes.
2. Preheat air fryer at 350ºF. Using a slotted spoon, transfer chicken thighs to the frying basket, reserve marinade, and Air Fry for 10-12 minutes, shaking once. Place chicken over a rice bed on serving plates and scatter with scallion greens and sesame seeds. Serve with pickled carrots.

Popcorn Chicken Tenders With Vegetables

Servings: 4
Cooking Time: 30 Minutes
Ingredients:
- 2 tbsp cooked popcorn, ground
- Salt and pepper to taste
- 1 lb chicken tenders
- ½ cup bread crumbs
- ½ tsp dried thyme
- 1 tbsp olive oil
- 2 carrots, sliced
- 12 baby potatoes

Directions:
1. Preheat air fryer to 380°F. Season the chicken tenders with salt and pepper. In a shallow bowl, mix the crumbs, popcorn, thyme, and olive oil until combined. Coat the chicken with mixture. Press firmly, so the crumbs adhere.Arrange the carrots and baby potatoes in the greased frying basket and top them with the chicken tenders. Bake for 9-10 minutes. Shake the basket and

continue cooking for another 9-10 minutes, until the vegetables are tender. Serve and enjoy!

Duck Breast With Figs

Servings: 2 Servings
Cooking Time: 40 Minutes
Ingredients:
- 1 pound of boneless duck breast
- 6 halved fresh figs
- 2 cups of pomegranate juice
- 3 tablespoons of brown sugar
- 2 tablespoons of lemon juice
- Pinch of black pepper and salt, to taste

Directions:
1. Add juice, sugar, and lemon to a saucepan. Bring it to a boil, then lower to low heat and simmer for about 25 minutes until thick consistency.
2. Preheat your air fryer to 400ºF. Spray the air fryer basket with some oil.
3. Dry the duck breast with a paper towel. Make 4 slits across the skin diagonally with a knife, then make another 4 slits in the opposite diagonal direction. Rub both sides generously with salt and black pepper.
4. Put the prepared duck breast skin-side down in the preheated air fryer basket and cook at 400ºF for 8 minutes. Flip it and continue cooking for 5 minutes. Flip it again and cook for 1 minute to make crispy skin. Remove from the air fryer.
5. Drizzle the fig halves with oil, season them with black pepper and salt. Put the figs into the air fryer and cook for 5 minutes.
6. Meanwhile, cut the cooked duck breast into slices, pour over pomegranate sauce, and add some roasted figs on the top.
7. Serve warm and enjoy your Duck Breast with Figs!

Chicken Drumettes With Mustard

Servings: 3
Cooking Time: 12 Minutes
Ingredients:
- ¼ cup soy sauce
- 1 teaspoon brown mustard
- 1 teaspoon garlic paste
- 2 tablespoons tomato paste
- 2 tablespoons sesame oil
- 1 tablespoon brown sugar
- 2 tablespoons rice vinegar
- 1 pound chicken drumettes

Directions:
1. Add all the ingredients in a resealable bag and let it marinate for 2 hours.
2. Transfer the chicken drumettes to the air fryer basket and reserve the rest mixture.
3. Cook in your air fryer at 400 degrees F/ 205 degrees C for 12 minutes. Shake the basket once or twice to cook evenly.

4. Meanwhile, in a small saucepan, boil the reserved marinade and reduce heat to low to simmer until the sauce thickens.
5. Pour the sauce over the chicken drumettes.
6. Serve immediately.

Goat Cheese Stuffed Turkey Roulade
Servings: 4
Cooking Time: 55 Minutes
Ingredients:
- 1 boneless turkey breast, skinless
- Salt and pepper to taste
- 4 oz goat cheese
- 1 tbsp marjoram
- 1 tbsp sage
- 2 garlic cloves, minced
- 2 tbsp olive oil
- 2 tbsp chopped cilantro

Directions:
1. Preheat air fryer to 380°F. Butterfly the turkey breast with a sharp knife and season with salt and pepper. Mix together the goat cheese, marjoram, sage, and garlic in a bowl. Spread the cheese mixture over the turkey breast, then roll it up tightly, tucking the ends underneath.
2. Put the turkey breast roulade onto a piece of aluminum foil, wrap it up, and place it into the air fryer. Bake for 30 minutes. Turn the turkey breast, brush the top with oil, and then continue to cook for another 10-15 minutes. Slice and serve sprinkled with cilantro.

Southern-style Chicken Legs
Servings: 6
Cooking Time: 20 Minutes
Ingredients:
- 2 cups buttermilk
- 1 tablespoon hot sauce
- 12 chicken legs
- ½ teaspoon salt
- ½ teaspoon pepper
- 1 teaspoon paprika
- ½ teaspoon onion powder
- 1 teaspoon garlic powder
- 1 cup all-purpose flour

Directions:
1. In an airtight container, place the buttermilk, hot sauce, and chicken legs and refrigerate for 4 to 8 hours.
2. In a medium bowl, whisk together the salt, pepper, paprika, onion powder, garlic powder, and flour. Drain the chicken legs from the buttermilk and dip the chicken legs into the flour mixture, stirring to coat well.
3. Preheat the air fryer to 390°F.
4. Place the chicken legs in the air fryer basket and spray with cooking spray. Cook for 10 minutes, turn the chicken legs over, and cook for another 8 to 10 minutes. Check for an internal temperature of 165°F.

Israeli Chicken Schnitzel
Servings:4

Cooking Time: 10 Minutes
Ingredients:
- 2 large boneless, skinless chicken breasts, each weighing about 1 pound (454 g)
- 1 cup all-purpose flour
- 2 teaspoons garlic powder
- 2 teaspoons kosher salt
- 1 teaspoon black pepper
- 1 teaspoon paprika
- 2 eggs beaten with 2 tablespoons water
- 2 cups panko bread crumbs
- Vegetable oil spray
- Lemon juice, for serving

Directions:
1. Preheat the air fryer to 375ºF (191ºC).
2. Place 1 chicken breast between 2 pieces of plastic wrap. Use a mallet or a rolling pin to pound the chicken until it is ¼ inch thick. Set aside. Repeat with the second breast. Whisk together the flour, garlic powder, salt, pepper, and paprika on a large plate. Place the panko in a separate shallow bowl or pie plate.
3. Dredge 1 chicken breast in the flour, shaking off any excess, then dip it in the egg mixture. Dredge the chicken breast in the panko, making sure to coat it completely. Shake off any excess panko. Place the battered chicken breast on a plate. Repeat with the second chicken breast.
4. Spray the air fryer basket with oil spray. Place 1 of the battered chicken breasts in the basket and spray the top with oil spray. Air fry until the top is browned, about 5 minutes. Flip the chicken and spray the second side with oil spray. Air fry until the second side is browned and crispy and the internal temperature reaches 165ºF (74ºC). Remove the first chicken breast from the air fryer and repeat with the second chicken breast.
5. Serve hot with lemon juice.

Crispy Chicken Cordon Bleu
Servings:4
Cooking Time: 13 To 15 Minutes
Ingredients:
- 4 chicken breast fillets
- ¼ cup chopped ham
- ⅓ cup grated Swiss or Gruyère cheese
- ¼ cup flour
- Pinch salt
- Freshly ground black pepper, to taste
- ½ teaspoon dried marjoram
- 1 egg
- 1 cup panko bread crumbs
- Olive oil for misting

Directions:
1. Preheat the air fryer to 380ºF (193ºC).
2. Put the chicken breast fillets on a work surface and gently press them with the palm of your hand to make them a bit thinner. Don't tear the meat.
3. In a small bowl, combine the ham and cheese. Divide this mixture among the chicken fillets. Wrap the

chicken around the filling to enclose it, using toothpicks to hold the chicken together.

4. In a shallow bowl, mix the flour, salt, pepper, and marjoram. In another bowl, beat the egg. Spread the bread crumbs out on a plate.

5. Dip the chicken into the flour mixture, then into the egg, then into the bread crumbs to coat thoroughly.

6. Put the chicken in the air fryer basket and mist with olive oil.

7. Bake for 13 to 15 minutes or until the chicken is thoroughly cooked to 165°F (74°C). Carefully remove the toothpicks and serve.

Chicken Wellington

Servings: 2
Cooking Time: 31 Minutes
Ingredients:

- 2 (5-ounce) boneless, skinless chicken breasts
- ½ cup White Worcestershire sauce
- 3 tablespoons butter
- ½ cup finely diced onion (about ½ onion)
- 8 ounces button mushrooms, finely chopped
- ¼ cup chicken stock
- 2 tablespoons White Worcestershire sauce (or white wine)
- salt and freshly ground black pepper
- 1 tablespoon chopped fresh tarragon
- 2 sheets puff pastry, thawed
- 1 egg, beaten
- vegetable oil

Directions:

1. Place the chicken breasts in a shallow dish. Pour the White Worcestershire sauce over the chicken coating both sides and marinate for 30 minutes.

2. While the chicken is marinating, melt the butter in a large skillet over medium-high heat on the stovetop. Add the onion and sauté for a few minutes, until it starts to soften. Add the mushrooms and sauté for 5 minutes until the vegetables are brown and soft. Deglaze the skillet with the chicken stock, scraping up any bits from the bottom of the pan. Add the White Worcestershire sauce and simmer for 3 minutes until the mixture reduces and starts to thicken. Season with salt and freshly ground black pepper. Remove the mushroom mixture from the heat and stir in the fresh tarragon. Let the mushroom mixture cool.

3. Preheat the air fryer to 360°F.

4. Remove the chicken from the marinade and transfer it to the air fryer basket. Tuck the small end of the chicken breast under the thicker part to shape it into a circle rather than an oval. Pour the marinade over the chicken and air-fry for 10 minutes.

5. Roll out the puff pastry and cut out two 6-inch squares. Brush the perimeter of each square with the egg wash. Place half of the mushroom mixture in the center of each puff pastry square. Place the chicken breasts, top side down on the mushroom mixture. Starting with one corner of puff pastry and working in one direction, pull

the pastry up over the chicken to enclose it and press the ends of the pastry together in the middle. Brush the pastry with the egg wash to seal the edges. Turn the Wellingtons over and set aside.

6. To make a decorative design with the remaining puff pastry, cut out four 10-inch strips. For each Wellington, twist two of the strips together, place them over the chicken breast wrapped in puff pastry, and tuck the ends underneath to seal it. Brush the entire top and sides of the Wellingtons with the egg wash.

7. Preheat the air fryer to 350°F.

8. Spray or brush the air fryer basket with vegetable oil. Air-fry the chicken Wellingtons for 13 minutes. Carefully turn the Wellingtons over. Air-fry for another 8 minutes. Transfer to serving plates, light a candle and enjoy!

Roasted Turkey Thighs And Cauliflower

Servings: 4
Cooking Time: 53 Minutes
Ingredients:

- 1 tablespoon butter, room temperature
- 2 pounds turkey thighs
- ½ teaspoon smoked paprika
- ½ teaspoon dried marjoram
- ¼ teaspoon dried dill
- Sea salt, to taste
- Ground black pepper, to taste
- 1 pound cauliflower, broken into small florets
- ⅓ cup Pecorino Romano cheese, freshly grated
- 1 teaspoon garlic, minced

Directions:

1. Before cooking, heat your air fryer to 360 degrees F/ 180 degrees C. Toss the turkey thighs with butter. To season, rub the turkey thighs with marjoram, smoked paprika, salt, black pepper, and dill.

2. Roast the turkey thighs at 360 degrees F/ 180 degrees C for about 20 minutes.

3. Then flip to cook the other side for 20 minutes.

4. Mix the cauliflower, garlic, and Pecorino Romano, and salt together. Toss well.

5. Cook in your air fryer at 400 degrees F/ 205 degrees C for 12 to 13 minutes.

6. When cooked, serve the turkey with the cauliflower. Enjoy!

Cajun Chicken Drumsticks

Servings: 5
Cooking Time: 40 Minutes
Ingredients:

- 10 chicken drumsticks
- 1½ tablespoons Louisiana Cajun Seasoning
- Salt
- Pepper
- Cooking oil

Directions:

1. Season the drumsticks with the Cajun seasoning and salt and pepper to taste.
2. Spray the air fryer basket with cooking oil.
3. Place 5 drumsticks in the air fryer. Do not stack. Spray the drumsticks with cooking oil. Cook for 10 minutes.
4. Open the air fryer and flip the chicken. Cook for an additional 8 minutes.
5. Remove the cooked chicken from the air fryer, then repeat steps 3 and 4 for the remaining 5 drumsticks.
6. Cool before serving.

Broccoli And Cheese-stuffed Chicken

Servings:4
Cooking Time: 20 Minutes
Ingredients:
- 2 ounces cream cheese, softened
- 1 cup chopped fresh broccoli, steamed
- ½ cup shredded sharp Cheddar cheese
- 4 boneless, skinless chicken breasts
- 2 tablespoons mayonnaise
- ¼ teaspoon salt
- ¼ teaspoon garlic powder
- ⅛ teaspoon ground black pepper

Directions:
1. In a medium bowl, combine cream cheese, broccoli, and Cheddar. Cut a 4" pocket into each chicken breast. Evenly divide mixture between chicken breasts; stuff the pocket of each chicken breast with the mixture.
2. Spread ¼ tablespoon mayonnaise per side of each chicken breast, then sprinkle both sides of breasts with salt, garlic powder, and pepper.
3. Place stuffed chicken breasts into ungreased air fryer basket so that the open seams face up. Adjust the temperature to 350°F and set the timer for 20 minutes, turning chicken halfway through cooking. When done, chicken will be golden and have an internal temperature of at least 165°F. Serve warm.

Baked Chicken With Parmesan Cheese

Servings: 2
Cooking Time: 12 Minutes
Ingredients:
- 2 chicken fillets
- 1 egg, beaten
- 2 tablespoons milk
- 1 teaspoon garlic paste
- 1 tablespoon fresh cilantro, chopped
- ½ cup seasoned breadcrumbs
- 4 tablespoons marinara sauce
- 4 slices parmesan cheese

Directions:
1. Before cooking, heat your air fryer to 380 degrees F/ 195 degrees C.
2. Using a nonstick cooking oil, spritz the air fryer basket.

3. Beat the egg in a medium shallow bowl, and add milk, cilantro, and garlic paste.
4. Place the seasoned breadcrumbs in a separate bowl.
5. Dredge the chicken fillet in the egg mixture and then in the seasoned breadcrumbs to coat well the fillet. Press to ensure the fillet is well coated.
6. Set the temperature to 380 degrees F/ 195 degrees C and the timer to 6 minutes. Turn the chicken over halfway cooking.
7. Drizzle the marinara sauce and parmesan cheese over the chicken fillet and cook again in the air fryer for 6 minutes.
8. Serve immediately and enjoy!

Mexican Chicken Roll-ups

Servings: 4
Cooking Time: 35 Minutes
Ingredients:
- ½ red bell pepper, cut into strips
- ½ green bell pepper, cut into strips
- 2 chicken breasts
- ½ lime, juiced
- 2 tbsp taco seasoning
- 1 spring onion, thinly sliced

Directions:
1. Preheat air fryer to 400°F. Cut the chicken into cutlets by slicing the chicken breast in half horizontally in order to have 4 thin cutlets. Drizzle with lime juice and season with taco seasoning. Divide the red pepper, green pepper, and spring onion equally between the 4 cutlets. Roll up the cutlets. Secure with toothpicks. Place the chicken roll-ups in the air fryer and lightly spray with cooking oil. Bake for 12 minutes, turning once. Serve warm.

Nacho Chicken Fries

Servings: 4
Cooking Time: 7 Minutes
Ingredients:
- 1 pound chicken tenders
- salt
- ¼ cup flour
- 2 eggs
- ¾ cup panko breadcrumbs
- ¾ cup crushed organic nacho cheese tortilla chips
- oil for misting or cooking spray
- Seasoning Mix
- 1 tablespoon chili powder
- 1 teaspoon ground cumin
- ½ teaspoon garlic powder
- ½ teaspoon onion powder

Directions:
1. Stir together all seasonings in a small cup and set aside.
2. Cut chicken tenders in half crosswise, then cut into strips no wider than about ½ inch.
3. Preheat air fryer to 390°F.

4. Salt chicken to taste. Place strips in large bowl and sprinkle with 1 tablespoon of the seasoning mix. Stir well to distribute seasonings.

5. Add flour to chicken and stir well to coat all sides.

6. Beat eggs together in a shallow dish.

7. In a second shallow dish, combine the panko, crushed chips, and the remaining 2 teaspoons of seasoning mix.

8. Dip chicken strips in eggs, then roll in crumbs. Mist with oil or cooking spray.

9. Chicken strips will cook best if done in two batches. They can be crowded and overlapping a little but not stacked in double or triple layers.

10. Cook for 4minutes. Shake basket, mist with oil, and cook 3 moreminutes, until chicken juices run clear and outside is crispy.

11. Repeat step 10 to cook remaining chicken fries.

Crispy Parmesan Chicken Breasts

Servings: 3
Cooking Time: 15 Minutes
Ingredients:
- 2 6-ounces boneless chicken breasts, cut into tenders
- ¾ cup buttermilk
- 1½ teaspoons Worcestershire sauce, divided
- ½ teaspoon smoked paprika, divided
- Salt and black pepper, as required
- ½ cup all-purpose flour
- 1½ cups panko breadcrumbs
- ¼ cup Parmesan cheese, finely grated
- 2 tablespoons butter, melted
- 2 large eggs

Directions:
1. In a suitable bowl, mix together buttermilk, ¾ teaspoon of Worcestershire sauce, ¼ teaspoon of paprika, salt, and black pepper.

2. Add in the chicken tenders and refrigerate overnight.

3. In a suitable bowl, mix the flour, remaining paprika, salt, and black pepper.

4. Place the remaining Worcestershire sauce and eggs in a third bowl and beat until well combined.

5. Mix well the panko, Parmesan, and butter in a fourth bowl.

6. Remove the chicken tenders from bowl and discard the buttermilk.

7. Coat the chicken tenders with flour mixture, then dip into egg mixture and finally coat with the panko mixture.

8. At 400 degrees F/ 205 degrees C, preheat your Air Fryer. Oil its air fryer basket.

9. Arrange chicken tenders into the prepared air fryer basket in 2 batches in a single layer.

10. Air fry for about 13-15 minutes, flipping once halfway through.

11. Remove from Air Fryer and transfer the chicken tenders onto a serving platter.

12. Serve hot.

Barbecue Chicken Drumsticks

Servings:4

Cooking Time: 25 Minutes
Ingredients:
- 1 teaspoon salt
- 1 teaspoon chili powder
- 1 teaspoon garlic powder
- ½ teaspoon ground black pepper
- ½ teaspoon onion powder
- 8 chicken drumsticks
- 1 cup barbecue sauce, divided

Directions:
1. Preheat the air fryer to 375°F.

2. In a large bowl, combine salt, chili powder, garlic powder, pepper, and onion powder. Add drumsticks and toss to fully coat.

3. Brush drumsticks with ¾ cup barbecue sauce to coat.

4. Place in the air fryer basket and cook 25 minutes, turning three times during cooking, until drumsticks are brown and internal temperature reaches at least 165°F.

5. Before serving, brush remaining ¼ cup barbecue sauce over drumsticks. Serve warm.

Chicken & Fruit Biryani

Servings: 4
Cooking Time: 30 Minutes
Ingredients:
- 3 chicken breasts, cubed
- 2 tsp olive oil
- 2 tbsp cornstarch
- 1 tbsp curry powder
- 1 apple, chopped
- ½ cup chicken broth
- 1/3 cup dried cranberries
- 1 cooked basmati rice

Directions:
1. Preheat air fryer to 380°F. Combine the chicken and olive oil, then add some corn starch and curry powder. Mix to coat, then add the apple and pour the mix in a baking pan. Put the pan in the air fryer and Bake for 8 minutes, stirring once. Add the chicken broth, cranberries, and 2 tbsp of water and continue baking for 10 minutes, letting the sauce thicken. The chicken should be lightly charred and cooked through. Serve warm with basmati rice.

Granny Pesto Chicken Caprese

Servings: 4
Cooking Time: 30 Minutes
Ingredients:
- 2 tbsp grated Parmesan cheese
- 4 oz fresh mozzarella cheese, thinly sliced
- 16 grape tomatoes, halved
- 4 garlic cloves, minced
- 1 tsp olive oil
- Salt and pepper to taste
- 4 chicken cutlets
- 1 tbsp prepared pesto
- 1 large egg, beaten
- ½ cup bread crumbs

- 2 tbsp Italian seasoning
- 1 tsp balsamic vinegar
- 2 tbsp chopped fresh basil

Directions:

1. Preheat air fryer to 400°F. In a bowl, coat the tomatoes with garlic, olive oil, salt and pepper. Air Fry for 5 minutes, shaking them twice. Set aside when soft.

2. Place the cutlets between two sheets of parchment paper. Pound the chicken to ¼-inch thickness using a meat mallet. Season on both sides with salt and pepper. Spread an even coat of pesto. Put the beaten egg in a shallow bowl. Mix the crumbs, Italian seasoning, and Parmesan in a second shallow bowl. Dip the chicken in the egg bowl, and then in the crumb mix. Press the crumbs so that they stick to the chicken.

3. Place the chicken in the greased frying basket. Air Fry the chicken for 6-8 minutes, flipping once until golden and cooked through. Put 1 oz of mozzarella and ¼ of the tomatoes on top of each cutlet. When all of the cutlets are cooked, return them to the frying basket and melt the cheese for 2 minutes. Remove from the fryer, drizzle with balsamic vinegar and basil on top.

Simple Chicken Burgers

Servings: 4
Cooking Time: 11 Minutes

Ingredients:

- 1 ¼ pounds chicken white meat, ground
- ½ white onion, finely chopped
- 1 teaspoon fresh garlic, finely chopped
- Sea salt, to taste
- Ground black pepper, to taste
- 1 teaspoon paprika
- ½ cup cornmeal
- 1 ½ cups breadcrumbs
- 4 burger buns
- 4 lettuce leaves
- 2 small pickles, sliced
- 2 tablespoons ketchup
- 1 teaspoon yellow mustard

Directions:

1. In a mixing dish, combine thoroughly the onion, salt, black pepper, garlic, and chicken. Then make 4 equal patties from the mixture.

2. Mix cornmeal, breadcrumbs, and paprika in a shallow bowl.

3. Dredge the patties in the breadcrumb mixture. Press the patties to coat the both sides.

4. Using a non-stick cooking spray, spritz an air fryer basket.

5. Place the coated patties inside the air fryer basket.

6. Cook the patties in your air fryer at 370 degrees F/ 185 degrees C for 11 minutes or until it reaches the doneness as you desired.

7. When cooked, remove from the air fryer and place on burger buns. Serve with toppings. Enjoy!

8. Place your burgers on burger buns and serve with toppings. Bon appétit!

15-minute Chicken

Servings:4
Cooking Time: 15 Minutes

Ingredients:

- 4 boneless, skinless chicken breasts
- 2 tablespoons olive oil
- 1 teaspoon salt
- 1 teaspoon garlic powder
- 1 teaspoon paprika
- ½ teaspoon ground black pepper

Directions:

1. Preheat the air fryer to 375°F.

2. Carefully butterfly chicken breasts lengthwise, leaving the two halves connected. Drizzle chicken with oil, then sprinkle with salt, garlic powder, paprika, and pepper.

3. Place in the air fryer basket and cook 15 minutes, turning halfway through cooking time, until chicken is golden brown and the internal temperature reaches at least 165°F. Serve warm.

Whole Roasted Chicken

Servings:6
Cooking Time: 1 Hour

Ingredients:

- Olive oil
- 1 teaspoon salt
- 1 teaspoon Italian seasoning
- ½ teaspoon freshly ground black pepper
- ½ teaspoon paprika
- ½ teaspoon garlic powder
- ½ teaspoon onion powder
- 2 tablespoons olive oil
- 1 (4-pound) fryer chicken

Directions:

1. Spray a fryer basket lightly with olive oil.

2. In a small bowl, mix together the salt, Italian seasoning, pepper, paprika, garlic powder, and onion powder.

3. Remove any giblets from the chicken. Pat the chicken dry very thoroughly with paper towels, including the cavity.

4. Brush the chicken all over with the olive oil and rub it with the seasoning mixture.

5. Truss the chicken or tie the legs with butcher's twine. This will make it easier to flip the chicken during cooking.

6. Place the chicken in the fryer basket, breast side down. Air fry for 30 minutes. Flip the chicken over and baste it with any drippings collected in the bottom drawer of the air fryer. Lightly spray the chicken with olive oil.

7. Air fry for 20 minutes. Flip the chicken over one last time and cook until a thermometer inserted into the thickest part of the thigh reaches at least 165°F and it's crispy and golden, 10 more minutes. Continue to cook, checking every 5 minutes until the chicken reaches the correct internal temperature.

8. Let the chicken rest for 10 minutes before carving.

Piri-piri Chicken Thighs

Servings:4
Cooking Time: 25 Minutes
Ingredients:
- ¼ cup piri-piri sauce
- 1 tablespoon freshly squeezed lemon juice
- 2 tablespoons brown sugar, divided
- 2 cloves garlic, minced
- 1 tablespoon extra-virgin olive oil
- 4 bone-in, skin-on chicken thighs, each weighing approximately 7 to 8 ounces (198 to 227 g)
- ½ teaspoon cornstarch

Directions:
1. To make the marinade, whisk together the piri-piri sauce, lemon juice, 1 tablespoon of brown sugar, and the garlic in a small bowl. While whisking, slowly pour in the oil in a steady stream and continue to whisk until emulsified. Using a skewer, poke holes in the chicken thighs and place them in a small glass dish. Pour the marinade over the chicken and turn the thighs to coat them with the sauce. Cover the dish and refrigerate for at least 15 minutes and up to 1 hour.
2. Preheat the air fryer to 375°F (191°C). Remove the chicken thighs from the dish, reserving the marinade, and place them skin-side down in the air fryer basket. Air fry until the internal temperature reaches 165°F (74°C), 15 to 20 minutes.
3. Meanwhile, whisk the remaining brown sugar and the cornstarch into the marinade and microwave it on high power for 1 minute until it is bubbling and thickened to a glaze.
4. Once the chicken is cooked, turn the thighs over and brush them with the glaze. Air fry for a few additional minutes until the glaze browns and begins to char in spots.
5. Remove the chicken to a platter and serve with additional piri-piri sauce, if desired.

Cheesy Chicken Nuggets

Servings:4
Cooking Time: 15 Minutes
Ingredients:
- 1 pound ground chicken thighs
- ½ cup shredded mozzarella cheese
- 1 large egg, whisked
- ½ teaspoon salt
- ¼ teaspoon dried oregano
- ¼ teaspoon garlic powder

Directions:
1. In a large bowl, combine all ingredients. Form mixture into twenty nugget shapes, about 2 tablespoons each.
2. Place nuggets into ungreased air fryer basket, working in batches if needed. Adjust the temperature to 375°F and set the timer for 15 minutes, turning nuggets halfway through cooking. Let cool 5 minutes before serving.

Crusted Chicken Tenders

Servings: 3
Cooking Time: 10 Minutes
Ingredients:
- 1 pound chicken tenders
- Sea salt and black pepper, to taste
- ½ teaspoon shallot powder
- ½ teaspoon porcini powder
- ½ teaspoon dried rosemary
- ⅓ cup tortilla chips, crushed

Directions:
1. Before cooking, heat your air fryer to 360 degrees F/ 180 degrees C.
2. Rub salt, shallot powder, dried rosemary, pepper, tortilla chips, and porcini powder over the chicken tenders.
3. Using a nonstick cooking spray, spritz the air fryer basket.
4. Transfer the chicken tenders inside the air fryer basket.
5. Cook the coated chicken in your air fryer for 10 minutes. Flip halfway through cooking.
6. Serve warm with your favorite dipping sauce.

Greek Chicken Meatballs

Servings: 12 Meatballs
Cooking Time: 30 Minutes
Ingredients:
- 1 pound of ground chicken
- 1 large egg
- 4–5 minced garlic cloves
- 1 tablespoon of dried oregano
- 1 teaspoon of onion powder
- 1 teaspoon of lemon zest
- ¾ teaspoon of salt
- ¼ teaspoon of black pepper

Directions:
1. Preheat your air fryer to 390°F. Spray the air fryer basket with some oil.
2. Put all the ingredients in a large mixing bowl. Mix it well by hands or a spoon.
3. Divide the prepared mixture in half, then repeatedly in half. Make 3 meatballs from each of the halves, so in total you will have 12 meatballs of the same size.
4. Put about 6 meatballs (depends on your air fryer size) in a single layer; avoid them touching. Spray the tops with a little oil and cook at 390°F for 8–9 minutes until golden-brown. Repeat with the remaining part of meatballs.
5. Serve* warm and enjoy your Greek Chicken Meatballs!

Spicy Honey Mustard Chicken

Servings: 4
Cooking Time: 30 Minutes
Ingredients:
- 1/3 cup tomato sauce
- 2 tbsp yellow mustard

- 2 tbsp apple cider vinegar
- 1 tbsp honey
- 2 garlic cloves, minced
- 1 Fresno pepper, minced
- 1 tsp onion powder
- 4 chicken breasts

Directions:

1. Preheat air fryer to 370°F. Mix the tomato sauce, mustard, apple cider vinegar, honey, garlic, Fresno pepper, and onion powder in a bowl, then use a brush to rub the mix over the chicken breasts. Put the chicken in the air fryer and Grill for 10 minutes. Remove it, turn it, and rub with more sauce. Cook further for about 5 minutes. Remove the basket and flip the chicken. Add more sauce, return to the fryer, and cook for 3-5 more minutes or until the chicken is cooked through. Serve warm.

Jerk Turkey Meatballs

Servings: 7
Cooking Time: 8 Minutes
Ingredients:

- 1 pound lean ground turkey
- ¼ cup chopped onion
- 1 teaspoon minced garlic
- ½ teaspoon dried thyme
- ¼ teaspoon ground cinnamon
- 1 teaspoon cayenne pepper
- ½ teaspoon paprika
- ½ teaspoon salt
- ⅛ teaspoon black pepper
- ¼ teaspoon red pepper flakes
- 2 teaspoons brown sugar
- 1 large egg, whisked
- ⅓ cup panko breadcrumbs
- 2⅓ cups cooked brown Jasmine rice
- 2 green onions, chopped
- ¾ cup sweet onion dressing

Directions:

1. Preheat the air fryer to 350°F.
2. In a medium bowl, mix the ground turkey with the onion, garlic, thyme, cinnamon, cayenne pepper, paprika, salt, pepper, red pepper flakes, and brown sugar. Add the whisked egg and stir in the breadcrumbs until the turkey starts to hold together.
3. Using a 1-ounce scoop, portion the turkey into meatballs. You should get about 28 meatballs.
4. Spray the air fryer basket with olive oil spray.
5. Place the meatballs into the air fryer basket and cook for 5 minutes, shake the basket, and cook another 2 to 4 minutes (or until the internal temperature of the meatballs reaches 165°F).
6. Remove the meatballs from the basket and repeat for the remaining meatballs.
7. Serve warm over a bed of rice with chopped green onions and spicy Caribbean jerk dressing.

Fried Chicken Halves

Servings: 4
Cooking Time: 75 Minutes
Ingredients:

- 16 oz whole chicken
- 1 tablespoon dried thyme
- 1 teaspoon ground cumin
- 1 teaspoon salt
- 1 tablespoon avocado oil

Directions:

1. Cut the chicken into halves and sprinkle it with dried thyme, cumin, and salt. Then brush the chicken halves with avocado oil. Preheat the air fryer to 365°F. Put the chicken halves in the air fryer and cook them for 60 minutes. Then flip the chicken halves on another side and cook them for 15 minutes more.

Turkey Scotch Eggs

Servings: 4
Cooking Time: 30 Minutes
Ingredients:

- 1 ½ lb ground turkey
- 1 tbsp ground cumin
- 1 tsp ground coriander
- 2 garlic cloves, minced
- 3 raw eggs
- 1 ½ cups bread crumbs
- 6 hard-cooked eggs, peeled
- ½ cup flour

Directions:

1. Preheat air fryer to 370°F. Place the ground turkey, cumin, coriander, garlic, one egg, and ½ cup of bread crumbs in a large bowl and mix until well incorporated.
2. Divide into 6 equal portions, then flatten each into long ovals. Set aside. In a shallow bowl, beat the remaining raw eggs. In another shallow bowl, add flour. Do the same with another plate for bread crumbs. Roll each cooked egg in flour, then wrap with one oval of chicken sausage until completely covered.
3. Roll again in flour, then coat in the beaten egg before rolling in bread crumbs. Arrange the eggs in the greased frying basket. Air Fry for 12-14 minutes, flipping once until the sausage is cooked and the eggs are brown. Serve.

Rotisserie Whole Chicken

Servings: 6 Servings
Cooking Time: 1 Hour 5 Minutes
Ingredients:

- 1 whole chicken without giblets (about 5 pounds)
- 1 tablespoon of salt
- 1 teaspoon of garlic powder
- 1 teaspoon of black pepper
- 1 teaspoon of smoked paprika
- ½ teaspoon of dried oregano
- ½ teaspoon of dried basil
- ½ teaspoon of dried thyme
- 2 tablespoons of olive oil

Directions:
1. Preheat your air fryer to 360ºF.
2. Mix all seasonings with oil in a mixing bowl and spread it over the chicken.
3. Spray the air fryer basket with cooking spray. Put the chicken breast-side down in the air fryer basket and cook for 50 minutes. Flip it and cook at 360ºF for 10 minutes more. If chicken is not 165ºF internally, cook for additional 5–10 minutes.
4. Serve warm and enjoy your Rotisserie Whole Chicken!

Chicken Pinchos Morunos

Servings: 4
Cooking Time: 35 Minutes
Ingredients:
- 1 yellow summer squash, sliced
- 3 chicken breasts
- ¼ cup plain yogurt
- 2 tbsp olive oil
- 1 tsp sweet pimentón
- 1 tsp dried thyme
- ½ tsp sea salt
- ½ tsp garlic powder
- ½ tsp ground cumin
- 2 red bell peppers
- 3 scallions
- 16 large green olives

Directions:
1. Preheat the air fryer to 400°F. Combine yogurt, olive oil, pimentón, thyme, cumin, salt, and garlic in a bowl and add the chicken. Stir to coat. Cut the bell peppers and scallions into 1-inch pieces. Remove the chicken from the marinade; set aside the rest of the marinade. Thread the chicken, peppers, scallions, squash, and olives onto the soaked skewers. Brush the kebabs with marinade. Discard any remaining marinade. Lay the kebabs in the frying basket. Add a raised rack and put the rest of the kebabs on it. Bake for 18-23 minutes, flipping once around minute 10. Serve hot.

Roasted Whole Chicken

Servings: 4
Cooking Time: 20 Minutes
Ingredients:
- 3 pounds' whole chicken, remove giblets and pat dry chicken
- 1 teaspoon Italian seasoning
- ½ teaspoon garlic powder
- ½ teaspoon onion powder
- ¼ teaspoon paprika
- ¼ teaspoon black pepper
- 1 ½ teaspoon salt

Directions:
1. In a suitable bowl, mix together Italian seasoning, garlic powder, onion powder, paprika, black pepper, and salt.

2. Rub spice mixture from inside and outside of the chicken.
3. Place chicken breast side down in air fryer basket.
4. Roast chicken for 30 minutes at 360 degrees F/ 180 degrees C.
5. Turn chicken and roast for 20 minutes more or internal temperature of chicken reaches at 165 degrees F/ 75 degrees C.
6. Serve and enjoy.

Gingery Turkey Meatballs

Servings: 4
Cooking Time: 25 Minutes
Ingredients:
- ¼ cup water chestnuts, chopped
- ¼ cup panko bread crumbs
- 1 lb ground turkey
- ½ tsp ground ginger
- 2 tbsp fish sauce
- 1 tbsp sesame oil
- 1 small onion, minced
- 1 egg, beaten

Directions:
1. Preheat air fryer to 400°F. Place the ground turkey, water chestnuts, ground ginger, fish sauce, onion, egg, and bread crumbs in a bowl and stir to combine. Form the turkey mixture into 1-inch meatballs. Arrange the meatballs in the baking pan. Drizzle with sesame oil. Bake until the meatballs are cooked through, 10-12 minutes, flipping once. Serve and enjoy!

Buffalo Chicken Meatballs

Servings:5
Cooking Time: 12 Minutes
Ingredients:
- 1 pound ground chicken breast
- 1 packet dry ranch seasoning
- ⅓ cup plain bread crumbs
- 3 tablespoons mayonnaise
- 5 tablespoons buffalo sauce, divided

Directions:
1. Preheat the air fryer to 370°F.
2. In a large bowl, mix chicken, ranch seasoning, bread crumbs, and mayonnaise. Pour in 2 tablespoons buffalo sauce and stir to combine.
3. Roll meat mixture into balls, about 2 tablespoons for each, to make twenty meatballs.
4. Place meatballs in the air fryer basket and cook 12 minutes, shaking the basket twice during cooking, until brown and internal temperature reaches at least 165°F.
5. Toss meatballs in remaining buffalo sauce and serve.

Paprika Chicken Drumettes

Servings: 2
Cooking Time: 30 Minutes
Ingredients:
- 1 lb chicken drumettes
- 1 cup buttermilk

- 3/4 cup bread crumbs
- ½ tsp smoked paprika
- 1 tsp chicken seasoning
- ½ tsp garlic powder
- Salt and pepper to taste
- 3 tsp of lemon juice

Directions:
1. Mix drumettes and buttermilk in a bowl and let sit covered in the fridge overnight. Preheat air fryer at 350ºF. In a shallow bowl, combine the remaining ingredients. Shake excess buttermilk off drumettes and dip them in the breadcrumb mixture. Place breaded drumettes in the greased frying basket and Air Fry for 12 minutes. Increase air fryer temperature to 400ºF, toss chicken, and cook for 8 minutes. Let rest for 5 minutes before serving.

Sesame Chicken Tenders

Servings:4
Cooking Time: 15 Minutes
Ingredients:
- Olive oil
- ¼ cup soy sauce
- 2 tablespoons white vinegar
- 1 tablespoon honey
- 1 tablespoon toasted sesame oil
- 1 tablespoon lime juice
- 1 teaspoon ground ginger
- 1 pound boneless skinless, chicken tenderloins
- 2 teaspoon toasted sesame seeds

Directions:
1. Spray a fryer basket lightly with olive oil.
2. In a large zip-top plastic bag, combine the soy sauce, white vinegar, honey, sesame oil, lime juice, and ginger to make a marinade.
3. Add the chicken tenderloins to the bag, seal, and marinate the chicken in the refrigerator for at least 2 hours or overnight.
4. If using wooden skewers, soak them in water for at least 30 minutes before using.
5. Thread 1 chicken tenderloin onto each skewer. Sprinkle with sesame seeds. Reserve the marinade.
6. Place the skewers in the fryer basket in a single layer. You may need to cook the chicken in batches.
7. Air fry for 6 minutes. Flip the chicken over, baste with more marinade, and cook until crispy, an additional 5 to 8 minutes.

Yellow Curry Chicken Thighs With Peanuts

Servings:6
Cooking Time: 20 Minutes
Ingredients:
- ½ cup unsweetened full-fat coconut milk
- 2 tablespoons yellow curry paste
- 1 tablespoon minced fresh ginger
- 1 tablespoon minced garlic
- 1 teaspoon kosher salt

- 1 pound (454 g) boneless, skinless chicken thighs, halved crosswise
- 2 tablespoons chopped peanuts

Directions:
1. In a large bowl, stir together the coconut milk, curry paste, ginger, garlic, and salt until well blended. Add the chicken; toss well to coat. Marinate at room temperature for 30 minutes, or cover and refrigerate for up to 24 hours.
2. Preheat the air fryer to 375ºF (191ºC).
3. Place the chicken (along with marinade) in a baking pan. Place the pan in the air fryer basket. Bake for 20 minutes, turning the chicken halfway through the cooking time. Use a meat thermometer to ensure the chicken has reached an internal temperature of 165ºF (74ºC).
4. Sprinkle the chicken with the chopped peanuts and serve.

Easy Tandoori Chicken

Servings:4
Cooking Time: 18 To 23 Minutes
Ingredients:
- ⅔ cup plain low-fat yogurt
- 2 tablespoons freshly squeezed lemon juice
- 2 teaspoons curry powder
- ½ teaspoon ground cinnamon
- 2 garlic cloves, minced
- 2 teaspoons olive oil
- 4 (5-ounce / 142-g) low-sodium boneless, skinless chicken breasts

Directions:
1. In a medium bowl, whisk the yogurt, lemon juice, curry powder, cinnamon, garlic, and olive oil.
2. With a sharp knife, cut thin slashes into the chicken. Add it to the yogurt mixture and turn to coat. Let stand for 10 minutes at room temperature. You can also prepare this ahead of time and marinate the chicken in the refrigerator for up to 24 hours.
3. Preheat the air fryer to 360ºF (182ºC).
4. Remove the chicken from the marinade and shake off any excess liquid. Discard any remaining marinade.
5. Roast the chicken for 10 minutes. With tongs, carefully turn each piece. Roast for 8 to 13 minutes more, or until the chicken reaches an internal temperature of 165ºF (74ºC) on a meat thermometer. Serve immediately.

Spiced Chicken With Pork Rind

Servings: 6
Cooking Time: 12 Minutes
Ingredients:
- 4 eggs
- 1 ½ pounds chicken breasts, diced into small chunks
- 1 teaspoon paprika
- ½ teaspoon garlic powder
- 1 teaspoon onion powder
- 2 ½ cups pork rind, crushed
- ¼ cup coconut flour
- Black pepper

- Salt

Directions:

1. In a suitable bowl, mix together coconut flour, black pepper, and salt.
2. In another bowl, whisk eggs until combined.
3. Take 1 more bowl and mix together pork panko, paprika, garlic powder, and onion powder.
4. Add chicken pieces in a suitable mixing bowl. Sprinkle coconut flour mixture over chicken and toss well.
5. Dip chicken pieces in the prepared egg mixture and coat with pork panko mixture and place on a plate.
6. Grease its air fryer basket with cooking spray.
7. At 400 degrees F/ 205 degrees C, preheat your Air fryer.
8. Add ½ prepared chicken in air fryer basket and cook for almost 10-12 minutes. Shake basket halfway through.
9. Cook remaining ½ using the same method.
10. Serve and enjoy.

Apricot-glazed Chicken

Servings:2
Cooking Time: 12 Minutes

Ingredients:

- 2 tablespoons apricot preserves
- ½ teaspoon minced fresh thyme or ⅛ teaspoon dried
- 2 (8-ounce / 227-g) boneless, skinless chicken breasts, trimmed
- 1 teaspoon vegetable oil
- Salt and pepper, to taste

Directions:

1. Preheat the air fryer to 400°F (204°C).
2. Microwave apricot preserves and thyme in bowl until fluid, about 30 seconds; set aside. Pound chicken to uniform thickness as needed. Pat dry with paper towels, rub with oil, and season with salt and pepper.
3. Arrange breasts skin-side down in air fryer basket, spaced evenly apart, alternating ends. Air fry the chicken for 4 minutes. Flip chicken and brush skin side with apricot-thyme mixture. Air fry until chicken registers 160°F (71°C), 8 to 12 minutes more.
4. Transfer chicken to serving platter, tent loosely with aluminum foil, and let rest for 5 minutes. Serve.

Garlic Chicken

Servings: 4
Cooking Time: 30 Minutes

Ingredients:

- 4 bone-in skinless chicken thighs
- 1 tbsp olive oil
- 1 tbsp lemon juice
- 3 tbsp cornstarch
- 1 tsp dried sage
- Black pepper to taste
- 20 garlic cloves, unpeeled

Directions:

1. Preheat air fryer to 370°F. Brush the chicken with olive oil and lemon juice, then drizzle cornstarch, sage, and pepper.Put the chicken in the frying basket and

scatter the garlic cloves on top. Roast for 25 minutes or until the garlic is soft, and the chicken is cooked through. Serve.

Chicken Tenders With Italian Seasoning

Servings: 2
Cooking Time: 10 Minutes

Ingredients:

- 2 eggs, lightly beaten
- 1 ½ pounds chicken tenders
- ½ teaspoon onion powder
- ½ teaspoon garlic powder
- 1 teaspoon paprika
- 1 teaspoon Italian seasoning
- 2 tablespoons' ground flax seed
- 1 cup almond flour
- ½ teaspoon black pepper
- 1 teaspoon salt

Directions:

1. At 400 degrees F/ 205 degrees C, preheat your Air fryer.
2. Season chicken with black pepper and salt.
3. In a suitable bowl, whisk eggs to combine.
4. In a shallow dish, mix together almond flour, all seasonings, and flaxseed.
5. Dip chicken into the egg then coats with almond flour mixture and place on a plate.
6. Grease its air fryer basket with cooking spray.
7. Place ½ chicken tenders in air fryer basket and cook for almost 10 minutes, turning halfway through.
8. Cook remaining chicken tenders using same steps.
9. Serve and enjoy.

Fried Buffalo Chicken Taquitos

Servings:6
Cooking Time: 5 To 10 Minutes

Ingredients:

- 8 ounces (227 g) fat-free cream cheese, softened
- ⅛ cup Buffalo sauce
- 2 cups shredded cooked chicken
- 12 (7-inch) low-carb flour tortillas
- Olive oil spray

Directions:

1. Preheat the air fryer to 360°F (182°C). Spray the air fryer basket lightly with olive oil spray.
2. In a large bowl, mix together the cream cheese and Buffalo sauce until well combined. Add the chicken and stir until combined.
3. Place the tortillas on a clean workspace. Spoon 2 to 3 tablespoons of the chicken mixture in a thin line down the center of each tortilla. Roll up the tortillas.
4. Place the tortillas in the air fryer basket, seam-side down. Spray each tortilla lightly with olive oil spray. You may need to cook the taquitos in batches.
5. Air fry until golden brown, 5 to 10 minutes. Serve hot.

Lemon Chicken And Spinach Salad

Servings:4
Cooking Time: 16 To 20 Minutes
Ingredients:
- 3 (5-ounce / 142-g) low-sodium boneless, skinless chicken breasts, cut into 1-inch cubes
- 5 teaspoons olive oil
- ½ teaspoon dried thyme
- 1 medium red onion, sliced
- 1 red bell pepper, sliced
- 1 small zucchini, cut into strips
- 3 tablespoons freshly squeezed lemon juice
- 6 cups fresh baby spinach

Directions:
1. Preheat the air fryer to 400ºF (204ºC).
2. In a large bowl, mix the chicken with the olive oil and thyme. Toss to coat. Transfer to a medium metal bowl and roast for 8 minutes in the air fryer.
3. Add the red onion, red bell pepper, and zucchini. Roast for 8 to 12 minutes more, stirring once during cooking, or until the chicken reaches an internal temperature of 165ºF (74ºC) on a meat thermometer.
4. Remove the bowl from the air fryer and stir in the lemon juice.
5. Put the spinach in a serving bowl and top with the chicken mixture. Toss to combine and serve immediately.

Chicken Hand Pies

Servings: 8
Cooking Time: 10 Minutes Per Batch
Ingredients:
- ¾ cup chicken broth
- ¾ cup frozen mixed peas and carrots
- 1 cup cooked chicken, chopped
- 1 tablespoon cornstarch
- 1 tablespoon milk
- salt and pepper
- 1 8-count can organic flaky biscuits
- oil for misting or cooking spray

Directions:
1. In a medium saucepan, bring chicken broth to a boil. Stir in the frozen peas and carrots and cook for 5minutes over medium heat. Stir in chicken.
2. Mix the cornstarch into the milk until it dissolves. Stir it into the simmering chicken broth mixture and cook just until thickened.
3. Remove from heat, add salt and pepper to taste, and let cool slightly.
4. Lay biscuits out on wax paper. Peel each biscuit apart in the middle to make 2 rounds so you have 16 rounds total. Using your hands or a rolling pin, flatten each biscuit round slightly to make it larger and thinner.
5. Divide chicken filling among 8 of the biscuit rounds. Place remaining biscuit rounds on top and press edges all around. Use the tines of a fork to crimp biscuit edges and make sure they are sealed well.
6. Spray both sides lightly with oil or cooking spray.

7. Cook in a single layer, 4 at a time, at 330°F for 10minutes or until biscuit dough is cooked through and golden brown.

Simple Buttermilk Fried Chicken

Servings: 4
Cooking Time: 27 Minutes
Ingredients:
- 1 (4-pound) chicken, cut into 8 pieces
- 2 cups buttermilk
- hot sauce (optional)
- 1½ cups flour*
- 2 teaspoons paprika
- 1 teaspoon salt
- freshly ground black pepper
- 2 eggs, lightly beaten
- vegetable oil, in a spray bottle

Directions:
1. Cut the chicken into 8 pieces and submerge them in the buttermilk and hot sauce, if using. A zipper-sealable plastic bag works well for this. Let the chicken soak in the buttermilk for at least one hour or even overnight in the refrigerator.
2. Set up a dredging station. Mix the flour, paprika, salt and black pepper in a clean zipper-sealable plastic bag. Whisk the eggs and place them in a shallow dish. Remove four pieces of chicken from the buttermilk and transfer them to the bag with the flour. Shake them around to coat on all sides. Remove the chicken from the flour, shaking off any excess flour, and dip them into the beaten egg. Return the chicken to the bag of seasoned flour and shake again. Set the coated chicken aside and repeat with the remaining four pieces of chicken.
3. Preheat the air fryer to 370°F.
4. Spray the chicken on all sides with the vegetable oil and then transfer one batch to the air fryer basket. Air-fry the chicken at 370°F for 20 minutes, flipping the pieces over halfway through the cooking process, taking care not to knock off the breading. Transfer the chicken to a plate, but do not cover. Repeat with the second batch of chicken.
5. Lower the temperature on the air fryer to 340°F. Flip the chicken back over and place the first batch of chicken on top of the second batch already in the basket. Air-fry for another 7 minutes and serve warm.

Dill Pickle-ranch Wings

Servings:4
Cooking Time: 2 Hours 20 Minutes
Ingredients:
- 1 cup pickle juice
- 2 pounds chicken wings, flats and drums separated
- ½ teaspoon salt
- ½ teaspoon ground black pepper
- 2 teaspoons dry ranch seasoning

Directions:

1. In a large bowl or resealable plastic bag, combine pickle juice and wings. Cover and let marinate in refrigerator 2 hours.
2. Preheat the air fryer to 400°F.
3. In a separate bowl, mix salt, pepper, and ranch seasoning. Remove wings from marinade and toss in dry seasoning.
4. Place wings in the air fryer basket in a single layer, working in batches as necessary. Cook 20 minutes, turning halfway through cooking time, until wings reach an internal temperature of at least 165°F. Cool 5 minutes before serving.

Chicken And Onion Sausages

Servings: 4
Cooking Time: 10 Minutes
Ingredients:
- 1 garlic clove, diced
- 1 spring onion, chopped
- 1 cup ground chicken
- ½ teaspoon salt
- ½ teaspoon ground black pepper
- 4 sausage links
- 1 teaspoon olive oil

Directions:
1. Mix together the ground chicken, ground black pepper, onion, and the diced garlic clove in a mixing dish to make the filling.
2. Fill the sausage links with the chicken mixture.
3. Then cut the sausages into halves and make sure the endings of the sausage halves are secured.
4. Before cooking, heat your air fryer to 365 degrees F/ 185 degrees C.
5. Brush olive oil over the sausages. Arrange the chicken and onion sausage in the air fryer basket and cook in the preheated air fryer for 10 minutes.

6. Then flip the sausage to ensure even cook. Cook again for 5 minutes or more. Or increase the temperature to 390 degrees F/ 200 degrees C and cook for 8 minutes for a faster result.

French Mustard Chicken Thighs

Servings: 4
Cooking Time: 15 Minutes
Ingredients:
- 1-pound bone-in or boneless, skinless chicken thighs
- Black pepper and salt to taste
- 2 garlic cloves, minced
- ½ cup honey
- ¼ cup French mustard
- 2 tablespoons butter
- 2 tablespoon dill, chopped
- Herbs de Provence seasoning, as needed

Directions:
1. At 390 degrees F/ 200 degrees C, preheat your Air fryer.
2. Grease its air fryer basket with cooking spray.
3. In a suitable bowl, mix the Herbs de Provence seasoning, salt, and black pepper. Rub the chicken with this mixture.
4. Transfer to the cooking basket.
5. Cook for almost 15 minutes, flipping once halfway through.
6. Meanwhile, melt the butter in a suitable saucepan over medium heat.
7. Add honey, French mustard, and garlic; cook until reduced to a thick consistency, about 3 minutes.
8. Serve the chicken drizzled with the honey-mustard sauce.

Chapter 8: Fish And Seafood Recipes

Shrimp Patties

Servings: 4
Cooking Time: 10 Minutes
Ingredients:
- ½ pound shelled and deveined raw shrimp
- ¼ cup chopped red bell pepper
- ¼ cup chopped green onion
- ¼ cup chopped celery
- 2 cups cooked sushi rice
- ½ teaspoon garlic powder
- ½ teaspoon Old Bay Seasoning
- ½ teaspoon salt
- 2 teaspoons Worcestershire sauce
- ½ cup plain breadcrumbs
- oil for misting or cooking spray

Directions:
1. Finely chop the shrimp. You can do this in a food processor, but it takes only a few pulses. Be careful not to overprocess into mush.
2. Place shrimp in a large bowl and add all other ingredients except the breadcrumbs and oil. Stir until well combined.
3. Preheat air fryer to 390°F.
4. Shape shrimp mixture into 8 patties, no more than ½-inch thick. Roll patties in breadcrumbs and mist with oil or cooking spray.
5. Place 4 shrimp patties in air fryer basket and cook at 390°F for 10 minutes, until shrimp cooks through and outside is crispy.
6. Repeat step 5 to cook remaining shrimp patties.

Sinaloa Fish Fajitas

Servings: 4
Cooking Time: 30 Minutes
Ingredients:
- 1 lemon, thinly sliced
- 16 oz red snapper filets
- 1 tbsp olive oil
- 1 tbsp cayenne pepper
- ½ tsp salt
- 2 cups shredded coleslaw
- 1 carrot, shredded
- 2 tbsp orange juice
- ½ cup salsa
- 4 flour tortillas
- ½ cup sour cream
- 2 avocados, sliced

Directions:
1. Preheat the air fryer to 350°F. Lay the lemon slices at the bottom of the basket. Drizzle the fillets with olive oil and sprinkle with cayenne pepper and salt. Lay the fillets on top of the lemons and Bake for 6-9 minutes or until the fish easily flakes. While the fish cooks, toss the coleslaw, carrot, orange juice, and salsa in a bowl. When the fish is done, remove it and cover. Toss the lemons. Air Fry the tortillas for 2-3 minutes to warm up. Add the fish to the tortillas and top with a cabbage mix, sour cream, and avocados. Serve and enjoy!

Chunky Fish With Mustard

Servings: 4
Cooking Time: 10 Minutes
Ingredients:
- 2 cans canned fish
- 2 celery stalks, trimmed and finely chopped
- 1 egg, whisked
- 1 cup bread crumbs
- 1 teaspoon whole-grain mustard
- ½-teaspoon sea salt
- ¼-teaspoon freshly cracked black peppercorns
- ½ teaspoon paprika

Directions:
1. Add all of the ingredients one by one and combine well.
2. Form four equal-sized cakes from the mixture, then leave to chill in the refrigerator for 50 minutes.
3. Spray all sides of each cake after putting them on the cooking pan of your air fryer.
4. Arrange the pan to the air fryer and grill at 360 degrees F/ 180 degrees C for 5 minutes.
5. After 5 minutes, turn the cakes over and resume cooking for an additional 3 minutes.
6. Serve with mashed potatoes if desired.

Fish Sticks With Tartar Sauce

Servings: 2
Cooking Time: 6 Minutes
Ingredients:
- 12 ounces cod or flounder
- ½ cup flour
- ½ teaspoon paprika
- 1 teaspoon salt
- lots of freshly ground black pepper
- 2 eggs, lightly beaten
- 1½ cups panko breadcrumbs
- 1 teaspoon salt
- vegetable oil
- Tartar Sauce:
- ¼ cup mayonnaise
- 2 teaspoons lemon juice
- 2 tablespoons finely chopped sweet pickles
- salt and freshly ground black pepper

Directions:
1. Cut the fish into ¾-inch wide sticks or strips. Set up a dredging station. Combine the flour, paprika, salt and pepper in a shallow dish. Beat the eggs lightly in a second shallow dish. Finally, mix the breadcrumbs and salt in a third shallow dish. Coat the fish sticks by dipping the fish into the flour, then the egg and finally the breadcrumbs, coating on all sides in each step and pressing the crumbs firmly onto the fish. Place the finished sticks on a plate or baking sheet while you finish all the sticks.
2. Preheat the air fryer to 400°F.

3. Spray the fish sticks with the oil and spray or brush the bottom of the air fryer basket. Place the fish into the basket and air-fry at 400°F for 4 minutes, turn the fish sticks over, and air-fry for another 2 minutes.

4. While the fish is cooking, mix the tartar sauce ingredients together.

5. Serve the fish sticks warm with the tartar sauce and some French fries on the side.

Spicy Mackerel

Servings: 2
Cooking Time: 20 Minutes
Ingredients:
- 2 mackerel fillets
- 2 tbsp. red chili flakes
- 2 tsp. garlic, minced
- 1 tsp. lemon juice

Directions:
1. Season the mackerel fillets with the red pepper flakes, minced garlic, and a drizzle of lemon juice. Allow to sit for five minutes.

2. Preheat your fryer at 350°F.

3. Cook the mackerel for five minutes, before opening the drawer, flipping the fillets, and allowing to cook on the other side for another five minutes.

4. Plate the fillets, making sure to spoon any remaining juice over them before serving.

Shrimp Tempura

Servings: 6 Servings
Cooking Time: 30 Minutes
Ingredients:
- 2 pounds of peeled raw shrimp
- 2 eggs
- 2 ½ cups of panko bread crumbs
- 1 cup of all-purpose flour
- 2 tablespoons of olive oil
- 2 teaspoons of water

Directions:
1. Preheat your air fryer to 350ºF. Spray some oil inside the air fryer basket.

2. Whisk eggs with 2 teaspoons of water in a small bowl. Put flour in a separate bowl. Add bread crumbs in a third bowl.

3. First, coat the shrimp with the flour (shake off the excess flour), then dip into the egg mixture, and finally roll in the bread crumbs until fully covered. Put them in the air fryer basket in a single layer; avoid them touching.

4. Cook at 350ºF for 4 minutes, spray tops with some oil, flip them, and cook for extra 4 minutes. Repeat the last 2 steps until all shrimp are cooked.

5. Serve warm with any sauce you like. Enjoy your Shrimp Tempura!

Fish Sticks For Grown-ups

Servings: 4
Cooking Time: 6 Minutes
Ingredients:
- 1 pound fish fillets
- ½ teaspoon hot sauce

- 1 tablespoon coarse brown mustard
- 1 teaspoon Worcestershire sauce
- salt
- Crumb Coating
- ¾ cup panko breadcrumbs
- ¼ cup stone-ground cornmeal
- ¼ teaspoon salt
- oil for misting or cooking spray

Directions:
1. Cut fish fillets crosswise into slices 1-inch wide.

2. Mix the hot sauce, mustard, and Worcestershire sauce together to make a paste and rub on all sides of the fish. Season to taste with salt.

3. Mix crumb coating ingredients together and spread on a sheet of wax paper.

4. Roll the fish fillets in the crumb mixture.

5. Spray all sides with olive oil or cooking spray and place in air fryer basket in a single layer.

6. Cook at 390°F for 6 minutes, until fish flakes easily.

Cheese & Crab Stuffed Mushrooms

Servings: 2
Cooking Time: 30 Minutes
Ingredients:
- 6 oz lump crabmeat, shells discarded
- 6 oz mascarpone cheese, softened
- 2 jalapeño peppers, minced
- ¼ cup diced red onions
- 2 tsp grated Parmesan cheese
- 2 portobello mushroom caps
- 2 tbsp butter, divided
- ½ tsp prepared horseradish
- ¼ tsp Worcestershire sauce
- ¼ tsp smoked paprika
- Salt and pepper to taste
- ¼ cup bread crumbs

Directions:
1. Melt 1 tbsp of butter in a skillet over heat for 30 seconds. Add in onion and cook for 3 minutes until tender. Stir in mascarpone cheese, Parmesan cheese, horseradish, jalapeño peppers, Worcestershire sauce, paprika, salt and pepper and cook for 2 minutes until smooth. Fold in crabmeat. Spoon mixture into mushroom caps. Set aside.

2. Preheat air fryer at 350ºF. Microwave the remaining butter until melted. Stir in breadcrumbs. Scatter over stuffed mushrooms. Place mushrooms in the greased frying basket and Bake for 8 minutes. Serve immediately.

Potato-crusted Cod

Servings: 4
Cooking Time: 15 Minutes
Ingredients:
- 4 boneless, skinless cod fillets
- 2 tablespoons olive oil
- ½ teaspoon salt, divided
- 1 teaspoon dried dill
- 2 cups mashed potato flakes

Directions:

1. Preheat the air fryer to 350°F.
2. Place cod fillets on a work surface and brush with oil. Sprinkle with ¼ teaspoon salt and dill.
3. In a large bowl, combine mashed potato flakes with remaining salt.
4. Roll each fillet in the potato mixture and spritz with cooking spray.
5. Place in the air fryer basket and cook 15 minutes, turning halfway through cooking time. Cod will be golden brown and have an internal temperature of at least 145°F when done. Serve warm.

Crab Cakes On A Budget

Servings: 4
Cooking Time: 12 Minutes
Ingredients:
- 8 ounces imitation crabmeat
- 4 ounces leftover cooked fish (such as cod, pollock, or haddock)
- 2 tablespoons minced green onion
- 2 tablespoons minced celery
- ¾ cup crushed saltine cracker crumbs
- 2 tablespoons light mayonnaise
- 1 teaspoon prepared yellow mustard
- 1 tablespoon Worcestershire sauce, plus 2 teaspoons
- 2 teaspoons dried parsley flakes
- ½ teaspoon dried dill weed, crushed
- ½ teaspoon garlic powder
- ½ teaspoon Old Bay Seasoning
- ½ cup panko breadcrumbs
- oil for misting or cooking spray

Directions:
1. Use knives or a food processor to finely shred crabmeat and fish.
2. In a large bowl, combine all ingredients except panko and oil. Stir well.
3. Shape into 8 small, fat patties.
4. Carefully roll patties in panko crumbs to coat. Spray both sides with oil or cooking spray.
5. Place patties in air fryer basket and cook at 390°F for 12 minutes or until golden brown and crispy.

Lemon-dill Salmon Burgers

Servings: 4
Cooking Time: 8 Minutes
Ingredients:
- 2 (6-ounce) fillets of salmon, finely chopped by hand or in a food processor
- 1 cup fine breadcrumbs
- 1 teaspoon freshly grated lemon zest
- 2 tablespoons chopped fresh dill weed
- 1 teaspoon salt
- freshly ground black pepper
- 2 eggs, lightly beaten
- 4 brioche or hamburger buns
- lettuce, tomato, red onion, avocado, mayonnaise or mustard, to serve

Directions:
1. Preheat the air fryer to 400°F.

2. Combine all the ingredients in a bowl. Mix together well and divide into four balls. Flatten the balls into patties, making an indentation in the center of each patty with your thumb (this will help the burger stay flat as it cooks) and flattening the sides of the burgers so that they fit nicely into the air fryer basket.
3. Transfer the burgers to the air fryer basket and air-fry for 4 minutes. Flip the burgers over and air-fry for another 3 to 4 minutes, until nicely browned and firm to the touch.
4. Serve on soft brioche buns with your choice of topping – lettuce, tomato, red onion, avocado, mayonnaise or mustard.

Lime Trout With Parsley

Servings: 4
Cooking Time: 12 Minutes
Ingredients:
- 4 trout fillets, boneless
- 4 tablespoons butter, melted
- Black pepper and salt to the taste
- Juice of 1 lime
- 1 tablespoon chives, chopped
- 1 tablespoon parsley, chopped

Directions:
1. Mix the fish fillets with the melted butter, black pepper and salt, rub gently, put the trout fillets in your air fryer basket and cook at almost 390 degrees F/ 200 degrees C for 6 minutes per side.
2. Divide between plates and serve with lime juice drizzled on top and with parsley and chives sprinkled at the end.

Chinese Firecracker Shrimp

Servings: 4
Cooking Time: 20 Minutes
Ingredients:
- 1 lb peeled shrimp, deveined
- 2 green onions, chopped
- 2 tbsp sesame seeds
- Salt and pepper to taste
- 1 egg
- ½ cup all-purpose flour
- ¾ cup panko bread crumbs
- 1/3 cup sour cream
- 2 tbsp Sriracha sauce
- ¼ cup sweet chili sauce

Directions:
1. Preheat air fryer to 400°F. Set out three small bowls. In the first, add flour. In the second, beat the egg. In the third, add the crumbs. Season the shrimp with salt and pepper. Dip the shrimp in the flour, then dredge in the egg, and finally in the bread crumbs. Place the shrimp in the greased frying basket and Air Fry for 8 minutes, flipping once until crispy. Combine sour cream, Sriracha, and sweet chili sauce in a bowl. Top the shrimp with sesame seeds and green onions and serve with the chili sauce.

Cajun Flounder Fillets

Servings:2
Cooking Time: 5 Minutes
Ingredients:
- 2 4-ounce skinless flounder fillet(s)
- 2 teaspoons Peanut oil
- 1 teaspoon Purchased or homemade Cajun dried seasoning blend

Directions:
1. Preheat the air fryer to 400°F.
2. Oil the fillet(s) by drizzling on the peanut oil, then gently rubbing in the oil with your clean, dry fingers. Sprinkle the seasoning blend evenly over both sides of the fillet(s).
3. When the machine is at temperature, set the fillet(s) in the basket. If working with more than one fillet, they should not touch, although they may be quite close together, depending on the basket's size. Air-fry undisturbed for 5 minutes, or until lightly browned and cooked through.
4. Use a nonstick-safe spatula to transfer the fillets to a serving platter or plate(s). Serve at once.

Hazelnut-crusted Fish

Servings: 4
Cooking Time: 30 Minutes
Ingredients:
- ½ cup hazelnuts, ground
- 1 scallion, finely chopped
- 1 lemon, juiced and zested
- ½ tbsp olive oil
- Salt and pepper to taste
- 3 skinless sea bass fillets
- 1 tsp Dijon mustard

Directions:
1. Place the hazelnuts in a small bowl along with scallion, lemon zest, olive oil, salt and pepper. Mix everything until combined. Spray only the top of the fish with cooking oil, then squeeze lemon juice onto the fish. Coat the top of the fish with mustard. Spread with hazelnuts and press gently so that it stays on the fish.
2. Preheat air fryer to 375°F. Air Fry the fish in the greased frying basket for 7-8 minutes or it starts browning and the fish is cooked through. Serve hot.

Tuna Patties With Dill Sauce

Servings: 6
Cooking Time: 10 Minutes
Ingredients:
- Two 5-ounce cans albacore tuna, drained
- ½ teaspoon garlic powder
- 2 teaspoons dried dill, divided
- ½ teaspoon black pepper
- ½ teaspoon salt, divided
- ¼ cup minced onion
- 1 large egg
- 7 tablespoons mayonnaise, divided
- ¼ cup panko breadcrumbs

- 1 teaspoon fresh lemon juice
- ¼ teaspoon fresh lemon zest
- 6 pieces butterleaf lettuce
- 1 cup diced tomatoes

Directions:
1. In a large bowl, mix the tuna with the garlic powder, 1 teaspoon of the dried dill, the black pepper, ¼ teaspoon of the salt, and the onion. Make sure to use the back of a fork to really break up the tuna so there are no large chunks.
2. Mix in the egg and 1 tablespoon of the mayonnaise; then fold in the breadcrumbs so the tuna begins to form a thick batter that holds together.
3. Portion the tuna mixture into 6 equal patties and place on a plate lined with parchment paper in the refrigerator for at least 30 minutes. This will help the patties hold together in the air fryer.
4. When ready to cook, preheat the air fryer to 350°F.
5. Liberally spray the metal trivet that sits inside the air fryer basket with olive oil mist and place the patties onto the trivet.
6. Cook for 5 minutes, flip, and cook another 5 minutes.
7. While the patties are cooking, make the dill sauce by combining the remaining 6 tablespoons of mayonnaise with the remaining 1 teaspoon of dill, the lemon juice, the lemon zest, and the remaining ¼ teaspoon of salt. Set aside.
8. Remove the patties from the air fryer.
9. Place 1 slice of lettuce on a plate and top with the tuna patty and a tomato slice. Repeat to form the remaining servings. Drizzle the dill dressing over the top. Serve immediately.

Lemon Salmon Fillets

Servings: 2
Cooking Time: 15 Minutes
Ingredients:
- 2 salmon fillets
- ½ teaspoon garlic powder
- ¼ cup plain yogurt
- 1 teaspoon fresh lemon juice
- 1 tablespoon fresh dill, chopped
- 1 lemon, sliced
- Black pepper
- Salt

Directions:
1. Place lemon slices into the air fryer basket.
2. Season salmon with black pepper and salt and place on top of lemon slices into the air fryer basket.
3. Cook salmon at 330 degrees F/ 165 degrees C for almost 15 minutes.
4. Meanwhile, in a suitable bowl, mix together yogurt, garlic powder, lemon juice, dill, black pepper, and salt.
5. Place the prepared salmon on serving plate and top with yogurt mixture.
6. Serve and enjoy.

Cajun Fish Sticks

Servings: 4
Cooking Time: 10 Minutes
Ingredients:
- 1-pound white fish, cut into pieces
- ¾ teaspoon Cajun seasoning
- 1 ½ cups pork rind, crushed
- 2 tablespoons water
- 2 tablespoons Dijon mustard
- ¼ cup mayonnaise
- Black pepper
- Salt

Directions:
1. Grease its air fryer basket with cooking spray.
2. In a suitable bowl, whisk water, mayonnaise, and mustard.
3. In a shallow bowl, mix black pepper, pork rind, Cajun seasoning, and salt.
4. Dip fish pieces in mayo mixture and coat well with pork rind mixture them set in the air fryer basket evenly.
5. Cook at almost 400 degrees F/ 205 degrees C for 5 minutes.
6. Flip the fish sticks and continue cooking for 5 minutes more.
7. Serve and enjoy.

Haddock Cakes

Servings: 3
Cooking Time: 10 Minutes
Ingredients:
- 1 pound haddock
- 1 egg
- 2 tablespoons milk
- 1 bell pepper, deveined and finely chopped
- 2 stalks fresh scallions, minced
- ½ teaspoon fresh garlic, minced
- Sea salt, to taste
- Ground black pepper, to taste
- ½ teaspoon cumin seeds
- ¼ teaspoon celery seeds
- ½ cup breadcrumbs
- 1 teaspoon olive oil

Directions:
1. In addition to the breadcrumbs and olive oil, thoroughly combine the other ingredients.
2. Form 3 patties from the mixture and coat them with breadcrumbs, pressing to adhere.
3. Place the patties on the cooking basket and then drizzle the olive oil on them.
4. Arrange the basket to the air fryer and cook at 400 degrees F/ 205 degrees C for 10 minutes, flipping halfway through.
5. Bon appétit!

Easy Lobster Tail With Salted Butetr

Servings:4
Cooking Time: 6 Minutes
Ingredients:
- 2 tablespoons melted butter
- 4 lobster tails
- Salt and pepper to taste

Directions:
1. Preheat the air fryer to 390°F.
2. Place the grill pan accessory.
3. Cut the lobster through the tail section using a pair of kitchen scissors.
4. Brush the lobster tails with melted butter and season with salt and pepper to taste.
5. Place on the grill pan and cook for 6 minutes.

Italian Baked Cod

Servings:4
Cooking Time: 12 Minutes
Ingredients:
- 4 cod fillets
- 2 tablespoons salted butter, melted
- 1 teaspoon Italian seasoning
- ¼ teaspoon salt
- ½ cup low-carb marinara sauce

Directions:
1. Place cod into an ungreased 6" round nonstick baking dish. Pour butter over cod and sprinkle with Italian seasoning and salt. Top with marinara.
2. Place dish into air fryer basket. Adjust the temperature to 350°F and set the timer for 12 minutes. Fillets will be lightly browned, easily flake, and have an internal temperature of at least 145°F when done. Serve warm.

Lemon Pepper-breaded Tilapia

Servings:4
Cooking Time: 10 Minutes
Ingredients:
- 1 large egg
- ⅓ cup all-purpose flour
- ¼ cup grated Parmesan cheese
- ½ tablespoon lemon pepper seasoning
- 4 boneless, skinless tilapia fillets

Directions:
1. Preheat the air fryer to 375°F.
2. In a medium bowl, whisk egg. On a large plate, mix flour, Parmesan, and lemon pepper seasoning.
3. Pat tilapia dry. Dip each fillet into egg, gently shaking off excess. Press into flour mixture, then spritz both sides with cooking spray.
4. Place in the air fryer basket and cook 10 minutes, turning halfway through cooking, until fillets are golden and crispy and internal temperature reaches at least 145°F. Serve warm.

Delicious Grouper Filets

Servings: 3
Cooking Time: 10 Minutes
Ingredients:
- 1 pound grouper filets
- ¼ teaspoon shallot powder

- ¼ teaspoon porcini powder
- 1 teaspoon fresh garlic, minced
- ½ teaspoon cayenne pepper
- ½ teaspoon hot paprika
- ¼ teaspoon oregano
- ½ teaspoon marjoram
- ½ teaspoon sage
- 1 tablespoon butter, melted
- Sea salt and black pepper, to taste

Directions:
1. Use the kitchen towels to pat dry the grouper filets.
2. Mix up the remaining ingredients until well incorporated, then rub the grouper filets on all sides with the mixture.
3. Cook the grouper filets in the preheated Air Fryer at 400 degrees F/ 205 degrees C for 10 minutes, flipping halfway through.
4. Serve over hot rice if desired. Bon appétit!

Dijon Shrimp Cakes

Servings: 4
Cooking Time: 30 Minutes
Ingredients:
- 1 cup cooked shrimp, minced
- ¾ cup saltine cracker crumbs
- 1 cup lump crabmeat
- 3 green onions, chopped
- 1 egg, beaten
- ¼ cup mayonnaise
- 2 tbsp Dijon mustard
- 1 tbsp lemon juice

Directions:
1. Preheat the air fryer to 375°F. Combine the crabmeat, shrimp, green onions, egg, mayonnaise, mustard, ¼ cup of cracker crumbs, and the lemon juice in a bowl and mix gently. Make 4 patties, sprinkle with the rest of the cracker crumbs on both sides, and spray with cooking oil. Line the frying basket with a round parchment paper with holes poked in it. Coat the paper with cooking spray and lay the patties on it. Bake for 10-14 minutes or until the patties are golden brown. Serve warm.

Crunchy Coconut Shrimp

Servings:2
Cooking Time: 8 Minutes
Ingredients:
- 8 ounces jumbo shrimp, peeled and deveined
- 2 tablespoons salted butter, melted
- ½ teaspoon Old Bay Seasoning
- ¼ cup unsweetened shredded coconut
- ¼ cup coconut flour

Directions:
1. In a large bowl, toss shrimp in butter and Old Bay Seasoning.
2. In a medium bowl, combine shredded coconut with coconut flour. Coat each piece of shrimp in coconut mixture.

3. Place shrimp into ungreased air fryer basket. Adjust the temperature to 400°F and set the timer for 8 minutes, gently turning shrimp halfway through cooking. Shrimp will be pink and C-shaped when done. Serve warm.

Thai Coconut Fish

Servings: 2
Cooking Time: 20 Minutes
Ingredients:
- 1 cup coconut milk
- 1 tablespoon lime juice
- 1 tablespoon Shoyu sauce
- Salt and white pepper, to taste
- 1 teaspoon turmeric powder
- ½-teaspoon ginger powder
- ½ Thai Bird's Eye chili
- 1 lb. tilapia
- 1 tablespoon olive oil

Directions:
1. Remove the seeds from the chili and finely chop them. Prepare a mixing bowl, thoroughly combine the coconut milk with the lime juice, Shoyu sauce, salt, pepper, turmeric, ginger, and chili pepper.
2. Coat the tilapia with the mixture and let it marinate for 1 hour.
3. Brush the basket of your air fryer with olive oil.
4. Take the tilapia fillets out of the marinade and place them in the basket.
5. Cook the tilapia fillets in the preheated Air Fryer at 400 degrees F/ 205 degrees C for 12 minutes, flipping halfway through.
6. Working in batches is suggested.
7. Serve with some extra lime wedges if desired. Enjoy!

Creamy Tuna With Zucchinis

Servings: 4
Cooking Time: 20 Minutes
Ingredients:
- 4 medium zucchinis
- 120g of tuna in oil canned drained
- 30g grated cheese
- 1 teaspoon pine nuts
- Salt, black pepper to taste

Directions:
1. Cut the zucchini in ½ laterally and empty it with a small spoon set aside the pulp that will be used for filling; place them in the basket.
2. In a food processor, put the zucchini pulp, drained tuna, pine nuts and grated cheese.
3. Mix until you get a homogeneous and dense mixture.
4. Fill the zucchini. Set the air fryer to 360 degrees F/ 180 degrees C.
5. Air fry for almost 20 minutes depending on the size of the zucchini. Let cool before serving.

Crumbed Fish Fillets With Parmesan Cheese

Servings: 4
Cooking Time: 25 Minutes
Ingredients:

- 2 eggs, beaten
- ½-teaspoon tarragon
- 4 fish fillets, halved
- ½ tablespoon dry white wine
- ⅓ cup Parmesan cheese, grated
- 1 teaspoon seasoned salt
- ⅓-teaspoon mixed peppercorns
- ½-teaspoon fennel seed

Directions:
1. Add the Parmesan cheese, salt, peppercorns, fennel seeds, and tarragon to your food processor; blitz for about 20 seconds.
2. Drizzle dry white wine on the top of these fish fillets.
3. In a shallow dish, dump the egg.
4. Now, coat the fish fillets with the beaten egg on all sides, then coat them with the seasoned cracker mix.
5. Air-fry at 345 degrees F/ 175 degrees C for about 17 minutes. Bon appétit!

Tender Salmon

Servings: 4 Servings
Cooking Time: 30 Minutes
Ingredients:

- 4 salmon fillets
- 4 teaspoons of soy sauce
- 3 tablespoons of maple syrup
- 1 teaspoon of minced garlic
- 1/8 teaspoon of black pepper

Directions:
1. Add soy sauce, maple syrup, black pepper, and garlic to a bowl. Mix it until well combined. Put the salmon fillets in a Ziplock bag and pour in the prepared marinade. Leave it for 10–30 minutes for good flavor.
2. Preheat your air fryer to 350ºF. Spray some oil inside the air fryer basket.
3. Transfer the marinated filets into the air fryer basket in a single layer.* Cook at 350ºF for 8–10 minutes if you like medium-rare. Cook for 10–12 minutes, if you prefer well done.** The internal temperature for medium-rare should be 120–125ºF, and for well-done will be 140ºF.
4. Serve warm*** and enjoy your Tender Salmon!

Flavor Moroccan Harissa Shrimp

Servings: 3
Cooking Time: 10 Minutes
Ingredients:

- 1-pound breaded shrimp, frozen
- 1 teaspoon extra-virgin olive oil
- Sea salt, to taste
- Ground black pepper, to taste
- 1 teaspoon coriander seeds
- 1 teaspoon caraway seeds
- 1 teaspoon crushed red pepper

- 1 teaspoon fresh garlic, minced

Directions:
1. Arrange the breaded shrimp tossed with olive oil to the cooking basket and then arrange the basket to the air fryer.
2. Cook the shrimp at 400 degrees F/ 205 degrees C for 5 minutes.
3. After 5 minutes, shake the basket and cook an additional 4 minutes.
4. During cooking, mix the remaining ingredients until well combined.
5. Taste and adjust seasonings.
6. Toss the warm shrimp with the harissa sauce and serve immediately. Enjoy!

Mediterranean Salmon Cakes

Servings:4
Cooking Time: 30 Minutes
Ingredients:

- ¼ cup heavy cream
- 5 tbsp mayonnaise
- 2 cloves garlic, minced
- ¼ tsp caper juice
- 2 tsp lemon juice
- 1 tbsp capers
- 1 can salmon
- 2 tsp lemon zest
- 1 egg
- ¼ minced red bell peppers
- ½ cup flour
- ⅛ tsp salt
- 2 tbsp sliced green olives

Directions:
1. Combine heavy cream, 2 tbsp of mayonnaise, garlic, caper juices, capers, and lemon juice in a bowl. Place the resulting caper sauce in the fridge until ready to use.
2. Preheat air fryer to 400ºF. Combine canned salmon, lemon zest, egg, remaining mayo, bell peppers, flour, and salt in a bowl. Form into 8 patties. Place the patties in the greased frying basket and Air Fry for 10 minutes, turning once. Let rest for 5 minutes before drizzling with lemon sauce. Garnish with green olives to serve.

Old Bay Fish `n´ Chips

Servings: 4
Cooking Time: 40 Minutes
Ingredients:

- 2 russet potatoes, peeled
- 2 tbsp olive oil
- 4 tilapia filets
- ¼ cup flour
- Salt and pepper to taste
- 1 tsp Old Bay seasoning
- 1 lemon, zested
- 1 egg, beaten
- 1 cup panko bread crumbs
- 3 tbsp tartar sauce

Directions:

1. Preheat the air fryer to 400°F. Slice the potatoes into ½-inch-thick chips and drizzle with olive oil. Sprinkle with salt. Add the fries to the frying basket and Air Fry for 12-16 minutes, shaking once. Remove the potatoes to a plate. Cover loosely with foil to keep warm. Sprinkle the fish with salt and season with black pepper, lemon zest, and Old Bay seasoning, then lay on a plate. Put the egg in a shallow bowl and spread the panko on a separate plate. Dip the fish in the flour, then the egg, then the panko. Press to coat completely. Add half the fish to the frying basket and spray with cooking oil. Set a raised rack on the frying basket, top with the other half of the fish, and spray with cooking oil. Air Fry for 8-10 minutes until the fish flakes. Serve the fish and chips with tartar sauce.

Cheesy Tuna Tower

Servings:2
Cooking Time: 15 Minutes
Ingredients:
- ½ cup grated mozzarella
- 1 can tuna in water
- ¼ cup mayonnaise
- 2 tsp yellow mustard
- 1 tbsp minced dill pickle
- 1 tbsp minced celery
- 1 tbsp minced green onion
- Salt and pepper to taste
- 4 tomato slices
- 8 avocado slices

Directions:
1. Preheat air fryer to 350ºF. In a bowl, combine tuna, mayonnaise, mustard, pickle, celery, green onion, salt, and pepper. Cut a piece of parchment paper to fit the bottom of the frying basket. Place tomato slices on paper in a single layer and top with 2 avocado slices. Share tuna salad over avocado slices and top with mozzarella cheese. Place the towers in the frying basket and Bake for 4 minutes until the cheese starts to brown. Serve warm.

Thyme Scallops

Servings: 1
Cooking Time: 12 Minutes
Ingredients:
- 1 lb. scallops
- Salt and pepper
- ½ tbsp. butter
- ½ cup thyme, chopped

Directions:
1. Wash the scallops and dry them completely. Season with pepper and salt, then set aside while you prepare the pan.
2. Grease a foil pan in several spots with the butter and cover the bottom with the thyme. Place the scallops on top.
3. Pre-heat the fryer at 400°F and set the rack inside.

4. Place the foil pan on the rack and allow to cook for seven minutes.
5. Take care when removing the pan from the fryer and transfer the scallops to a serving dish. Spoon any remaining butter in the pan over the fish and enjoy.

Creole Tilapia With Garlic Mayo

Servings: 4
Cooking Time: 20 Minutes
Ingredients:
- 4 tilapia fillets
- 2 tbsp olive oil
- 1 tsp paprika
- 1 tsp garlic powder
- 1 tsp dried basil
- ½ tsp Creole seasoning
- ½ tsp chili powder
- 2 garlic cloves, minced
- 1 tbsp mayonnaise
- 1 tsp olive oil
- ½ lemon, juiced
- Salt and pepper to taste

Directions:
1. Preheat air fryer to 400°F. Coat the tilapia with some olive oil, then season with paprika, garlic powder, basil, and Creole seasoning. Bake in the greased frying basket for 15 minutes, flipping once during cooking.
2. While the fish is cooking, whisk together garlic, mayonnaise, olive oil, lemon juice, chili powder, salt and pepper in a bowl. Serve the cooked fish with the aioli.

Butternut Squash-wrapped Halibut Fillets

Servings:3
Cooking Time: 11 Minutes
Ingredients:
- 15 Long spiralized peeled and seeded butternut squash strands
- 3 5- to 6-ounce skinless halibut fillets
- 3 tablespoons Butter, melted
- ¾ teaspoon Mild paprika
- ¾ teaspoon Table salt
- ¾ teaspoon Ground black pepper

Directions:
1. Preheat the air fryer to 375°F .
2. Hold 5 long butternut squash strands together and wrap them around a fillet. Set it aside and wrap any remaining fillet(s).
3. Mix the melted butter, paprika, salt, and pepper in a small bowl. Brush this mixture over the squash-wrapped fillets on all sides.
4. When the machine is at temperature, set the fillets in the basket with as much air space between them as possible. Air-fry undisturbed for 10 minutes, or until the squash strands have browned but not burned. If the machine is at 360°F, you may need to add 1 minute to the cooking time. In any event, watch the fish carefully after the 8-minute mark.

5. Use a nonstick-safe spatula to gently transfer the fillets to a serving platter or plates. Cool for only a minute or so before serving.

Bang Bang Shrimp

Servings: 4 Servings
Cooking Time: 30 Minutes
Ingredients:
- 1 pound of peeled jumbo shrimp
- 1 cup of mayonnaise
- 1 cup of bread crumbs
- ¾ cup of corn starch
- ½ cup of buttermilk
- ¼ cup of sweet chili sauce
- ½ teaspoon of sriracha
- Chopped fresh parsley, for garnishing

Directions:
1. Preheat your air fryer to 400ºF. Spray some oil inside the air fryer basket.
2. Add mayonnaise, sweet chili sauce, and sriracha in a small bowl. Mix it well until combined.
3. Take 6–8 shrimp at a time, generously coat in cornstarch. Then dip in buttermilk and finally roll them in bread crumbs until fully covered. Transfer the coated shrimp in the air fryer in a single layer; avoid them touching.
4. Cook at 400ºF for 5 minutes, spray tops with some oil, flip them, and cook for extra 5 minutes. Remove and set aside. Repeat the last 2 steps with the remaining part of the shrimp.
5. Put all cooked shrimp in a medium mixing bowl, pour in the mayonnaise-chili sauce, and toss* until the shrimp are fully covered.
6. Top with fresh parsley, serve warm,** and enjoy your Bang Bang Shrimp!

Cajun Shrimp With Veggie

Servings: 4
Cooking Time: 20 Minutes
Ingredients:
- 50 small shrimp
- 1 tablespoon Cajun seasoning
- 1 bag of frozen mix vegetables
- 1 tablespoon olive oil

Directions:
1. Line air fryer basket with aluminum foil.
2. Add all the recipe ingredients into the suitable mixing bowl and toss well.
3. Transfer shrimp and vegetable mixture into the air fryer basket and cook at almost 350 degrees F/ 175 degrees C for almost 10 minutes.
4. Toss well and cook for almost 10 minutes more.
5. Serve and enjoy.

Salty German-style Shrimp Pancakes

Servings: 4
Cooking Time: 15 Minutes
Ingredients:
- 1 tbsp butter

- 3 eggs, beaten
- ½ cup flour
- ½ cup milk
- ⅛ tsp salt
- 1 cup salsa
- 1 cup cooked shrimp, minced
- 2 tbsp cilantro, chopped

Directions:
1. Preheat air fryer to 390°F. Mix the eggs, flour, milk, and salt in a bowl until frothy. Pour the batter into a greased baking pan and place in the air fryer. Bake for 15 minutes or until the pancake is puffed and golden. Flip the pancake onto a plate. Mix salsa, shrimp, and cilantro. Top the pancake and serve.

Easy Air Fried Salmon

Servings: 2
Cooking Time: 10 Minutes
Ingredients:
- 2 salmon fillets, skinless and boneless
- 1 teaspoon olive oil
- Black pepper
- Salt

Directions:
1. Coat boneless salmon fillets with olive oil and season with black pepper and salt.
2. Place salmon fillets in air fryer basket and Cook at almost 360 degrees F/ 180 degrees C for 8-10 minutes.
3. Serve and enjoy.

Homestyle Catfish Strips

Servings:4
Cooking Time: 20 Minutes
Ingredients:
- 1 cup buttermilk
- 5 catfish fillets, cut into 1½-inch strips
- Olive oil
- 1 cup cornmeal
- 1 tablespoon Creole, Cajun, or Old Bay seasoning

Directions:
1. Pour the buttermilk into a shallow baking dish. Place the catfish in the dish and refrigerate for at least 1 hour to help remove any fishy taste.
2. Spray a fryer basket lightly with olive oil.
3. In a shallow bowl, combine cornmeal and Creole seasoning.
4. Shake any excess buttermilk off the catfish. Place each strip in the cornmeal mixture and coat completely. Press the cornmeal into the catfish gently to help it stick.
5. Place the strips in the fryer basket in a single layer. Lightly spray the catfish with olive oil. You may need to cook the catfish in more than one batch.
6. Air fry for 8 minutes. Turn the catfish strips over and lightly spray with olive oil. Cook until golden brown and crispy, 8 to 10 more minutes.

Simple Salmon

Servings:2
Cooking Time:10 Minutes
Ingredients:
- 2 salmon fillets
- Salt and black pepper, as required
- 1 tablespoon olive oil

Directions:
1. Preheat the Air fryer to 390°F and grease an Air fryer basket.
2. Season each salmon fillet with salt and black pepper and drizzle with olive oil.
3. Arrange salmon fillets into the Air fryer basket and cook for about 10 minutes.
4. Remove from the Air fryer and dish out the salmon fillets onto the serving plates.

Crunchy And Buttery Cod With Ritz® Cracker Crust

Servings: 2
Cooking Time: 10 Minutes
Ingredients:
- 4 tablespoons butter, melted
- 8 to 10 RITZ® crackers, crushed into crumbs
- 2 (6-ounce) cod fillets
- salt and freshly ground black pepper
- 1 lemon

Directions:
1. Preheat the air fryer to 380°F.
2. Melt the butter in a small saucepan on the stovetop or in a microwavable dish in the microwave, and then transfer the butter to a shallow dish. Place the crushed RITZ® crackers into a second shallow dish.
3. Season the fish fillets with salt and freshly ground black pepper. Dip them into the butter and then coat both sides with the RITZ® crackers.
4. Place the fish into the air fryer basket and air-fry at 380°F for 10 minutes, flipping the fish over halfway through the cooking time.
5. Serve with a wedge of lemon to squeeze over the top.

Crabmeat-stuffed Flounder

Servings:3
Cooking Time: 12 Minutes
Ingredients:
- 4½ ounces Purchased backfin or claw crabmeat, picked over for bits of shell and cartilage
- 6 Saltine crackers, crushed into fine crumbs
- 2 tablespoons plus 1 teaspoon Regular or low-fat mayonnaise (not fat-free)
- ¾ teaspoon Yellow prepared mustard

- 1½ teaspoons Worcestershire sauce
- ⅛ teaspoon Celery salt
- 3 5- to 6-ounce skinless flounder fillets
- Vegetable oil spray
- Mild paprika

Directions:
1. Preheat the air fryer to 400°F.
2. Gently mix the crabmeat, crushed saltines, mayonnaise, mustard, Worcestershire sauce, and celery salt in a bowl until well combined.
3. Generously coat the flat side of a fillet with vegetable oil spray. Set the fillet sprayed side down on your work surface. Cut the fillet in half widthwise, then cut one of the halves in half lengthwise. Set a scant ⅓ cup of the crabmeat mixture on top of the undivided half of the fish fillet, mounding the mixture to make an oval that somewhat fits the shape of the fillet with at least a ¼-inch border of fillet beyond the filling all around.
4. Take the two thin divided quarters (that is, the halves of the half) and lay them lengthwise over the filling, overlapping at each end and leaving a little space in the middle where the filling peeks through. Coat the top of the stuffed flounder piece with vegetable oil spray, then sprinkle paprika over the stuffed flounder fillet. Set aside and use the remaining fillet(s) to make more stuffed flounder "packets," repeating steps 3 and
5. Use a nonstick-safe spatula to transfer the stuffed flounder fillets to the basket. Leave as much space between them as possible. Air-fry undisturbed for 12 minutes, or until lightly brown and firm (but not hard).
6. Use that same spatula, plus perhaps another one, to transfer the fillets to a serving platter or plates. Cool for a minute or two, then serve hot.

Garlic Lobster With Herbs

Servings: 3
Cooking Time: 10 Minutes
Ingredients:
- 1 teaspoon garlic, minced
- 1 tablespoon butter
- Black pepper and salt to taste
- ½ tablespoon lemon Juice

Directions:
1. Add all the recipe ingredients to a food processor, except shrimp, and blend well.
2. Clean the skin of the lobster and cover with the marinade.
3. At 380 degrees F/ 195 degrees C, preheat your air fryer.
4. Place the lobster in your air fryer basket and cook for almost 10 minutes.
5. Serve with fresh herbs and enjoy!

Chapter 9: Beef, pork & Lamb Recipes

Cheese Crusted Chops

Servings:6
Cooking Time: 12 Minutes
Ingredients:
- ¼ teaspoon pepper
- ½ teaspoons salt
- 4 to 6 thick boneless pork chops
- 1 cup pork rind crumbs
- ¼ teaspoon chili powder
- ½ teaspoons onion powder
- 1 teaspoon smoked paprika
- 2 beaten eggs
- 3 tablespoons grated Parmesan cheese
- Cooking spray

Directions:
1. Preheat the air fryer to 400ºF (205ºC).
2. Rub the pepper and salt on both sides of pork chops.
3. In a food processor, pulse pork rinds into crumbs. Mix crumbs with chili powder, onion powder, and paprika in a bowl.
4. Beat eggs in another bowl.
5. Dip pork chops into eggs then into pork rind crumb mixture.
6. Spritz the air fryer with cooking spray and add pork chops to the basket.
7. Air fry for 12 minutes.
8. Serve garnished with the Parmesan cheese.

Chicken Fried Steak

Servings: 4
Cooking Time: 15 Minutes
Ingredients:
- 2 eggs
- ½ cup buttermilk
- 1½ cups flour
- ¾ teaspoon salt
- ½ teaspoon pepper
- 1 pound beef cube steaks
- salt and pepper
- oil for misting or cooking spray

Directions:
1. Beat together eggs and buttermilk in a shallow dish.
2. In another shallow dish, stir together the flour, ½ teaspoon salt, and ¼ teaspoon pepper.
3. Season cube steaks with remaining salt and pepper to taste. Dip in flour, buttermilk egg wash, and then flour again.
4. Spray both sides of steaks with oil or cooking spray.
5. Cooking in 2 batches, place steaks in air fryer basket in single layer. Cook at 360°F for 10minutes. Spray tops of steaks with oil and cook 5minutes or until meat is well done.
6. Repeat to cook remaining steaks.

Beef Brazilian Empanadas

Servings: 6
Cooking Time: 40 Minutes
Ingredients:
- 1 cup shredded Pepper Jack cheese
- 1/3 minced green bell pepper
- 1 cup shredded mozzarella
- 2 garlic cloves, chopped
- 1/3 onion, chopped
- 8 oz ground beef
- 1 tsp allspice
- ½ tsp paprika
- ½ teaspoon chili powder
- Salt and pepper to taste
- 15 empanada wrappers
- 1 tbsp butter

Directions:
1. Spray a skillet with cooking oil. Over medium heat, stir-fry garlic, green pepper, and onion for 2 minutes or until aromatic. Add beef, allspice, chili, paprika, salt and pepper. Use a spoon to break up the beef. Cook until brown. Drain the excess fat. On a clean work surface, glaze each empanada wrapper edge with water using a basting brush to soften the crust. Mound 2-3 tbsp of meat onto each wrapper. Top with mozzarella and pepper Jack cheese. Fold one side of the wrapper to the opposite side. Press the edges with the back of a fork to seal.
2. Preheat air fryer to 400°F. Place the empanadas in the air fryer and spray with cooking oil. Bake for 8 minutes, then flip the empanadas. Cook for another 4 minutes.Melt butter in a microwave-safe bowl for 20 seconds. Brush melted butter over the top of each empanada. Serve warm.

Stuffed Pork Chops

Servings: 4
Cooking Time: 12 Minutes
Ingredients:
- 4 boneless pork chops
- ½ teaspoon salt
- ½ teaspoon black pepper
- ¼ teaspoon paprika
- 1 cup frozen spinach, defrosted and squeezed dry
- 2 cloves garlic, minced
- 2 ounces cream cheese
- ¼ cup grated Parmesan cheese
- 1 tablespoon extra-virgin olive oil

Directions:
1. Pat the pork chops with a paper towel. Make a slit in the side of each pork chop to create a pouch.
2. Season the pork chops with the salt, pepper, and paprika.
3. In a small bowl, mix together the spinach, garlic, cream cheese, and Parmesan cheese.
4. Divide the mixture into fourths and stuff the pork chop pouches. Secure the pouches with toothpicks.
5. Preheat the air fryer to 400°F.
6. Place the stuffed pork chops in the air fryer basket and spray liberally with cooking spray. Cook for 6 minutes, flip and coat with more cooking spray, and cook another 6 minutes. Check to make sure the meat is cooked to an internal temperature of 145°F. Cook the pork chops in batches, as needed.

Traditional Moo Shu Pork Lettuce Wraps

Servings: 4
Cooking Time: 40 Minutes
Ingredients:
- ½ cup sliced shiitake mushrooms
- 1 lb boneless pork loin, cubed
- 3 tbsp cornstarch
- 2 tbsp rice vinegar
- 3 tbsp hoisin sauce
- 1 tsp oyster sauce
- 3 tsp sesame oil
- 1 tsp sesame seeds
- ¼ tsp ground ginger
- 1 egg
- 2 tbsp flour
- 1 bag coleslaw mix
- 1 cup chopped baby spinach
- 3 green onions, sliced
- 8 iceberg lettuce leaves

Directions:
1. Preheat air fryer at 350ºF. Make a slurry by whisking 1 tbsp of cornstarch and 1 tbsp of water in a bowl. Set aside. Warm a saucepan over heat, add in rice vinegar, hoisin sauce, oyster sauce, 1 tsp of sesame oil, and ginger, and cook for 3 minutes, stirring often. Add in cornstarch slurry and cook for 1 minute. Set aside and let the mixture thicken. Beat the egg, flour, and the remaining cornstarch in a bowl. Set aside.
2. Dredge pork cubes in the egg mixture. Shake off any excess. Place them in the greased frying basket and Air Fry for 8 minutes, shaking once. Warm the remaining sesame oil in a skillet over medium heat. Add in coleslaw mix, baby spinach, green onions, and mushrooms and cook for 5 minutes until the coleslaw wilts. Turn the heat off. Add in cooked pork, pour in oyster sauce mixture, and toss until coated. Divide mixture between lettuce leaves, sprinkle with sesame seed, roll them up, and serve.

Steak Fingers

Servings: 4
Cooking Time: 8 Minutes
Ingredients:
- 4 small beef cube steaks
- salt and pepper
- ½ cup flour
- oil for misting or cooking spray

Directions:
1. Cut cube steaks into 1-inch-wide strips.
2. Sprinkle lightly with salt and pepper to taste.
3. Roll in flour to coat all sides.
4. Spray air fryer basket with cooking spray or oil.
5. Place steak strips in air fryer basket in single layer, very close together but not touching. Spray top of steak strips with oil or cooking spray.

6. Cook at 390°F for 4minutes, turn strips over, and spray with oil or cooking spray.
7. Cook 4 more minutes and test with fork for doneness. Steak fingers should be crispy outside with no red juices inside. If needed, cook an additional 4 minutes or until well done.
8. Repeat steps 5 through 7 to cook remaining strips.

Glazed Tender Pork Chops

Servings: 3
Cooking Time: 14 Minutes
Ingredients:
- 3 pork chops, rinsed and pat dry
- ¼ teaspoon smoked paprika
- ½ teaspoon garlic powder
- 2 teaspoons olive oil
- Black pepper
- Salt

Directions:
1. Coat pork chops with paprika, olive oil, garlic powder, black pepper, and salt.
2. Place the prepared pork chops in air fryer basket and cook at almost 380 degrees F/ 195 degrees C for almost 10-14 minutes. Turn halfway through the cooking time.
3. Serve and enjoy.

Bacon, Blue Cheese And Pear Stuffed Pork Chops

Servings: 3
Cooking Time: 24 Minutes
Ingredients:
- 4 slices bacon, chopped
- 1 tablespoon butter
- ½ cup finely diced onion
- ⅓ cup chicken stock
- 1½ cups seasoned stuffing cubes
- 1 egg, beaten
- ½ teaspoon dried thyme
- ½ teaspoon salt
- ⅛ teaspoon black pepper
- 1 pear, finely diced
- ⅓ cup crumbled blue cheese
- 3 boneless center-cut pork chops (2-inch thick)
- olive oil
- salt and freshly ground black pepper

Directions:
1. Preheat the air fryer to 400°F.
2. Place the bacon into the air fryer basket and air-fry for 6 minutes, stirring halfway through the cooking time. Remove the bacon and set it aside on a paper towel. Pour out the grease from the bottom of the air fryer.
3. To make the stuffing, melt the butter in a medium saucepan over medium heat on the stovetop. Add the onion and sauté for a few minutes, until it starts to soften. Add the chicken stock and simmer for 1 minute. Remove the pan from the heat and add the stuffing cubes. Stir until the stock has been absorbed. Add the egg, dried thyme, salt and freshly ground black pepper, and stir

until combined. Fold in the diced pear and crumbled blue cheese.

4. Place the pork chops on a cutting board. Using the palm of your hand to hold the chop flat and steady, slice into the side of the pork chop to make a pocket in the center of the chop. Leave about an inch of chop uncut and make sure you don't cut all the way through the pork chop. Brush both sides of the pork chops with olive oil and season with salt and freshly ground black pepper. Stuff each pork chop with a third of the stuffing, packing the stuffing tightly inside the pocket.

5. Preheat the air fryer to 360°F.

6. Spray or brush the sides of the air fryer basket with oil. Place the pork chops in the air fryer basket with the open stuffed edge of the pork chop facing the outside edges of the basket.

7. Air-fry the pork chops for 18 minutes, turning the pork chops over halfway through the cooking time. When the chops are done, let them rest for 5 minutes and then transfer to a serving platter.

Mozzarella Beef Brisket

Servings:6
Cooking Time: 25 Minutes
Ingredients:
- 12 ounces (340 g) beef brisket
- 2 teaspoons Italian herbs
- 2 teaspoons butter
- 1 onion, sliced
- 7 ounces (198 g) Mozzarella cheese, sliced

Directions:
1. Preheat the air fryer to 365ºF (185ºC).
2. Cut up the brisket into four equal slices and season with the Italian herbs.
3. Allow the butter to melt in the air fryer. Put the slices of beef inside along with the onion. Air fry for 25 minutes. Flip the brisket halfway through. Put a piece of Mozzarella on top of each piece of brisket in the last 5 minutes.
4. Serve immediately.

Korean-style Lamb Shoulder Chops

Servings: 3
Cooking Time: 28 Minutes
Ingredients:
- ⅓ cup Regular or low-sodium soy sauce or gluten-free tamari sauce
- 1½ tablespoons Toasted sesame oil
- 1½ tablespoons Granulated white sugar
- 2 teaspoons Minced peeled fresh ginger
- 1 teaspoon Minced garlic
- ¼ teaspoon Red pepper flakes
- 3 6-ounce bone-in lamb shoulder chops, any excess fat trimmed
- ⅔ cup Tapioca flour
- Vegetable oil spray

Directions:

1. Put the soy or tamari sauce, sesame oil, sugar, ginger, garlic, and red pepper flakes in a large, heavy zip-closed plastic bag. Add the chops, seal, and rub the marinade evenly over them through the bag. Refrigerate for at least 2 hours or up to 6 hours, turning the bag at least once so the chops move around in the marinade.

2. Set the bag out on the counter as the air fryer heats. Preheat the air fryer to 375°F .

3. Pour the tapioca flour on a dinner plate or in a small pie plate. Remove a chop from the marinade and dredge it on both sides in the tapioca flour, coating it evenly and well. Coat both sides with vegetable oil spray, set it in the basket, and dredge and spray the remaining chop(s), setting them in the basket in a single layer with space between them. Discard the bag with the marinade.

4. Air-fry, turning once, for 25 minutes, or until the chops are well browned and tender when pierced with the point of a paring knife. If the machine is at 360°F, you may need to add up to 3 minutes to the cooking time.

5. Use kitchen tongs to transfer the chops to a wire rack. Cool for just a couple of minutes before serving.

Beef Burgers With Worcestershire Sauce

Servings: 4
Cooking Time: 15 Minutes
Ingredients:
- 1 ½ pound ground beef
- Black pepper and salt to season
- ¼ teaspoon liquid smoke
- 2 teaspoons onion powder
- 1 teaspoon garlic powder
- 1 ½ tablespoon Worcestershire sauce
- Burgers:
- 4 buns
- 4 trimmed lettuce leaves
- 4 tablespoons mayonnaise
- 1 large tomato, sliced
- 4 slices Cheddar cheese

Directions:
1. At 370 degrees F/ 185 degrees C, preheat your air fryer.
2. In a suitable bowl, combine the beef, salt, black pepper, liquid smoke, onion powder, garlic powder and Worcestershire sauce using your hands.
3. Form 3 to 4 patties out of the mixture.
4. Place the patties in the fryer basket making sure to leave enough space between them.
5. Ideally, work with 2 patties at a time.
6. Close the air fryer and cook for 10 minutes.
7. Turn the beef with kitchen tongs, reduce the temperature to 350 degrees F/ 175 degrees C, and cook further for 5 minutes.
8. Remove the patties onto a plate.
9. Assemble burgers with the lettuce, mayonnaise, sliced cheese, and sliced tomato.

Better-than-chinese-take-out Pork Ribs

Servings: 3
Cooking Time: 35 Minutes
Ingredients:
- 1½ tablespoons Hoisin sauce (see here; gluten-free, if a concern)
- 1½ tablespoons Regular or low-sodium soy sauce or gluten-free tamari sauce
- 1½ tablespoons Shaoxing (Chinese cooking rice wine), dry sherry, or white grape juice
- 1½ teaspoons Minced garlic
- ¾ teaspoon Ground dried ginger
- ¾ teaspoon Ground white pepper
- 1½ pounds Pork baby back rib rack(s), cut into 2-bone pieces

Directions:
1. Mix the hoisin sauce, soy or tamari sauce, Shaoxing or its substitute, garlic, ginger, and white pepper in a large bowl. Add the rib sections and stir well to coat. Cover and refrigerate for at least 2 hours or up to 24 hours, stirring the rib sections in the marinade occasionally.
2. Preheat the air fryer to 350°F . Set the ribs in their bowl on the counter as the machine heats.
3. When the machine is at temperature, set the rib pieces on their sides in a single layer in the basket with as much air space between them as possible. Air-fry for 35 minutes, turning and rearranging the pieces once, until deeply browned and sizzling.
4. Use kitchen tongs to transfer the rib pieces to a large serving bowl or platter. Wait a minute or two before serving them so the meat can reabsorb some of its own juices.

Pork Schnitzel

Servings: 4
Cooking Time: 14 Minutes
Ingredients:
- 4 boneless pork chops, pounded to ¼-inch thickness
- 1 teaspoon salt, divided
- 1 teaspoon black pepper, divided
- ½ cup all-purpose flour
- 2 eggs
- 1 cup breadcrumbs
- ¼ teaspoon paprika
- 1 lemon, cut into wedges

Directions:
1. Season both sides of the pork chops with ½ teaspoon of the salt and ½ teaspoon of the pepper.
2. On a plate, place the flour.
3. In a large bowl, whisk the eggs.
4. In another large bowl, place the breadcrumbs.
5. Season the flour with the paprika and season the breadcrumbs with the remaining ½ teaspoon of salt and ½ teaspoon of pepper.
6. To bread the pork, place a pork chop in the flour, then into the whisked eggs, and then into the breadcrumbs. Place the breaded pork onto a plate and finish breading the remaining pork chops.
7. Preheat the air fryer to 390°F.
8. Place the pork chops into the air fryer, not overlapping and working in batches as needed. Spray the pork chops with cooking spray and cook for 8 minutes; flip the pork and cook for another 4 to 6 minutes or until cooked to an internal temperature of 145°F.
9. Serve with lemon wedges.

Flank Steak With Roasted Peppers And Chimichurri

Servings: 4
Cooking Time: 22 Minutes
Ingredients:
- 2 cups flat-leaf parsley leaves
- ¼ cup fresh oregano leaves
- 3 cloves garlic
- ½ cup olive oil
- ¼ cup red wine vinegar
- ½ teaspoon salt
- freshly ground black pepper
- ¼ teaspoon crushed red pepper flakes
- ½ teaspoon ground cumin
- 1 pound flank steak
- 1 red bell pepper, cut into strips
- 1 yellow bell pepper, cut into strips

Directions:
1. Make the chimichurri sauce by chopping the parsley, oregano and garlic in a food processor. Add the olive oil, vinegar and seasonings and process again. Pour half of the sauce into a shallow dish with the flank steak and set the remaining sauce aside. Pierce the flank steak with a needle-style meat tenderizer or a paring knife and marinate the steak for 2 to 24 hours in the refrigerator. When you are ready to cook, remove the steak from the refrigerator and let it sit at room temperature for 30 minutes.
2. Preheat the air fryer to 400°F.
3. Cut the flank steak in half so that it fits more easily into the air fryer and transfer both pieces to the air fryer basket. Air-fry for 14 minutes, depending on how you like your steak cooked (10 minutes will give you medium for a 1-inch thick flank steak). Flip the steak over halfway through the cooking time.
4. When the flank steak is cooked to your liking, transfer it to a cutting board, loosely tent with foil and let it rest while you cook the peppers.
5. Toss the peppers in a little olive oil, salt and freshly ground black pepper and transfer them to the air fryer basket. Air-fry at 400°F for 8 minutes, shaking the basket once or twice throughout the cooking process. To serve, slice the flank steak against the grain of the meat and top with the roasted peppers. Drizzle the reserved chimichurri sauce on top, thinning the sauce with another tablespoon of olive oil if desired.

Perfect Strip Steaks

Servings: 2
Cooking Time: 17 Minutes
Ingredients:
- 1½ tablespoons Olive oil
- 1½ tablespoons Minced garlic
- 2 teaspoons Ground black pepper
- 1 teaspoon Table salt
- 2 ¾-pound boneless beef strip steak(s)

Directions:
1. Preheat the air fryer to 375°F.
2. Mix the oil, garlic, pepper, and salt in a small bowl, then smear this mixture over both sides of the steak(s).
3. When the machine is at temperature, put the steak(s) in the basket with as much air space as possible between them for the larger batch. They should not overlap or even touch. That said, even just a ¼-inch between them will work. Air-fry for 12 minutes, turning once, until an instant-read meat thermometer inserted into the thickest part of a steak registers 127°F for rare. Or air-fry for 15 minutes, turning once, until an instant-read meat thermometer registers 145°F for medium. If the machine is at 390°F, the steaks may cook 2 minutes more quickly than the stated timing.
4. Use kitchen tongs to transfer the steak(s) to a wire rack. Cool for 5 minutes before serving.

City "chicken"

Servings: 3
Cooking Time: 10 Minutes
Ingredients:
- 1 pound Pork tenderloin, cut into 2-inch cubes
- ½ cup All-purpose flour or tapioca flour
- 1 Large egg(s)
- 1 teaspoon Dried poultry seasoning blend
- 1¼ cups Plain panko bread crumbs (gluten-free, if a concern)
- Vegetable oil spray

Directions:
1. Preheat the air fryer to 350°F .
2. Thread 3 or 4 pieces of pork on a 4-inch bamboo skewer. You'll need 2 or 3 skewers for a small batch, 3 or 4 for a medium, and up to 6 for a large batch.
3. Set up and fill three shallow soup plates or small pie plates on your counter: one for the flour; one for the egg(s), beaten with the poultry seasoning until foamy; and one for the bread crumbs.
4. Dip and roll one skewer into the flour, coating all sides of the meat. Gently shake off any excess flour, then dip and roll the skewer in the egg mixture. Let any excess egg mixture slip back into the rest, then set the skewer in the bread crumbs and roll it around, pressing gently, until the exterior surfaces of the meat are evenly coated. Generously coat the meat on the skewer with vegetable oil spray. Set aside and continue dredging, dipping, coating, and spraying the remaining skewers.
5. Set the skewers in the basket in one layer and air-fry undisturbed for 10 minutes, or until brown and crunchy.
6. Use kitchen tongs to transfer the skewers to a wire rack. Cool for a minute or two before serving.

Steak Bites And Spicy Dipping Sauce

Servings:4
Cooking Time: 8 Minutes
Ingredients:
- 2 pounds sirloin steak, cut into 2" cubes
- 2 teaspoons salt
- 1 teaspoon ground black pepper
- 1 teaspoon garlic powder
- ½ cup mayonnaise
- 2 tablespoons sriracha

Directions:
1. Preheat the air fryer to 400°F.
2. Sprinkle steak with salt, pepper, and garlic powder.
3. Place steak in the air fryer basket and cook 8 minutes, shaking the basket twice during cooking, until internal temperature reaches at least 160°F.
4. In a small bowl, combine mayonnaise and sriracha. Serve with steak bites for dipping.

Simple Rib-eye Steak

Servings: 2
Cooking Time: 14 Minutes
Ingredients:
- 2 medium-sized rib eye steaks
- Salt & freshly ground black pepper, to taste

Directions:
1. Use the kitchen towels to pat dry the steaks.
2. Season the rib eye steaks with salt and pepper well on both sides.
3. Cook the steaks at 400 degrees F/ 205 degrees C for 14 minutes, flipping halfway through.
4. Let the steaks cool for 5 minutes before serving.

Lemon-butter Veal Cutlets

Servings: 2
Cooking Time: 4 Minutes
Ingredients:
- 3 strips Butter
- 3 Thinly pounded 2-ounce veal leg cutlets (less than ¼ inch thick)
- ¼ teaspoon Lemon-pepper seasoning

Directions:
1. Preheat the air fryer to 400°F.
2. Run a vegetable peeler lengthwise along a hard, cold stick of butter, making 2, 3, or 4 long strips as the recipe requires for the number of cutlets you're making.
3. Lay the veal cutlets on a clean, dry cutting board or work surface. Sprinkle about ⅛ teaspoon lemon-pepper seasoning over each. Set a strip of butter on top of each cutlet.
4. When the machine is at temperature, set the topped cutlets in the basket so that they don't overlap or even touch. Air-fry undisturbed for 4 minutes without turning.
5. Use a nonstick-safe spatula to transfer the cutlets to a serving plate or plates, taking care to keep as much of the butter on top as possible. Remove the basket from the drawer or from over the baking tray. Carefully pour the browned butter over the cutlets.

Pork Loin

Servings: 8
Cooking Time: 50 Minutes
Ingredients:
- 1 tablespoon lime juice
- 1 tablespoon orange marmalade
- 1 teaspoon coarse brown mustard
- 1 teaspoon curry powder
- 1 teaspoon dried lemongrass
- 2-pound boneless pork loin roast
- salt and pepper
- cooking spray

Directions:
1. Mix together the lime juice, marmalade, mustard, curry powder, and lemongrass.
2. Rub mixture all over the surface of the pork loin. Season to taste with salt and pepper.
3. Spray air fryer basket with nonstick spray and place pork roast diagonally in basket.
4. Cook at 360°F for approximately 50 minutes, until roast registers 130°F on a meat thermometer.
5. Wrap roast in foil and let rest for 10minutes before slicing.

Ritzy Skirt Steak Fajitas

Servings:4
Cooking Time: 30 Minutes
Ingredients:
- 2 tablespoons olive oil
- ¼ cup lime juice
- 1 clove garlic, minced
- ½ teaspoon ground cumin
- ½ teaspoon hot sauce
- ½ teaspoon salt
- 2 tablespoons chopped fresh cilantro
- 1 pound (454 g) skirt steak
- 1 onion, sliced
- 1 teaspoon chili powder
- 1 red pepper, sliced
- 1 green pepper, sliced
- Salt and freshly ground black pepper, to taste
- 8 flour tortillas
- Toppings:
- Shredded lettuce
- Crumbled Queso Fresco (or grated Cheddar cheese)
- Sliced black olives
- Diced tomatoes
- Sour cream
- Guacamole

Directions:
1. Combine the olive oil, lime juice, garlic, cumin, hot sauce, salt and cilantro in a shallow dish. Add the skirt steak and turn it over several times to coat all sides. Pierce the steak with a needle-style meat tenderizer or paring knife. Marinate the steak in the refrigerator for at least 3 hours, or overnight. When you are ready to cook, remove the steak from the refrigerator and let it sit at room temperature for 30 minutes.

2. Preheat the air fryer to 400ºF (204ºC).
3. Toss the onion slices with the chili powder and a little olive oil and transfer them to the air fryer basket. Air fry for 5 minutes. Add the red and green peppers to the air fryer basket with the onions, season with salt and pepper and air fry for 8 more minutes, until the onions and peppers are soft. Transfer the vegetables to a dish and cover with aluminum foil to keep warm.
4. Put the skirt steak in the air fryer basket and pour the marinade over the top. Air fry at 400ºF (204ºC) for 12 minutes. Flip the steak over and air fry for an additional 5 minutes. Transfer the cooked steak to a cutting board and let the steak rest for a few minutes. If the peppers and onions need to be heated, return them to the air fryer for just 1 to 2 minutes.
5. Thinly slice the steak at an angle, cutting against the grain of the steak. Serve the steak with the onions and peppers, the warm tortillas and the fajita toppings on the side.
6. Serve immediately.

Simple Air Fryer Steak

Servings: 2
Cooking Time: 18 Minutes
Ingredients:
- 12 oz steaks, 3/4-inch thick
- 1 tsp garlic powder
- 1 tsp olive oil
- Pepper
- Salt

Directions:
1. Coat steaks with oil and season with garlic powder, pepper, and salt.
2. Preheat the air fryer to 400°F.
3. Place steaks in air fryer basket and cook for 15-18 minutes. Turn halfway through.
4. Serve and enjoy.

Calf's Liver

Servings: 4
Cooking Time: 5 Minutes
Ingredients:
- 1 pound sliced calf's liver
- salt and pepper
- 2 eggs
- 2 tablespoons milk
- ½ cup whole wheat flour
- 1½ cups panko breadcrumbs
- ½ cup plain breadcrumbs
- ½ teaspoon salt
- ¼ teaspoon pepper
- oil for misting or cooking spray

Directions:
1. Cut liver slices crosswise into strips about ½-inch wide. Sprinkle with salt and pepper to taste.
2. Beat together egg and milk in a shallow dish.
3. Place wheat flour in a second shallow dish.
4. In a third shallow dish, mix together panko, plain breadcrumbs, ½ teaspoon salt, and ¼ teaspoon pepper.

5. Preheat air fryer to 390°F.

6. Dip liver strips in flour, egg wash, and then breadcrumbs, pressing in coating slightly to make crumbs stick.

7. Cooking half the liver at a time, place strips in air fryer basket in a single layer, close but not touching. Cook at 390°F for 5 minutes or until done to your preference.

8. Repeat step 7 to cook remaining liver.

Mustard And Rosemary Pork Tenderloin With Fried Apples

Servings: 2
Cooking Time: 26 Minutes
Ingredients:
- 1 pork tenderloin
- 2 tablespoons coarse brown mustard
- salt and freshly ground black pepper
- 1½ teaspoons finely chopped fresh rosemary, plus sprigs for garnish
- 2 apples, cored and cut into 8 wedges
- 1 tablespoon butter, melted
- 1 teaspoon brown sugar

Directions:
1. Preheat the air fryer to 370°F.
2. Cut the pork tenderloin in half so that you have two pieces that fit into the air fryer basket. Brush the mustard onto both halves of the pork tenderloin and then season with salt, pepper and the fresh rosemary. Place the pork tenderloin halves into the air fryer basket and air-fry for 10 minutes. Turn the pork over and air-fry for an additional 8 minutes or until the internal temperature of the pork registers 155°F on an instant read thermometer. If your pork tenderloin is especially thick, you may need to add a minute or two, but it's better to check the pork and add time, than to overcook it.
3. Let the pork rest for 5 minutes. In the meantime, toss the apple wedges with the butter and brown sugar and air-fry at 400°F for 8 minutes, shaking the basket once or twice during the cooking process so the apples cook and brown evenly.
4. Slice the pork on the bias. Serve with the fried apples scattered over the top and a few sprigs of rosemary as garnish.

Spicy Pork Belly Pieces

Servings: 4
Cooking Time: 50 Minutes
Ingredients:
- 1 ½ lbs. pork belly, cut into 4 pieces
- Kosher salt and ground black pepper, to taste
- 1 teaspoon smoked paprika
- ½-teaspoon turmeric powder
- 1 tablespoon oyster sauce
- 1 tablespoon green onions
- 4 cloves garlic, sliced
- 1 lb. new potatoes, scrubbed

Directions:

1. Heat your Air Fryer to 390 degrees F/ 200 degrees C in advance.
2. Use the kitchen to pat the pork belly pieces dry and season with the remaining spices.
3. Spray the coated pieces with a non-stick spray on all sides and add the oyster sauce.
4. Cook the pork belly pieces in the preheated Air Fryer for 30 minutes.
5. Turn them over every 10 minutes.
6. When the time is over, increase the temperature to 400 degrees F/ 205 degrees C.
7. Add the green onions, garlic, and new potatoes and cook for another 15 minutes, shaking regularly.
8. When done, serve warm and enjoy.

Blue Cheese Burgers

Servings:4
Cooking Time: 20 Minutes
Ingredients:
- Olive oil
- 1 pound lean ground beef
- ½ cup blue cheese, crumbled
- 1 teaspoon Worcestershire sauce
- ½ teaspoon freshly ground black pepper
- ½ teaspoon hot sauce
- ½ teaspoon minced garlic
- ¼ teaspoon salt
- 4 whole-wheat buns

Directions:
1. Spray a fryer basket lightly with olive oil.
2. In a large bowl, mix together the beef, blue cheese, Worcestershire sauce, pepper, hot sauce, garlic, and salt.
3. Form the mixture into 4 patties.
4. Place the patties in the fryer basket in a single layer, leaving a little room between them for even cooking.
5. Air fry for 10 minutes. Flip over and cook until the meat reaches an internal temperature of at least 160°F, an additional 7 to 10 minutes.
6. Place each patty on a bun and serve with low-calorie toppings like sliced tomatoes or onions.

Premium Steakhouse Salad

Servings:2
Cooking Time: 20 Minutes
Ingredients:
- 1 head iceberg lettuce, cut into thin strips
- 2 tbsp olive oil
- 1 tbsp white wine vinegar
- 1 tbsp Greek yogurt
- 1 tsp Dijon mustard
- 1 (¾-lb) strip steak
- Salt and pepper to taste
- 2 tbsp chopped walnuts
- ¼ cup blue cheese crumbles
- 4 cherry tomatoes, halved
- 4 fig wedges

Directions:
1. In a bowl, whisk the olive oil, vinegar, Greek yogurt, and mustard. Let chill covered in the fridge until ready to

use. Preheat air fryer to 400ºF. Sprinkle the steak with salt and pepper. Place it in the greased frying basket and Air Fry for 9 minutes or until you reach your desired doneness, flipping once. Let sit onto a cutting board for 5 minutes.

2. Combine lettuce and mustard dressing in a large bowl, then divide between 2 medium bowls. Thinly slice steak and add to salads. Scatter with walnuts, blue cheese, cherry tomatoes, and fig wedges. Serve immediately.

Flank Steak With Honey And Paprika

Servings: 4

Cooking Time: 15 Minutes

Ingredients:

- 1 ½ lb. flank steak
- 1 teaspoon salt
- ½ teaspoon pepper
- 2 tablespoons fresh thyme, chopped
- 2 teaspoons honey
- 3 garlic cloves, minced
- 1 ½ teaspoon paprika
- 1 ½ tablespoon fresh rosemary, finely chopped
- 4 tablespoons olive oil

Directions:

1. In a sealable bag, coat the flank steak with the honey, salt, thyme, paprika, garlic, rosemary, olive oil, and pepper, then refrigerate them for at least 2 hours.

2. Cook the coated and marinated flank steak in your air fryer at 390 degrees F/ 200 degrees C for 15 minutes, flipping halfway through.

3. Serve immediately. Bon appétit!

Crunchy Veal Cutlets

Servings: 2

Cooking Time: 5 Minutes

Ingredients:

- ½ cup All-purpose flour or tapioca flour
- 1 Large egg(s), well beaten
- ¾ cup Seasoned Italian-style dried bread crumbs (gluten-free, if a concern)
- 2 tablespoons Yellow cornmeal
- 4 Thinly pounded 2-ounce veal leg cutlets (less than ¼ inch thick)
- Olive oil spray

Directions:

1. Preheat the air fryer to 400°F.

2. Set up and fill three shallow soup plates or small pie plates on your counter: one for the flour; one for the egg(s); and one for the bread crumbs, whisked with the cornmeal until well combined.

3. Dredge a veal cutlet in the flour, coating it on both sides. Gently shake off any excess flour, then gently dip it in the beaten egg(s), coating both sides. Let the excess egg slip back into the rest. Dip the cutlet in the bread-crumb mixture, turning it several times and pressing gently to make an even coating on both sides. Coat it on both sides with olive oil spray, then set it aside and continue dredging and coating more cutlets.

4. When the machine is at temperature, set the cutlets in the basket so that they don't touch each other. Air-fry undisturbed for 5 minutes, or until crisp and brown. (If only some of the veal cutlets will fit in one layer for any selected batch—the sizes of air fryer baskets vary dramatically—work in batches as necessary.)

5. Use kitchen tongs to transfer the cutlets to a wire rack. Cool for only 1 to 2 minutes before serving.

Italian-style Honey Pork

Servings: 3

Cooking Time: 50 Minutes

Ingredients:

- 1 teaspoon Celtic sea salt
- ½-teaspoon black pepper, freshly cracked
- ¼ cup red wine
- 1 tablespoon mustard
- 1 tablespoon honey
- 2 garlic cloves, minced
- 1 lb. pork top loin
- 1 tablespoon Italian herb seasoning blend

Directions:

1. Prepare a suitable bowl, mix up the salt, black pepper, red wine, mustard, honey, garlic and the pork top loin, then marinate the pork top loin at least 30 minutes.

2. Spray the cooking basket of your air fryer with the non-stick cooking spray.

3. Sprinkle the Italian herb on the top of the pork top loin after transfer it to the basket.

4. Cook the pork top loin at 370 degrees F/ 185 degrees C for 10 minutes, flipping and spraying with cooking oil halfway through.

5. When cooked, serve and enjoy.

Barbecue-style Beef Cube Steak

Servings: 2

Cooking Time: 14 Minutes

Ingredients:

- 2 4-ounce beef cube steak(s)
- 2 cups Fritos (original flavor) or a generic corn chip equivalent, crushed to crumbs
- 6 tablespoons Purchased smooth barbecue sauce, any flavor (gluten-free, if a concern)

Directions:

1. Preheat the air fryer to 375°F.

2. Spread the Fritos crumbs in a shallow soup plate or a small pie plate. Rub the barbecue sauce onto both sides of the steak(s). Dredge the steak(s) in the Fritos crumbs to coat well and thoroughly, turning several times and pressing down to get the little bits to adhere to the meat.

3. When the machine is at temperature, set the steak(s) in the basket. Leave as much air space between them as possible if you're working with more than one piece of beef. Air-fry undisturbed for 12 minutes, or until lightly brown and crunchy. If the machine is at 360°F, you may need to add 2 minutes to the cooking time.

4. Use kitchen tongs to transfer the steak(s) to a wire rack. Cool for 5 minutes before serving.

Roasted Pork Tenderloin

Servings: 6
Cooking Time: 1 Hour
Ingredients:
- 1 (3-pound) pork tenderloin
- 2 tablespoons extra-virgin olive oil
- 2 garlic cloves, minced
- 1 teaspoon dried basil
- 1 teaspoon dried oregano
- 1 teaspoon dried thyme
- Salt
- Pepper

Directions:
1. Drizzle the pork tenderloin with the olive oil.
2. Rub the garlic, basil, oregano, thyme, and salt and pepper to taste all over the tenderloin.
3. Place the tenderloin in the air fryer. Cook for 45 minutes.
4. Use a meat thermometer to test for doneness. (See Cooking tip.)
5. Open the air fryer and flip the pork tenderloin. Cook for an additional 15 minutes.
6. Remove the cooked pork from the air fryer and allow it to rest for 10 minutes before cutting.

Flavor Beef Ribs

Servings: 4
Cooking Time: 12 Minutes
Ingredients:
- 1 cup coriander, finely chopped
- 1 tablespoon basil leaves, chopped
- 2 garlic cloves, finely chopped
- 1-pound meaty beef ribs
- 3 tablespoons apple cider vinegar
- 1 chipotle powder
- 1 teaspoon fennel seeds
- 1 teaspoon hot paprika
- Kosher salt and black pepper, as needed
- ½ cup vegetable oil

Directions:
1. Thoroughly mix the coriander, basil leaves, garlic cloves, meaty beef ribs, apple cider vinegar, chipotle powder, fennel seeds, hot paprika, salt, black pepper, and vegetable oil together in a medium-size bowl and then coat the ribs well. Cover and refrigerate for 3-4 hours.
2. Coat the cooking basket of your air fryer with cooking oil or spray.
3. Once marinated, take the ribs out of the marinade and place on the cooking basket.
4. Cook the ribs at 360 degrees F/ 180 degrees C for 8 minutes.
5. If the meat is not tender, then cook for 3-4 more minutes.
6. Top with the leftover marinade and serve warm!

Mediterranean-style Beef Steak

Servings: 4
Cooking Time: 12 Minutes

Ingredients:
- 1 ½ pounds beef steak
- 1-pound zucchini
- 1 teaspoon dried rosemary
- 1 teaspoon dried basil
- 1 teaspoon dried oregano
- 2 tablespoons extra-virgin olive oil
- 2 tablespoons fresh chives, chopped

Directions:
1. At 400 degrees F/ 205 degrees C, preheat your Air Fryer.
2. Toss the steak and zucchini with the spices and olive oil.
3. Transfer to the cooking basket and cook for 6 minutes.
4. Now, shale the basket and cook another 6 minutes.
5. Serve immediately garnished with fresh chives.
6. Enjoy!

Meat Loaves

Servings: 4
Cooking Time: 19 Minutes
Ingredients:
- Sauce
- ¼ cup white vinegar
- ¼ cup brown sugar
- 2 tablespoons Worcestershire sauce
- ½ cup ketchup
- Meat Loaves
- 1 pound very lean ground beef
- ⅔ cup dry bread (approx. 1 slice torn into small pieces)
- 1 egg
- ⅓ cup minced onion
- 1 teaspoon salt
- 2 tablespoons ketchup

Directions:
1. In a small saucepan, combine all sauce ingredients and bring to a boil. Remove from heat and stir to ensure that brown sugar dissolves completely.
2. In a large bowl, combine the beef, bread, egg, onion, salt, and ketchup. Mix well.
3. Divide meat mixture into 4 portions and shape each into a thick, round patty. Patties will be about 3 to 3½ inches in diameter, and all four should fit easily into the air fryer basket at once.
4. Cook at 360°F for 18 minutes, until meat is well done. Baste tops of mini loaves with a small amount of sauce, and cook 1 minute.
5. Serve hot with additional sauce on the side.

Easy Garlic Butter Steak

Servings: 2
Cooking Time: 6 Minutes
Ingredients:
- 2 steaks
- 2 tsp garlic butter
- 1/4 tsp Italian seasoning

- Pepper
- Salt

Directions:

1. Season steaks with Italian seasoning, pepper, and salt.
2. Rub steaks with garlic butter and place into the air fryer basket and cook at 350°F for 6 minutes.
3. Serve and enjoy.

Bjorn's Beef Steak

Servings: 1
Cooking Time: 15 Minutes
Ingredients:

- 1 steak, 1-inch thick
- 1 tbsp. olive oil
- Black pepper to taste
- Sea salt to taste

Directions:

1. Place the baking tray inside the Air Fryer and pre-heat for about 5 minutes at 390°F.
2. Brush or spray both sides of the steak with the oil.
3. Season both sides with salt and pepper.
4. Take care when placing the steak in the baking tray and allow to cook for 3 minutes. Flip the meat over, and cook for an additional 3 minutes.
5. Take it out of the fryer and allow to sit for roughly 3 minutes before serving.

Kentucky-style Pork Tenderloin

Servings:2
Cooking Time: 30 Minutes
Ingredients:

- 1 lb pork tenderloin, halved crosswise
- 1 tbsp smoked paprika
- 2 tsp ground cumin
- 1 tsp garlic powder
- 1 tsp shallot powder
- ¼ tsp chili pepper
- Salt and pepper to taste
- 1 tsp Italian seasoning
- 2 tbsp butter, melted
- 1 tsp Worcestershire sauce

Directions:

1. Preheat air fryer to 350ºF. In a shallow bowl, combine all spices. Set aside. In another bowl, whisk butter and Worcestershire sauce and brush over pork tenderloin. Sprinkle with the seasoning mix. Place pork in the lightly greased frying basket and Air Fry for 16 minutes, flipping once. Let sit onto a cutting board for 5 minutes before slicing. Serve immediately.

Cheeseburger Sliders With Pickle Sauce

Servings: 4
Cooking Time: 20 Minutes
Ingredients:

- 4 iceberg lettuce leaves, each halved lengthwise
- 2 red onion slices, rings separated

- ¼ cup shredded Swiss cheese
- 1 lb ground beef
- 1 tbsp Dijon mustard
- Salt and pepper to taste
- ¼ tsp shallot powder
- 2 tbsp mayonnaise
- 2 tsp ketchup
- ½ tsp mustard powder
- ½ tsp dill pickle juice
- ⅛ tsp onion powder
- ⅛ tsp garlic powder
- ⅛ tsp sweet paprika
- 8 tomato slices
- ½ cucumber, thinly sliced

Directions:

1. In a large bowl, use your hands to mix beef, Swiss cheese, mustard, salt, shallot, and black pepper. Do not overmix. Form 8 patties ½-inch thick. Mix together mayonnaise, ketchup, mustard powder, pickle juice, onion and garlic powder, and paprika in a medium bowl. Stir until smooth.
2. Preheat air fryer to 400°F. Place the sliders in the greased frying basket and Air Fry for about 8-10 minutes, flipping once until preferred doneness. Serve on top of lettuce halves with a slice of tomato, a slider, onion, a smear of special sauce, and cucumber.

Marinated Rib Eye

Servings:4
Cooking Time: 10 Minutes
Ingredients:

- 1 pound rib eye steak
- ¼ cup soy sauce
- 1 tablespoon Worcestershire sauce
- 1 tablespoon granular brown erythritol
- 2 tablespoons olive oil
- ½ teaspoon salt
- ¼ teaspoon ground black pepper

Directions:

1. Place rib eye in a large sealable bowl or bag and pour in soy sauce, Worcestershire sauce, erythritol, and olive oil. Seal and let marinate 30 minutes in the refrigerator.
2. Remove rib eye from marinade, pat dry, and sprinkle on all sides with salt and pepper. Place rib eye into ungreased air fryer basket. Adjust the temperature to 400°F and set the timer for 10 minutes. Steak will be done when browned at the edges and has an internal temperature of 150°F for medium or 180°F for well-done. Serve warm.

Rice And Meatball Stuffed Bell Peppers

Servings:4
Cooking Time: 11 To 17 Minutes
Ingredients:

- 4 bell peppers
- 1 tablespoon olive oil

- 1 small onion, chopped
- 2 cloves garlic, minced
- 1 cup frozen cooked rice, thawed
- 16 to 20 small frozen precooked meatballs, thawed
- ½ cup tomato sauce
- 2 tablespoons Dijon mustard

Directions:
1. To prepare the peppers, cut off about ½ inch of the tops. Carefully remove the membranes and seeds from inside the peppers. Set aside.
2. In a 6-by-6-by-2-inch pan, combine the olive oil, onion, and garlic. Bake in the air fryer for 2 to 4 minutes or until crisp and tender. Remove the vegetable mixture from the pan and set aside in a medium bowl.
3. Add the rice, meatballs, tomato sauce, and mustard to the vegetable mixture and stir to combine.
4. Stuff the peppers with the meat-vegetable mixture.
5. Place the peppers in the air fryer basket and bake for 9 to 13 minutes or until the filling is hot and the peppers are tender.

Mexican-style Shredded Beef

Servings:6
Cooking Time: 35 Minutes
Ingredients:
- 1 beef chuck roast, cut into 2" cubes
- 1 teaspoon salt
- ½ teaspoon ground black pepper
- ½ cup no-sugar-added chipotle sauce

Directions:
1. In a large bowl, sprinkle beef cubes with salt and pepper and toss to coat. Place beef into ungreased air fryer basket. Adjust the temperature to 400°F and set the timer for 30 minutes, shaking the basket halfway through cooking. Beef will be done when internal temperature is at least 160°F.
2. Place cooked beef into a large bowl and shred with two forks. Pour in chipotle sauce and toss to coat.
3. Return beef to air fryer basket for an additional 5 minutes at 400°F to crisp with sauce. Serve warm.

Quick & Easy Meatballs

Servings: 4
Cooking Time: 12 Minutes
Ingredients:
- 4 oz lamb meat, minced
- 1 tbsp oregano, chopped
- ½ tbsp lemon zest
- 1 egg, lightly beaten
- Pepper
- Salt

Directions:
1. Add all ingredients into the bowl and mix until well combined.
2. Spray air fryer basket with cooking spray.
3. Make balls from bowl mixture and place into the air fryer basket and cook at 400°F for 12 minutes.
4. Serve and enjoy.

Sweet And Spicy Pork Ribs

Servings:4
Cooking Time: 20 Minutes Per Batch
Ingredients:
- 1 rack pork spareribs, white membrane removed
- ¼ cup brown sugar
- 2 teaspoons salt
- 2 teaspoons ground black pepper
- 1 tablespoon chili powder
- 1 teaspoon garlic powder
- ½ teaspoon cayenne pepper

Directions:
1. Preheat the air fryer to 400°F.
2. Place ribs on a work surface and cut the rack into two pieces to fit in the air fryer basket.
3. In a medium bowl, whisk together brown sugar, salt, black pepper, chili powder, garlic powder, and cayenne to make a dry rub.
4. Massage dry rub onto both sides of ribs until well coated. Place a portion of ribs in the air fryer basket, working in batches as necessary.
5. Cook 20 minutes until internal temperature reaches at least 190°F and no pink remains. Let rest 5 minutes before cutting and serving.

Paprika Fried Beef

Servings: 4
Cooking Time: 30 Minutes
Ingredients:
- Celery salt to taste
- 4 beef cube steaks
- ½ cup milk
- 1 cup flour
- 2 tsp paprika
- 1 egg
- 1 cup bread crumbs
- 2 tbsp olive oil

Directions:
1. Preheat air fryer to 350°F. Place the cube steaks in a zipper sealed bag or between two sheets of cling wrap. Gently pound the steaks until they are slightly thinner. Set aside. In a bowl, mix together milk, flour, paprika, celery salt, and egg until just combined. In a separate bowl, mix together the crumbs and olive oil. Take the steaks and dip them into the buttermilk batter, shake off some of the excess, and return to a plate for 5 minutes. Next, dip the steaks in the bread crumbs, patting the crumbs into both sides. Air Fry the steaks until the crust is crispy and brown, 12-16 minutes. Serve warm.

Tender Steak With Salsa Verde

Servings:4
Cooking Time: 20 Minutes
Ingredients:
- 1 flank steak, halved
- 1 ½ cups salsa verde
- ½ tsp black pepper

Directions:

1. Toss steak and 1 cup of salsa verde in a bowl and refrigerate covered for 2 hours. Preheat air fryer to 400°F.Add steaks to the lightly greased frying basket and Air Fry for 10-12 minutes or until you reach your desired doneness, flipping once. Let sit onto a cutting board for 5 minutes. Thinly slice against the grain and divide between 4 plates. Spoon over the remaining salsa verde and serve sprinkled with black pepper to serve.

Hungarian Air Fryer Stew

Servings: 4
Cooking Time: 65 Minutes
Ingredients:
- 4 tablespoons all-purpose flour
- Salt and black pepper, to taste
- 1 teaspoon Hungarian paprika
- 1-pound beef chuck roast, boneless, cut into bite-sized cubes
- 2 teaspoons sunflower oil
- 1 medium-sized leek, chopped
- 2 garlic cloves, minced
- 2 bay leaves
- 1 teaspoon caraway seeds.
- 2 cups roasted vegetable broth
- 2 ripe tomatoes, pureed
- 2 tablespoons red wine
- 2 bell peppers, chopped
- 2 medium carrots, sliced
- 1 celery stalk, peeled and diced

Directions:
1. Add the flour, salt, black pepper, paprika, and beef to a re-sealable bag; shake to coat well.
2. Heat the oil in a Dutch Air Fryer over medium-high flame; sauté the leeks, garlic, bay leaves, and caraway seeds about 4 minutes or until fragrant.
3. Transfer to a lightly sprayed baking pan.
4. Then, brown the beef, with occasional stirring, working in batches. Add to the baking pan.
5. Add the vegetable broth, tomatoes, and red wine. Lower the pan onto the Air Fryer basket. Air fry at 325 degrees F/ 160 degrees C for 40 minutes.
6. Add the bell peppers, carrots, and celery.
7. Cook an additional 20 minutes.
8. Serve immediately and enjoy!

Aromatic Pork Tenderloin

Servings: 6
Cooking Time: 65 Minutes
Ingredients:
- 1 pork tenderloin
- 2 tbsp olive oil
- 2 garlic cloves, minced
- 1 tsp dried sage
- 1 tsp dried marjoram
- 1 tsp dried thyme
- 1 tsp paprika
- Salt and pepper to taste

Directions:

1. Preheat air fryer to 360°F. Drizzle oil over the tenderloin, then rub garlic, sage, marjoram, thyme, paprika, salt and pepper all over. Place the tenderloin in the greased frying basket and Bake for 45 minutes. Flip the pork and cook for another 15 minutes. Check the temperature for doneness. Let the cooked tenderloin rest for 10 minutes before slicing. Serve and enjoy!

Sirloin Steak Flatbread

Servings: 2
Cooking Time: 40 Minutes
Ingredients:
- 1 premade flatbread dough
- 1 sirloin steak, cubed
- 2 cups breadcrumbs
- 2 eggs, beaten
- Salt and pepper to taste
- 2 tsp onion powder
- 1 tsp garlic powder
- 1 tsp dried thyme
- ½ onion, sliced
- 2 Swiss cheese slices

Directions:
1. Preheat air fryer to 360°F. Place the breadcrumbs, onion powder, garlic powder, thyme, salt, and pepper in a bowl and stir to combine. Add in the steak cubes, coating all sides. Dip into the beaten eggs, then dip again into the crumbs. Lay the coated steak pieces on half of the greased fryer basket. Place the onion slices on the other half of the basket. Air Fry 6 minutes. Turn the onions over and flip the steak pieces. Continue cooking for another 6 minutes. Roll the flatbread out and pierce it several times with a fork. Cover with Swiss cheese slices.
2. When the steak and onions are ready, remove them to the cheese-covered flatbread dough. Fold the flatbread over. Arrange the folded flatbread on the frying basket. Bake for 10 minutes, flipping once until golden brown. Serve.

Bourbon Bacon Burgers

Servings: 2
Cooking Time: 23-28 Minutes
Ingredients:
- 1 tablespoon bourbon
- 2 tablespoons brown sugar
- 3 strips maple bacon, cut in half
- ¾ pound ground beef (80% lean)
- 1 tablespoon minced onion
- 2 tablespoons BBQ sauce
- ½ teaspoon salt
- freshly ground black pepper
- 2 slices Colby Jack cheese (or Monterey Jack)
- 2 Kaiser rolls
- lettuce and tomato, for serving
- Zesty Burger Sauce:
- 2 tablespoons BBQ sauce
- 2 tablespoons mayonnaise
- ¼ teaspoon ground paprika

- freshly ground black pepper

Directions:

1. Preheat the air fryer to 390°F and pour a little water into the bottom of the air fryer drawer. (This will help prevent the grease that drips into the bottom drawer from burning and smoking.)

2. Combine the bourbon and brown sugar in a small bowl. Place the bacon strips in the air fryer basket and brush with the brown sugar mixture. Air-fry at 390°F for 4 minutes. Flip the bacon over, brush with more brown sugar and air-fry at 390°F for an additional 4 minutes until crispy.

3. While the bacon is cooking, make the burger patties. Combine the ground beef, onion, BBQ sauce, salt and pepper in a large bowl. Mix together thoroughly with your hands and shape the meat into 2 patties.

4. Transfer the burger patties to the air fryer basket and air-fry the burgers at 370°F for 15 to 20 minutes, depending on how you like your burger cooked (15 minutes for rare to medium-rare; 20 minutes for well-done). Flip the burgers over halfway through the cooking process.

5. While the burgers are air-frying, make the burger sauce by combining the BBQ sauce, mayonnaise, paprika and freshly ground black pepper in a bowl.

6. When the burgers are cooked to your liking, top each patty with a slice of Colby Jack cheese and air-fry for an additional minute, just to melt the cheese. (You might want to pin the cheese slice to the burger with a toothpick to prevent it from blowing off in your air fryer.) Spread the sauce on the inside of the Kaiser rolls, place the burgers on the rolls, top with the bourbon bacon, lettuce and tomato and enjoy!

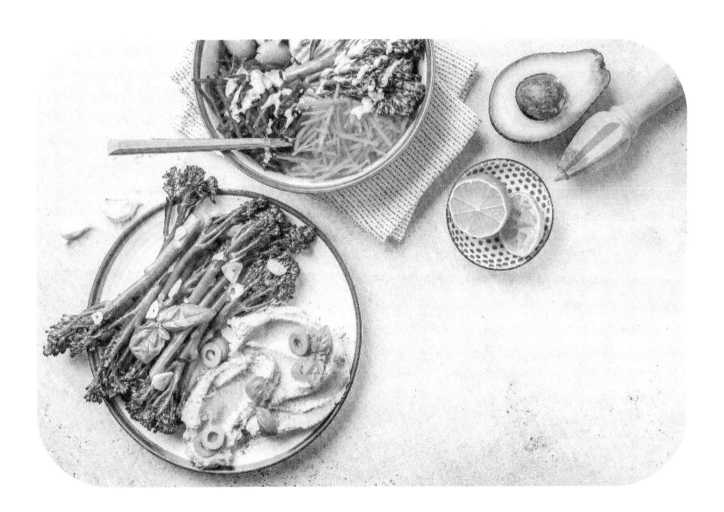

Chapter 10: Desserts And Sweets

Dark Chocolate Oatmeal Cookies

Servings:30
Cooking Time:8 To 13 Minutes
Ingredients:
- 3 tablespoons unsalted butter
- 2 ounces dark chocolate, chopped (see Tip)
- ½ cup packed brown sugar
- 2 egg whites
- 1 teaspoon pure vanilla extract
- 1 cup quick-cooking oatmeal
- ½ cup whole-wheat pastry flour
- ½ teaspoon baking soda
- ¼ cup dried cranberries

Directions:
1. In a medium metal bowl, mix the butter and dark chocolate. Bake in the air fryer for 1 to 3 minutes, or until the butter and chocolate melt. Stir until smooth.
2. Beat in the brown sugar, egg whites, and vanilla until smooth.
3. Stir in the oatmeal, pastry flour, and baking soda.
4. Stir in the cranberries. Form the dough into about 30 (1-inch) balls. Bake the dough balls, in batches of 8, in the air fryer basket for 7 to 10 minutes, or until set.
5. Carefully remove the cookies from the air fryer and cool on a wire rack. Repeat with the remaining dough balls.

Moon Pie

Servings:4
Cooking Time: 10 Minutes
Ingredients:
- 8 large marshmallows
- 8 squares each of dark, milk and white chocolate

Directions:
1. Arrange the cracker halves on a cutting board. Put 2 marshmallows onto half of the graham cracker halves. Place 2 squares of chocolate onto the cracker with the marshmallows. Put the remaining crackers on top to create 4 sandwiches. Wrap each one in the baking paper so it resembles a parcel. Cook in the fryer for 5 minutes at 340°F.

Fruit Turnovers

Servings: 6
Cooking Time: 25 Minutes
Ingredients:
- 1 sheet puff pastry dough
- 6 tsp peach preserves
- 3 kiwi, sliced
- 1 large egg, beaten
- 1 tbsp icing sugar

Directions:
1. Prepare puff pastry by cutting it into 6 rectangles. Roll out the pastry with a rolling pin into 5-inch squares. On your workspace, position one square so that it looks like a diamond with points to the top and bottom. Spoon 1 tsp of the preserves on the bottom half and spread it, leaving a ½-inch border from the edge. Place half of one kiwi on top of the preserves. Brush the clean edges with the egg, then fold the top corner over the filling to make a triangle. Crimp with a fork to seal the pastry. Brush the top of the pastry with egg. Preheat air fryer to 350°F. Put the pastries in the greased frying basket. Air Fry for 10 minutes, flipping once until golden and puffy. Remove from the fryer, let cool and dush with icing sugar. Serve.

Orange Marmalade

Servings: 4
Cooking Time: 20 Minutes
Ingredients:
- 4 oranges, peeled and chopped
- 3 cups sugar
- 1½ cups water

Directions:
1. In a pan that fits your air fryer, mix the oranges with the sugar and the water; stir.
2. Place the pan in the fryer and cook at 340°F for 20 minutes.
3. Stir well, divide into cups, refrigerate, and serve cold.

Air Fryer Reduced-sugar Cookies

Servings: 10
Cooking Time: 15 Minutes
Ingredients:
- 1 teaspoon of baking powder
- 1 cup of almond flour
- 3 tablespoons of natural low-calorie sweetener
- 1 large egg
- 3-½ tablespoons raspberry reduced-sugar pre-serves
- 4 tablespoons of softened cream cheese

Directions:
1. In a suitable bowl, add egg, baking powder, flour, sweetener, and cream cheese, mix well until a dough wet forms.
2. Then let the dough chill in the fridge for almost 20 minutes, until dough is cool enough.
3. And then form into balls.
4. Let the air fryer preheat to 400 degrees F/ 205 degrees C, add the parchment paper to the air fryer basket.
5. Make ten balls from the dough and put them in the prepared air fryer basket.
6. With your clean hands, make an indentation from your thumb in the center of every cookie. Add 1 teaspoon of the raspberry preserve in the thumb hole.
7. Air fry in the preheated Air Fryer for 7 minutes, or until light golden brown to your liking.
8. Let the cookies cool completely in the parchment paper for almost 15 minutes, or they will fall apart.

Keto Cheesecake Cups

Servings: 6
Cooking Time: 10 Minutes
Ingredients:
- 8 ounces cream cheese
- ¼ cup plain whole-milk Greek yogurt

- 1 large egg
- 1 teaspoon pure vanilla extract
- 3 tablespoons monk fruit sweetener
- ¼ teaspoon salt
- ½ cup walnuts, roughly chopped

Directions:
1. Preheat the air fryer to 315°F.
2. In a large bowl, use a hand mixer to beat the cream cheese together with the yogurt, egg, vanilla, sweetener, and salt. When combined, fold in the chopped walnuts.
3. Set 6 silicone muffin liners inside an air-fryer-safe pan. Note: This is to allow for an easier time getting the cheesecake bites in and out. If you don't have a pan, you can place them directly in the air fryer basket.
4. Evenly fill the cupcake liners with cheesecake batter.
5. Carefully place the pan into the air fryer basket and cook for about 10 minutes, or until the tops are lightly browned and firm.
6. Carefully remove the pan when done and place in the refrigerator for 3 hours to firm up before serving.

Almond Cherry Bars

Servings: 12
Cooking Time: 35 Minutes
Ingredients:
- 2 eggs, lightly beaten
- 1 cup erythritol
- ½ tsp vanilla
- ¼ cup water
- ½ cup butter, softened
- ¾ cup cherries, pitted
- 1 ½ cup almond flour
- 1 tablespoon xanthan gum
- ½ teaspoon salt

Directions:
1. Mix vanilla, butter, salt, almond flour, the beaten eggs, and erythritol together in a bowl to form a dough.
2. Transfer the dough to a baking dish that fits in your air fryer and press the dough to flatten the surface.
3. Bake in your air fryer at 375 degrees F/ 190 degrees C for 10 minutes.
4. While baking, stir together the xanthan gum, water, and cherries in a separate bowl.
5. When the cooking time is up, add the cherry mixture over the dough. Cook again for 25 minutes.
6. Once cooked, cut the dough into your desired size and serve.

Tasty Mozzarella Balls

Servings: 8
Cooking Time: 20 Minutes
Ingredients:
- 2 eggs, beaten
- 1 teaspoon almond butter, melted
- 7 oz. coconut flour
- 2 oz. almond flour
- 5 oz. Mozzarella, shredded
- 1 tablespoon butter

- 2 tablespoons swerve
- 1 teaspoon baking powder
- ½ teaspoon vanilla extract
- Cooking spray

Directions:
1. Mix up butter and Mozzarella in a suitable bowl, then microwave the mixture for 10 to 15 minutes or until it is melted.
2. Add the almond flour, coconut flour, swerve, baking powder and vanilla extract, then stir well. Knead the soft dough.
3. Microwave the mixture for 2-5 seconds more to melt better.
4. In the bowl, mix up almond butter and eggs. Form 8 balls from the mixture and coat them with the egg mixture.
5. Coat the cooking basket of your air fryer with cooking spray.
6. Cook the food at 400 degrees F/ 205 degrees C for 4 minutes.
7. Before serving, cool the food completely and sprinkle with Splenda if desired.

Coconut-carrot Cupcakes

Servings: 4
Cooking Time: 25 Minutes
Ingredients:
- 1 cup flour
- ½ tsp baking soda
- 1/3 cup light brown sugar
- ¼ tsp salt
- ¼ tsp ground cinnamon
- 1 ½ tsp vanilla extract
- 1 egg
- 1 tbsp buttermilk
- 1 tbsp vegetable oil
- ¼ cup grated carrots
- 2 tbsp coconut shreds
- 6 oz cream cheese
- 1 1/3 cups powdered sugar
- 2 tbsp butter, softened
- 1 tbsp milk
- 1 tbsp coconut flakes

Directions:
1. Preheat air fryer at 375°F. Combine flour, baking soda, brown sugar, salt, and cinnamon in a bowl. In another bowl, combine egg, 1 tsp of vanilla, buttermilk, and vegetable oil. Pour wet ingredients into dry ingredients and toss to combine. Do not overmix. Fold in carrots and coconut shreds. Spoon mixture into 8 greased silicone cupcake liners. Place cupcakes in the frying basket and Bake for 6-8 minutes. Let cool onto a cooling rack for 15 minutes. Whisk cream cheese, powdered sugar, remaining vanilla, softened butter, and milk in a bowl until smooth. Spread over cooled cupcakes. Garnish with coconut flakes and serve.

Vanilla Cobbler With Hazelnut

Servings: 4

Cooking Time: 30 Minutes

Ingredients:

- ¼ cup heavy cream
- 1 egg, beaten
- ½ cup almond flour
- 1 teaspoon vanilla extract
- 2 tablespoons butter, softened
- ¼ cup hazelnuts, chopped

Directions:

1. Mix up heavy cream, egg, almond flour, vanilla extract, and butter.
2. Then whisk the mixture gently. At 325 degrees F/ 160 degrees C, preheat your air fryer.
3. Layer its air fryer basket with baking paper.
4. Pour ½ part of the batter in the baking pan, flatten it gently and top with hazelnuts.
5. Then pour the remaining batter over the hazelnuts and place the pan in the air fryer.
6. Cook the cobbler for 30 minutes.

Hasselback Apple Crisp

Servings: 4

Cooking Time: 20 Minutes

Ingredients:

- 2 large Gala apples, peeled, cored and cut in half
- ¼ cup butter, melted
- ½ teaspoon ground cinnamon
- 2 tablespoons sugar
- Topping
- 3 tablespoons butter, melted
- 2 tablespoons brown sugar
- ¼ cup chopped pecans
- 2 tablespoons rolled oats*
- 1 tablespoon flour*
- vanilla ice cream
- caramel sauce

Directions:

1. Place the apples cut side down on a cutting board. Slicing from stem end to blossom end, make 8 to 10 slits down the apple halves but only slice three quarters of the way through the apple, not all the way through to the cutting board.
2. Preheat the air fryer to 330°F and pour a little water into the bottom of the air fryer drawer. (This will help prevent the grease that drips into the bottom drawer from burning and smoking.)
3. Transfer the apples to the air fryer basket, flat side down. Combine ¼ cup of melted butter, cinnamon and sugar in a small bowl. Brush this butter mixture onto the apples and air-fry at 330°F for 15 minutes. Baste the apples several times with the butter mixture during the cooking process.
4. While the apples are air-frying, make the filling. Combine 3 tablespoons of melted butter with the brown sugar, pecans, rolled oats and flour in a bowl. Stir with a fork until the mixture resembles small crumbles.

5. When the timer on the air fryer is up, spoon the topping down the center of the apples. Air-fry at 330°F for an additional 5 minutes.
6. Transfer the apples to a serving plate and serve with vanilla ice cream and caramel sauce.

Sweet Orange Muffins

Servings: 5

Cooking Time: 10 Minutes

Ingredients:

- 5 eggs, beaten
- 1 tablespoon poppy seeds
- 1 teaspoon vanilla extract
- ¼ teaspoon ground nutmeg
- ½ teaspoon baking powder
- 1 teaspoon orange juice
- 1 teaspoon orange zest, grated
- 5 tablespoons coconut flour
- 1 tablespoon Monk fruit
- 2 tablespoons coconut flakes
- Cooking spray

Directions:

1. After adding the eggs, poppy seeds, vanilla extract, ground nutmeg, baking powder, orange juice, orange zest, coconut flour, Monk fruit and coconut flakes, mix them well until homogenous and have no clumps.
2. Spray the inside of the muffin molds.
3. Pour the mixture batter in the molds and then arrange them to the air fryer.
4. Cook them at 360 degrees F/ 180 degrees C for 10 minutes.
5. When cooked, serve and enjoy.

Cheese Muffins With Cinnamon

Servings: 10

Cooking Time: 16 Minutes

Ingredients:

- 2 eggs
- ½ cup erythritol
- 8 ounces cream cheese
- 1 teaspoon ground cinnamon
- ½ tsp vanilla

Directions:

1. Before cooking, heat your air fryer to 325 degrees F/ 160 degrees C.
2. Mix together vanilla, erythritol, eggs, and cream cheese until smooth.
3. Divide the batter into the silicone muffin molds. Top the muffins with cinnamon.
4. In the air fryer basket, transfer the muffin molds.
5. Cook in your air fryer for 16 minutes.
6. Serve and enjoy!

Giant Buttery Chocolate Chip Cookie

Servings: 4

Cooking Time: 16 Minutes

Ingredients:

- ⅔ cup plus 1 tablespoon All-purpose flour

- ¼ teaspoon Baking soda
- ¼ teaspoon Table salt
- Baking spray (see the headnote)
- 4 tablespoons (¼ cup/½ stick) plus 1 teaspoon Butter, at room temperature
- ¼ cup plus 1 teaspoon Packed dark brown sugar
- 3 tablespoons plus 1 teaspoon Granulated white sugar
- 2½ tablespoons Pasteurized egg substitute, such as Egg Beaters
- ½ teaspoon Vanilla extract
- ¾ cup plus 1 tablespoon Semisweet or bittersweet chocolate chips

Directions:
1. Preheat the air fryer to 350°F .
2. Whisk the flour, baking soda, and salt in a bowl until well combined.
3. For a small air fryer, coat the inside of a 6-inch round cake pan with baking spray. For a medium air fryer, coat the inside of a 7-inch round cake pan with baking spray. And for a large air fryer, coat the inside of an 8-inch round cake pan with baking spray.
4. Using a hand electric mixer at medium speed, beat the butter, brown sugar, and granulated white sugar in a bowl until smooth and thick, about 3 minutes, scraping down the inside of the bowl several times.
5. Beat in the pasteurized egg substitute or egg (as applicable) and vanilla until uniform. Scrape down and remove the beaters. Fold in the flour mixture and chocolate chips with a rubber spatula, just until combined. Scrape and gently press this dough into the prepared pan, getting it even across the pan to the perimeter.
6. Set the pan in the basket and air-fry undisturbed for 16 minutes, or until the cookie is puffed, browned, and feels set to the touch.
7. Transfer the pan to a wire rack and cool for 10 minutes. Loosen the cookie from the perimeter with a spatula, then invert the pan onto a cutting board and let the cookie come free. Remove the pan and reinvert the cookie onto the wire rack. Cool for 5 minutes more before slicing into wedges to serve.

Cinnamon Tortilla Crisps

Servings: 4
Cooking Time: 8 Minutes
Ingredients:
- 1 tortilla
- 2 tsp muscovado sugar
- ½ tsp cinnamon

Directions:
1. Preheat air fryer to 350°F. Slice the tortilla into 8 triangles like a pizza. Put the slices on a plate and spray both sides with oil. Sprinkle muscovado sugar and cinnamon on top, then lightly spray the tops with oil. Place in the frying basket in a single layer. Air Fry for 5-6 minutes or until they are light brown. Enjoy warm.

Apple-peach Crisp

Servings: 4
Cooking Time:10 To 12 Minutes
Ingredients:
- 1 apple, peeled and chopped
- 2 peaches, peeled, pitted, and chopped
- 2 tablespoons honey
- ½ cup quick-cooking oatmeal
- ⅓ cup whole-wheat pastry flour
- 3 tablespoons packed brown sugar
- 2 tablespoons unsalted butter, at room temperature
- ½ teaspoon ground cinnamon

Directions:
1. In a 6-by-2-inch pan, thoroughly mix the apple, peaches, and honey.
2. In a medium bowl, stir together the oatmeal, pastry flour, brown sugar, butter, and cinnamon until crumbly. Sprinkle this mixture over the fruit.
3. Bake for 10 to 12 minutes, or until the fruit is bubbly and the topping is golden brown. Serve warm.

Honey-pecan Yogurt Cake

Servings: 6
Cooking Time: 18-24 Minutes
Ingredients:
- 1 cup plus 3½ tablespoons All-purpose flour
- ¼ teaspoon Baking powder
- ¼ teaspoon Baking soda
- ¼ teaspoon Table salt
- 5 tablespoons Plain full-fat, low-fat, or fat-free Greek yogurt
- 5 tablespoons Honey
- 5 tablespoons Pasteurized egg substitute, such as Egg Beaters
- 2 teaspoons Vanilla extract
- ⅔ cup Chopped pecans
- Baking spray (see here)

Directions:
1. Preheat the air fryer to 325°F (or 330°F, if the closest setting).
2. Mix the flour, baking powder, baking soda, and salt in a small bowl until well combined.
3. Using an electric hand mixer at medium speed , beat the yogurt, honey, egg substitute or egg, and vanilla in a medium bowl until smooth, about 2 minutes, scraping down the inside of the bowl once or twice.
4. Turn off the mixer; scrape down and remove the beaters. Fold in the flour mixture with a rubber spatula, just until all of the flour has been moistened. Fold in the pecans until they are evenly distributed in the mixture.
5. Use the baking spray to generously coat the inside of a 6-inch round cake pan for a small batch, a 7-inch round cake pan for a medium batch, or an 8-inch round cake pan for a large batch. Scrape and spread the batter into the pan, smoothing the batter out to an even layer.
6. Set the pan in the basket and air-fry for 18 minutes for a 6-inch layer, 22 minutes for a 7-inch layer, or 24 minutes for an 8-inch layer, or until a toothpick or cake

tester inserted into the center of the cake comes out clean. Start checking it at the 15-minute mark to know where you are.

7. Use hot pads or silicone baking mitts to transfer the cake pan to a wire rack. Cool for 5 minutes. To unmold, set a cutting board over the baking pan and invert both the board and the pan. Lift the still-warm pan off the cake layer. Set the wire rack on top of that layer and invert all of it with the cutting board so that the cake layer is now right side up on the wire rack. Remove the cutting board and continue cooling the cake for at least 10 minutes or to room temperature, about 30 minutes, before slicing into wedges.

Vanilla Custard

Servings: 2
Cooking Time: 25 Minutes
Ingredients:
*   5 eggs
*   2 tablespoons swerve
*   1 teaspoon vanilla
*   ½ cup unsweetened almond milk
*   ½ cup cream cheese

Directions:
1. Add eggs in a suitable bowl and beat using a hand mixer.
2. Add cream cheese, sweetener, vanilla, and almond milk and beat for 2 minutes more.
3. Spray 2 ramekins with cooking spray.
4. Pour batter into the prepared ramekins.
5. At 350 degrees F/ 175 degrees C, preheat your Air fryer.
6. Place ramekins into the air fryer and cook for 20 minutes.
7. Serve and enjoy.

Vanilla Spread

Servings: 4
Cooking Time: 5 Minutes
Ingredients:
*   2 oz. walnuts, chopped
*   5 teaspoons coconut oil
*   ½ teaspoon vanilla extract
*   1 tablespoon Erythritol
*   1 teaspoon of cocoa powder

Directions:
1. Preheat the air fryer to 350F.
2. Put the walnuts in the mason jar, then add the coconut oil, vanilla extract, Erythritol and cocoa powder.
3. Stir the walnut mixture with a spoon until smooth.
4. Arrange the mason jar with Nutella to your air fryer and cook at 350 degrees F/ 175 degrees C for 5 minutes.
5. Before serving, stir Nutella.

Brownies

Servings: 8
Cooking Time: 20 Minutes
Ingredients:
*   ½ cup all-purpose flour

*   1 cup granulated sugar
*   ¼ cup cocoa powder
*   ½ teaspoon baking powder
*   6 tablespoons salted butter, melted
*   1 large egg
*   ½ cup semisweet chocolate chips

Directions:
1. Preheat the air fryer to 350°F. Generously grease two 6" round cake pans.
2. In a large bowl, combine flour, sugar, cocoa powder, and baking powder.
3. Add butter, egg, and chocolate chips to dry ingredients. Stir until well combined.
4. Divide batter between prepared pans. Place in the air fryer basket and cook 20 minutes until a toothpick inserted into the center comes out clean. Cool 5 minutes before serving.

Lemony Apple Butter

Servings:1
Cooking Time: 1 Hour
Ingredients:
*   Cooking spray
*   2 cups unsweetened applesauce
*   ⅔ cup packed light brown sugar
*   3 tablespoons fresh lemon juice
*   ½ teaspoon kosher salt
*   ¼ teaspoon ground cinnamon
*   ⅛ teaspoon ground allspice

Directions:
1. Preheat the air fryer to 340ºF (171ºC).
2. Spray a metal cake pan with cooking spray. Whisk together all the ingredients in a bowl until smooth, then pour into the greased pan. Set the pan in the air fryer and bake until the apple mixture is caramelized, reduced to a thick purée, and fragrant, about 1 hour.
3. Remove the pan from the air fryer, stir to combine the caramelized bits at the edge with the rest, then let cool completely to thicken.
4. Serve immediately.

Gluten-free Chocolate Cake

Servings: 10 Servings
Cooking Time: 1 Hour 15 Minutes
Ingredients:
*   1 cup of almond flour
*   2/3 cup of sugar
*   3 large eggs
*   1/3 cup of heavy cream
*   ¼ cup of unsweetened cocoa powder
*   ¼ cup of melted coconut oil
*   1/8 cup of chopped pecans
*   1/8 cup of chopped walnuts
*   1 teaspoon of baking powder
*   ½ teaspoon of orange zest
*   Unsalted butter, for greasing

Directions:

1. Take a 7-inch round baking pan, cover the bottom with parchment paper and grease it with unsalted butter.
2. Put all the ingredients into a large mixing bowl. Blend the mixture on medium speed using a hand mixer until you receive the fluffy and light batter.
3. Gently fold in the walnuts and pecans. Transfer the prepared batter into the baking pan and cover it with a piece of aluminum foil.
4. Put the baking pan into the air fryer basket. Cook at 325ºF for 45 minutes. Take the foil out and cook for extra 10–15 minutes until done. To check the readiness, insert the toothpick in the center; it should come out clean.
5. Remove the pan from the air fryer. Let it cool for 10 minutes. Then take the cooked cake out from the pan and allow it to cool for extra 20 minutes.
6. Serve with berries and enjoy your Gluten-Free Chocolate Cake!

Low Carb Cheesecake Muffins

Servings: 18
Cooking Time: 30 Minutes
Ingredients:
*   ½ cup Splenda
*   1 ½ cup cream cheese
*   2 eggs
*   1 teaspoon vanilla Extract
Directions:
1. At 300 degrees F/ 150 degrees C, preheat your air fryer.
2. Spray the muffin pan with oil.
3. In a suitable bowl, add the sugar alternative, vanilla extract, and cream cheese. Mix well.
4. Add in the eggs gently, 1 at a time. Do not over mix the batter.
5. Let it air fry for 25 to 30 minutes, or until cooked.
6. Serve.

Lemon Butter Bars

Servings: 8
Cooking Time: 35 Minutes
Ingredients:
*   ½ cup butter, melted
*   1 cup Erythritol
*   1 and ¾ cups almond flour
*   3 eggs, whisked
*   Zest of 1 lemon, grated Juice of 3 lemons
Directions:
1. In a bowl, stir 1 cup flour, half of the Erythritol and butter well, then press the mixture into the cooking pan lined with parchment paper.
2. Cook the mixture at 350 degrees F/ 175 degrees C for 10 minutes.
3. While cooking, prepare a bowl, whisk the rest of flour, the remaining Erythritol and other ingredients well.
4. When the mixture cooked, spread the mixture over the it and cook at 350 degrees F/ 175 degrees C for 25 minutes more.
5. Cool down and cut into bars before enjoying.

Fried Oreos

Servings: 12
Cooking Time: 6 Minutes Per Batch
Ingredients:
*   oil for misting or nonstick spray
*   1 cup complete pancake and waffle mix
*   1 teaspoon vanilla extract
*   ½ cup water, plus 2 tablespoons
*   12 Oreos or other chocolate sandwich cookies
*   1 tablespoon confectioners' sugar
Directions:
1. Spray baking pan with oil or nonstick spray and place in basket.
2. Preheat air fryer to 390°F.
3. In a medium bowl, mix together the pancake mix, vanilla, and water.
4. Dip 4 cookies in batter and place in baking pan.
5. Cook for 6minutes, until browned.
6. Repeat steps 4 and 5 for the remaining cookies.
7. Sift sugar over warm cookies.

Orange Cornmeal Cake

Servings:8
Cooking Time: 23 Minutes
Ingredients:
*   Nonstick baking spray with flour
*   1¼ cups all-purpose flour
*   ⅓ cup yellow cornmeal
*   ¾ cup white sugar
*   1 teaspoon baking soda
*   ¼ cup safflower oil
*   1¼ cups orange juice, divided
*   1 teaspoon vanilla
*   ¼ cup powdered sugar
Directions:
1. Spray a 6-by-6-by-2-inch baking pan with nonstick spray and set aside.
2. In a medium bowl, combine the flour, cornmeal, sugar, baking soda, safflower oil, 1 cup of the orange juice, and vanilla, and mix well.
3. Pour the batter into the baking pan and place in the air fryer. Bake for 23 minutes or until a toothpick inserted in the center of the cake comes out clean.
4. Remove the cake from the basket and place on a cooling rack. Using a toothpick, make about 20 holes in the cake.
5. In a small bowl, combine remaining ¼ cup of orange juice and the powdered sugar and stir well. Drizzle this mixture over the hot cake slowly so the cake absorbs it.
6. Cool completely, then cut into wedges to serve.
7. Did You Know? To test for doneness when baking cakes, there are a few rules. A cake should spring back lightly when gently touched with a finger. Or, you can insert a clean toothpick into the cake; it should come out clean. Finally, when a cake is done, it starts to pull away from the sides of the baking pan slightly.

Enticing Chocolate Cake

Servings: 6
Cooking Time: 30 Minutes
Ingredients:

- 2 eggs, beaten
- ⅔ cup sour cream
- 1 cup almond flour
- ⅔ cup swerve
- ⅓ cup coconut oil, softened
- ¼ cup cocoa powder
- 2 tablespoons chocolate chips, unsweetened
- 1 ½ teaspoons baking powder
- 1 teaspoon vanilla extract
- ½ teaspoon pure rum extract
- Chocolate Frosting:
- ½ cup butter, softened
- ¼ cup cocoa powder
- 1 cup powdered swerve
- 2 tablespoons milk

Directions:

1. Mix all the recipe ingredients for the chocolate cake with a hand mixer on low speed.
2. Scrape the batter into a cake pan.
3. Air fry at 330 degrees F/ 165 degrees C for 25 to 30 minutes.
4. Then transfer the cake to a wire rack to cool.
5. Meanwhile, whip the butter and cocoa until smooth.
6. Add the powdered swerve. Slowly and gradually, pour in the milk until your frosting reaches desired consistency.
7. Whip until smooth and fluffy; then, frost the cooled cake.
8. Place the frosted cake in your refrigerator for a couple of hours.
9. Serve well chilled.

Honey-roasted Pears

Servings:4
Cooking Time: 20 Minutes
Ingredients:

- 2 large Bosc pears, halved and deseeded
- 3 tablespoons honey
- 1 tablespoon unsalted butter
- ½ teaspoon ground cinnamon
- ¼ cup walnuts, chopped
- ¼ cup part skim low-fat ricotta cheese, divided

Directions:

1. Preheat the air fryer to 350ºF (177ºC).
2. In a baking pan, place the pears, cut side up.
3. In a small microwave-safe bowl, melt the honey, butter, and cinnamon. Brush this mixture over the cut sides of the pears.
4. Pour 3 tablespoons of water around the pears in the pan. Roast the pears for 20 minutes, or until tender when pierced with a fork and slightly crisp on the edges, basting once with the liquid in the pan.
5. Carefully remove the pears from the pan and place on a serving plate. Drizzle each with some liquid from the pan, sprinkle the walnuts on top, and serve with a spoonful of ricotta cheese.

Apple Chips With Cinnamon

Servings: 4
Cooking Time: 12 Minutes
Ingredients:

- 1 apple, thinly slice using a mandolin slicer
- 1 tablespoon almond butter
- ¼ cup plain yogurt
- 2 teaspoons olive oil
- 1 teaspoon ground cinnamon
- 4 drops liquid stevia

Directions:

1. In a large bowl, toss together oil, cinnamon, and the apple slices.
2. Using cooking spray, spray the air fryer basket.
3. Transfer the apple slices in the air fryer basket.
4. Set the temperature to 375 degrees F/ 190 degrees C and timer for 12 minutes.
5. Turn over the apple slices every 4 minutes.
6. Then mix together the yogurt, sweetener, and the almond butter in a small bowl.
7. When cooked, remove the apple slices from the air fryer.
8. Serve the apple slices with the yogurt dip.

Maple Cinnamon Cheesecake

Servings: 4
Cooking Time: 12 Minutes
Ingredients:

- 6 sheets of cinnamon graham crackers
- 2 tablespoons butter
- 8 ounces Neufchâtel cream cheese
- 3 tablespoons pure maple syrup
- 1 large egg
- ½ teaspoon ground cinnamon
- ¼ teaspoon salt

Directions:

1. Preheat the air fryer to 350°F.
2. Place the graham crackers in a food processor and process until crushed into a flour. Mix with the butter and press into a mini air-fryer-safe pan lined at the bottom with parchment paper. Place in the air fryer and cook for 4 minutes.
3. In a large bowl, place the cream cheese and maple syrup. Use a hand mixer or stand mixer and beat together until smooth. Add in the egg, cinnamon, and salt and mix on medium speed until combined.
4. Remove the graham cracker crust from the air fryer and pour the batter into the pan.
5. Place the pan back in the air fryer, adjusting the temperature to 315°F. Cook for 18 minutes. Carefully remove when cooking completes. The top should be lightly browned and firm.
6. Keep the cheesecake in the pan and place in the refrigerator for 3 or more hours to firm up before serving.

Toasted Coconut Flakes

Servings: 1
Cooking Time: 5 Minutes
Ingredients:
- 1 cup unsweetened coconut flakes
- 2 tsp. coconut oil, melted
- ¼ cup granular erythritol
- Salt

Directions:
1. In a large bowl, combine the coconut flakes, oil, granular erythritol, and a pinch of salt, ensuring that the flakes are coated completely.
2. Place the coconut flakes in your fryer and cook at 300°F for three minutes, giving the basket a good shake a few times throughout the cooking time. Fry until golden and serve.

Pumpkin Cake

Servings:8
Cooking Time: 25 Minutes
Ingredients:
- 4 tablespoons salted butter, melted
- ½ cup granular brown erythritol
- ¼ cup pure pumpkin puree
- 1 cup blanched finely ground almond flour
- ½ teaspoon baking powder
- ⅛ teaspoon salt
- 1 teaspoon pumpkin pie spice

Directions:
1. Mix all ingredients in a large bowl. Pour batter into an ungreased 6" round nonstick baking dish.
2. Place dish into air fryer basket. Adjust the temperature to 300°F and set the timer for 25 minutes. The top will be dark brown, and a toothpick inserted in the center should come out clean when done. Let cool 30 minutes before serving.

Giant Vegan Chocolate Chip Cookie

Servings: 4
Cooking Time: 16 Minutes
Ingredients:
- ⅔ cup All-purpose flour
- 5 tablespoons Rolled oats (not quick-cooking or steel-cut oats)
- ¼ teaspoon Baking soda
- ¼ teaspoon Table salt
- 5 tablespoons Granulated white sugar
- ¼ cup Vegetable oil
- 2½ tablespoons Tahini (see here)
- 2½ tablespoons Maple syrup
- 2 teaspoons Vanilla extract
- ⅔ cup Vegan semisweet or bittersweet chocolate chips
- Baking spray

Directions:
1. Preheat the air fryer to 325°F (or 330°F, if that's the closest setting).

2. Whisk the flour, oats, baking soda, and salt in a bowl until well combined.
3. Using an electric hand mixer at medium speed, beat the sugar, oil, tahini, maple syrup, and vanilla until rich and creamy, about 3 minutes, scraping down the inside of the bowl occasionally.
4. Scrape down and remove the beaters. Fold in the flour mixture and chocolate chips with a rubber spatula just until all the flour is moistened and the chocolate chips are even throughout the dough.
5. For a small air fryer, coat the inside of a 6-inch round cake pan with baking spray. For a medium air fryer, coat the inside of a 7-inch round cake pan with baking spray. And for a large air fryer, coat the inside of an 8-inch round cake pan with baking spray. Scrape and gently press the dough into the prepared pan, spreading it into an even layer to the perimeter.
6. Set the pan in the basket and air-fry undisturbed for 16 minutes, or until puffed, browned, and firm to the touch.
7. Transfer the pan to a wire rack and cool for 10 minutes. Loosen the cookie from the perimeter with a spatula, then invert the pan onto a cutting board and let the cookie come free. Remove the pan and reinvert the cookie onto the wire rack. Cool for 5 minutes more before slicing into wedges to serve.

Pear And Almond Biscotti Crumble

Servings: 6
Cooking Time: 65 Minutes
Ingredients:
- 7-inch cake pan or ceramic dish
- 3 pears, peeled, cored and sliced
- ½ cup brown sugar
- ¼ teaspoon ground ginger
- 1 teaspoon ground cinnamon
- ⅛ teaspoon ground nutmeg
- 2 tablespoons cornstarch
- 1¼ cups (4 to 5) almond biscotti, coarsely crushed
- ¼ cup all-purpose flour
- ¼ cup sliced almonds
- ¼ cup butter, melted

Directions:
1. Combine the pears, brown sugar, ginger, cinnamon, nutmeg and cornstarch in a bowl. Toss to combine and then pour the pear mixture into a greased 7-inch cake pan or ceramic dish.
2. Combine the crushed biscotti, flour, almonds and melted butter in a medium bowl. Toss with a fork until the mixture resembles large crumbles. Sprinkle the biscotti crumble over the pears and cover the pan with aluminum foil.
3. Preheat the air fryer to 350°F.
4. Air-fry at 350°F for 60 minutes. Remove the aluminum foil and air-fry for an additional 5 minutes to brown the crumble layer.
5. Serve warm.

Lemon Mousse

Servings:6
Cooking Time:10 Minutes

Ingredients:
- 12-ounces cream cheese, softened
- ¼ teaspoon salt
- 1 teaspoon lemon liquid stevia
- 1/3 cup fresh lemon juice
- 1½ cups heavy cream

Directions:
1. Preheat the Air fryer to 345°F and grease a large ramekin lightly.
2. Mix all the ingredients in a large bowl until well combined.
3. Pour into the ramekin and transfer into the Air fryer.
4. Cook for about 10 minutes and pour into the serving glasses.
5. Refrigerate to cool for about 3 hours and serve chilled.

Molten Chocolate Almond Cakes

Servings: 3
Cooking Time: 13 Minutes

Ingredients:
- butter and flour for the ramekins
- 4 ounces bittersweet chocolate, chopped
- ½ cup (1 stick) unsalted butter
- 2 eggs
- 2 egg yolks
- ¼ cup sugar
- ½ teaspoon pure vanilla extract, or almond extract
- 1 tablespoon all-purpose flour
- 3 tablespoons ground almonds
- 8 to 12 semisweet chocolate discs (or 4 chunks of chocolate)
- cocoa powder or powdered sugar, for dusting
- toasted almonds, coarsely chopped

Directions:
1. Butter and flour three (6-ounce) ramekins. (Butter the ramekins and then coat the butter with flour by shaking it around in the ramekin and dumping out any excess.)
2. Melt the chocolate and butter together, either in the microwave or in a double boiler. In a separate bowl, beat the eggs, egg yolks and sugar together until light and smooth. Add the vanilla extract. Whisk the chocolate mixture into the egg mixture. Stir in the flour and ground almonds.
3. Preheat the air fryer to 330°F.
4. Transfer the batter carefully to the buttered ramekins, filling halfway. Place two or three chocolate discs in the center of the batter and then fill the ramekins to ½-inch below the top with the remaining batter. Place the ramekins into the air fryer basket and air-fry at 330°F for 13 minutes. The sides of the cake should be set, but the centers should be slightly soft. Remove the ramekins from the air fryer and let the cakes sit for 5 minutes. (If you'd like the cake a little less molten, air-fry for 14 minutes and let the cakes sit for 4 minutes.)
5. Run a butter knife around the edge of the ramekins and invert the cakes onto a plate. Lift the ramekin off the plate slowly and carefully so that the cake doesn't break. Dust with cocoa powder or powdered sugar and serve with a scoop of ice cream and some coarsely chopped toasted almonds.

Almond Pecan Muffins

Servings: 12
Cooking Time: 15 Minutes

Ingredients:
- 4 eggs
- 1 teaspoon vanilla
- ¼ cup almond milk
- 2 tablespoons butter, melted
- ½ cup swerve
- 1 teaspoon psyllium husk
- 1 tablespoon baking powder
- ½ cup pecans, chopped
- ½ teaspoon ground cinnamon
- 2 teaspoons allspice
- 1 ½ cups almond flour

Directions:
1. Before cooking, heat your air fryer to 370 degrees F/ 185 degrees C.
2. In a bowl, beat the butter, sweetener, almond milk, whisked eggs, and vanilla together with a hand mixer until smooth.
3. Then mix all the remaining ingredients together until well combined.
4. Divide the batter into the silicone muffin molds.
5. Cook in batches in the preheated air fryer for 15 minutes.
6. Serve and enjoy!

Grilled Pineapple Dessert

Servings: 4
Cooking Time: 12 Minutes

Ingredients:
- oil for misting or cooking spray
- 4 ½-inch-thick slices fresh pineapple, core removed
- 1 tablespoon honey
- ¼ teaspoon brandy
- 2 tablespoons slivered almonds, toasted
- vanilla frozen yogurt or coconut sorbet

Directions:
1. Spray both sides of pineapple slices with oil or cooking spray. Place on grill plate or directly into air fryer basket.
2. Cook at 390°F for 6minutes. Turn slices over and cook for an additional 6minutes.
3. Mix together the honey and brandy.
4. Remove cooked pineapple slices from air fryer, sprinkle with toasted almonds, and drizzle with honey mixture.
5. Serve with a scoop of frozen yogurt or sorbet on the side.

Vanilla Berry Cobbler

Servings: 6
Cooking Time: 10 Minutes
Ingredients:
- 1 egg, lightly beaten
- 1 tablespoon butter, melted
- 2 teaspoons swerve
- ½ teaspoon vanilla
- 1 cup almond flour
- ½ cup raspberries, sliced
- ½ cup strawberries, sliced

Directions:
1. Before cooking, heat your air fryer to 360 degrees F/ 180 degrees C.
2. Combine the sliced raspberries and strawberries in an air fryer baking dish that fits in your air fryer.
3. Pour the sweetener over the berries.
4. In a separate bowl, combine together vanilla, butter, and almond flour.
5. Combine the almond flour mixture with the beaten egg.
6. Top the sliced berries with the almond flour mixture and then use foil to cover the dish.
7. Then transfer the dish inside your air fryer and cook at 360 degrees F/ 180 degrees C for 10 minutes.
8. When cooked, remove from the air fryer and serve.

Holiday Pear Crumble

Servings: 4
Cooking Time: 40 Minutes
Ingredients:
- 2 tbsp coconut oil
- ¼ cup flour
- ¼ cup demerara sugar
- ⅛ tsp salt
- 2 cups finely chopped pears
- ½ tbsp lemon juice
- ¾ tsp cinnamon

Directions:
1. Combine the coconut oil, flour, sugar, and salt in a bowl and mix well. Preheat air fryer to 320°F. Stir the pears with 3 tbsp of water, lemon juice, and cinnamon into a baking pan until combined. Sprinkle the chilled topping over the pears. Bake for 30 minutes or until they are softened and the topping is crispy and golden. Serve.

Recipes Index

Printed in Great Britain
by Amazon

56083725R00064